THE NEW TEEN TITANS GAMES

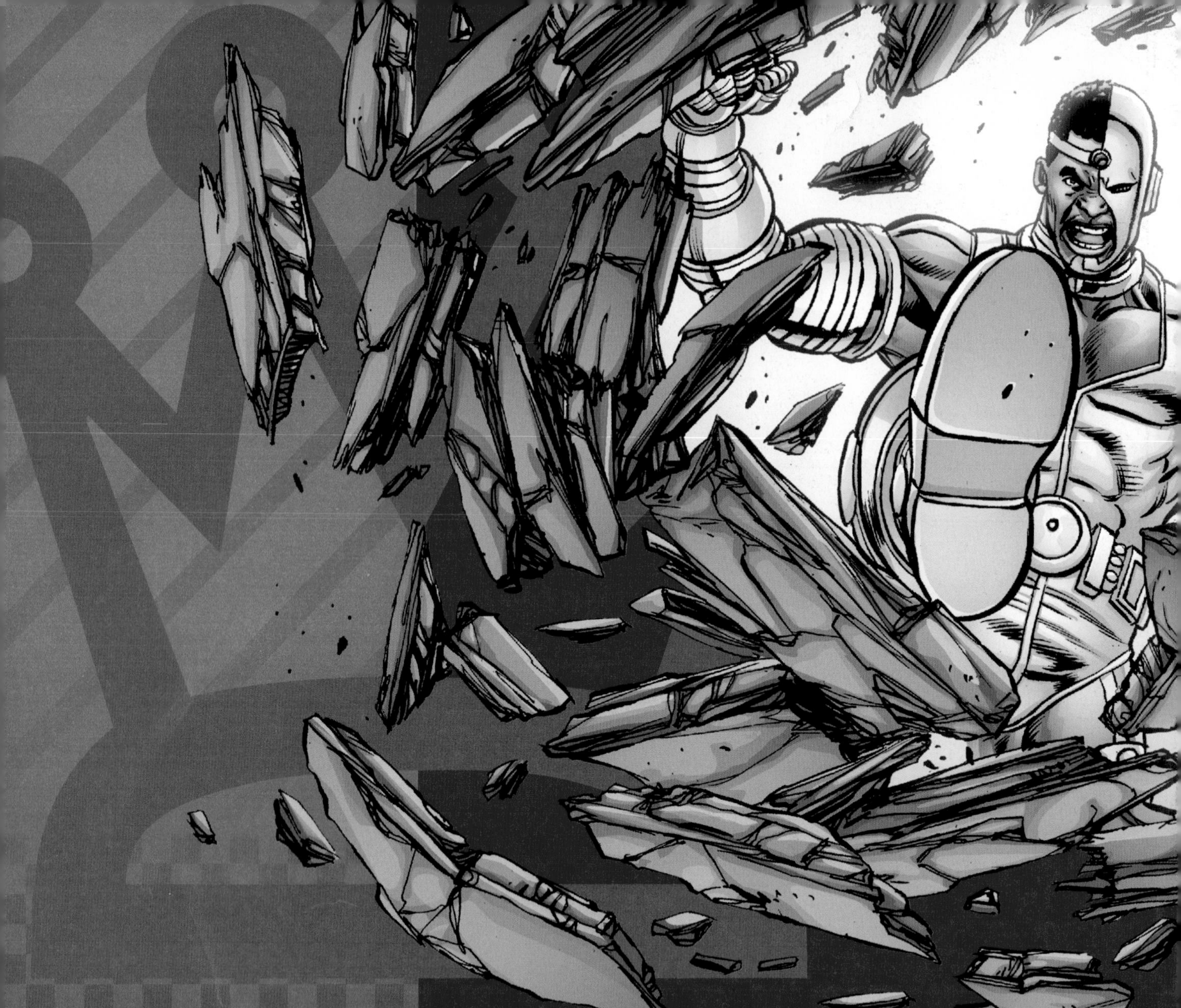

THE NEW TEEN TITANS®
GAMES

Written and plotted by

MARV WOLFMAN & GEORGE PÉREZ

Art and cover by

GEORGE PÉREZ

Inks by **MIKE PERKINS, AL VEY** and **GEORGE PÉREZ**

Colors by **HI-FI**

Lettered by **TRAVIS LANHAM**

New Teen Titans created by **MARV WOLFMAN** and **GEORGE PÉREZ**

Brian Cunningham *Editor*
Darren Shan *Assistant Editor*
Robbin Brosterman *Design Director-Books*
Curtis King Jr. *Publication Design*

Eddie Berganza *Executive Editor* / **Bob Harras** *VP - Editor in Chief*

Diane Nelson *President*
Dan DiDio and **Jim Lee** *Co-Publishers* / **Geoff Johns** *Chief Creative Officer*
John Rood *Executive VP - Sales, Marketing and Business Development*
Amy Genkins *Senior VP - Business and Legal Affairs*
Nairi Gardiner *Senior VP - Finance* / **Jeff Boison** *VP - Publishing Operations*
Mark Chiarello *VP - Art Direction and Design* / **John Cunningham** *VP - Marketing*
Terri Cunningham *VP - Talent Relations and Services*
Alison Gill *Senior VP - Manufacturing and Operations*
David Hyde *VP - Publicity* / **Hank Kanalz** *Senior VP - Digital*
Jay Kogan *VP - Business and Legal Affairs, Publishing*
Jack Mahan *VP - Business Affairs, Talent*
Nick Napolitano *VP - Manufacturing Administration* / **Ron Perazza** *VP - Online*
Sue Pohja *VP - Book Sales* / **Courtney Simmons** *Senior VP - Publicity*
Bob Wayne *Senior VP - Sales*

NEW TEEN TITANS: GAMES
Published by DC Comics, 1700 Broadway, New York, NY 10019. Copyright © 2011
DC Comics. All rights reserved. All characters, the distinctive likenesses thereof and
all related elements are trademarks of DC Comics. The stories, characters and
incidents mentioned in this book are entirely fictional. DC Comics does not read or
accept unsolicited submissions of ideas, stories or artwork.

SUSTAINABLE
FORESTRY
INITIATIVE
Certified Chain of Custody
Promoting Sustainable
Forest Management
www.sfiprogram.org
Fiber used in this product line meets the
sourcing requirements of the SFI program.
www.sfiprogram.org SGS-SFI/COC-US10/81072

DC COMICS 1700 Broadway, New York, NY 10019
A Warner Bros. Entertainment Company
Printed by RR Donnelley, Salem, VA, USA. 8/19/11.
First Printing. HC ISBN: 978-1-4012-3322-8
SC ISBN: 978-1-4012-0319-1

DEDICATIONS

To Noel and Jessica – Always.
To George, for making my words sing.
To all the previous Titans writers and artists,
for enriching my childhood.
And to all the fans who kept the dream.
Thank you.
                                    —Marv Wolfman

To my lovely, supportive and oh-so-patient wife
Carol Flynn, who, like the Titans themselves, seems
just as young as she was when I started this project over
two decades ago. I also dedicate this to all the Titans
fans who've patiently waited for this book since it was
first·announced and to all the new Titans fans who've been
born since then.
                                    —George Pérez

Special Thanks to the editors who helped shepherd GAMES along
the way: Barbara Randall Kesel, who started with it in 1988,
along with Mike Carlin and Eddie Berganza.

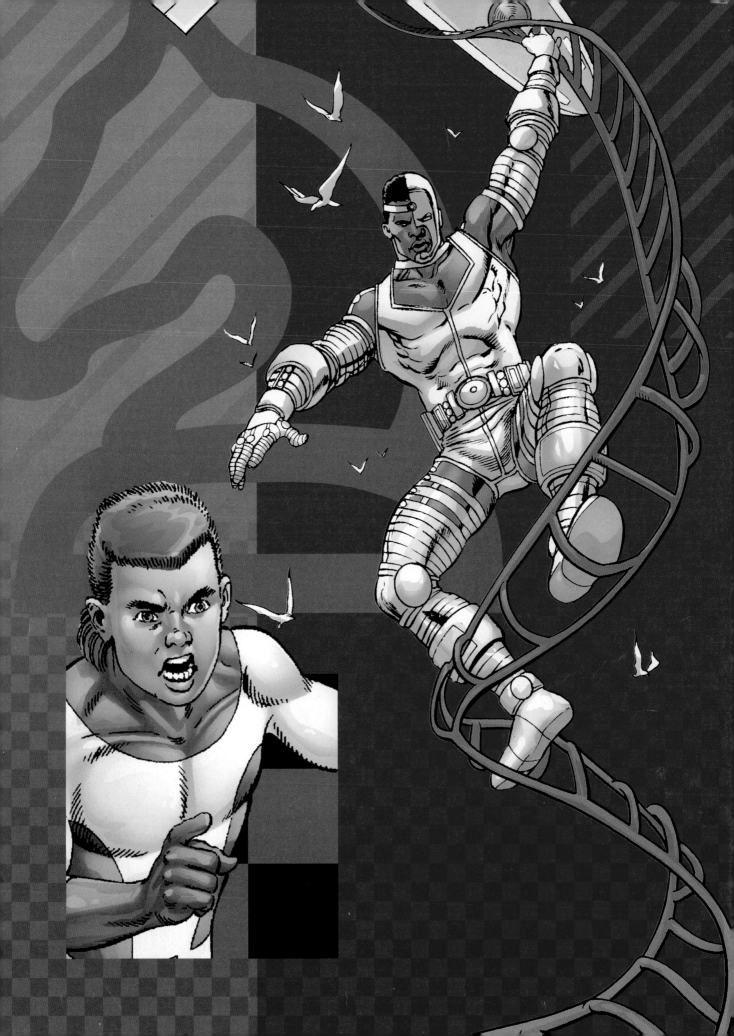

INTRODUCTION
BY MARV WOLFMAN

When I thought about writing this introduction, I wasn't sure where to begin. I could go back to 1987 or '88 (the mists of time and an awful memory for dates obscure the exact moment) when my brilliant NEW TEEN TITANS co-creator, George Pérez, and I got together with our original editor, Barbara Randall Kesel, and I mentioned my very, very initial rough idea. Or perhaps a few months later when the art, stunning beyond belief, started coming in. Or flash-forward a year or so later to my disappointment when the project, for so many reasons, stopped. Or perhaps slightly more than a decade and a half later when it started again, then stopped again, only to finally make it all the way to this lavish hardcover you're holding in your hands..

But talking solely about its ups and downs without proper context would diminish the absolute pleasure I have in finally saying, "TEEN TITANS: GAMES is here at last!" So please indulge me a bit.

I'd been a comics fan ever since that evening, centuries ago, it seems, when, watching TV at a friend's house, instead of changing the channel to a kids' show we both loved, we sat and watched a program we'd never heard of, "The Adventures of Superman." Thirty minutes later, when the show ended, we rushed to the corner candy store and bought our first comics. I may no longer walk down the block to buy a comic, but I still make a semi-regular pilgrimage to the comic shops for my latest multicolor fix. Oh, and Superman is still my favorite comic book character.

Some things never change.

Years and titles passed, and one day I picked up the 54th issue of DC's THE BRAVE AND THE BOLD, which featured the first team-up of three of DC's kid sidekicks. That issue was simply titled, "Kid Flash, Aqualad & Robin." Now, the truth of the matter is, even when I was a kid I never much liked the kid heroes because they all had to answer to their adult mentors. I always thought they had powers of their own and didn't need supervision. But that didn't stop me from buying B&B, or soon afterward the newly christened TEEN TITANS regular comic.

Although I bought every issue, I was a mild TEEN TITANS fan. Liked some issues, didn't like others. The stories were up and down but the art, which I later learned was by the amazing Nick Cardy, was just wonderful. And for a young teen boy, Nick's luscious rendering of Wonder Girl certainly was not a turn-off.

Somewhere between TEEN TITANS #1 and TEEN TITANS #14, I started writing comics professionally. Things were changing in the industry. The original creators were beginning to retire, and new writers, artists and even

editors were entering the field. My first major sale was for an issue of BLACKHAWK that was edited by the late Dick Giordano, a wonderful man, inker and editor who had just moved from Charlton Comics to DC. Dick also was given THE TEEN TITANS to edit, and he wanted to bring in new ideas and writers. Several of us young turks were given a chance to write on that original run, myself included. A few months later I helped plot a several-part story that Neal Adams wrote and drew, and then I wrote the very first real origin of Wonder Girl, a character who somehow was a member of the Titans despite the fact that she didn't actually exist as a character. Check out online reference sites as there's no room to explain Donna Troy's convoluted past here.

I moved out of comics for awhile, but a year later returned as an assistant editor at DC, then as an editor at Warren Publications and finally an editor and then Editor-in-Chief at Marvel. In 1980, after an eight-year stint at Marvel, I returned to DC and teamed up with George Pérez to create a brand-new version of the Titans. But George and I decided to do exactly the kind of comic we always wanted to see and, working out the stories and characters together, our Titans, all modesty aside, became a runaway hit.

Years passed, and the popularity of the Titans kept growing. But where a writer can usually write many scripts a month on very different titles, an artist is usually working on one single title full time. After five years, George needed to stretch and do new things, and he finally left the Titans and very soon afterward worked with me in putting together the DC maxiseries CRISIS ON INFINITE EARTHS.

Once CRISIS was done, George went on to writing and drawing a dynamic and very popular new take on Wonder Woman. I continued to write other comics. But somehow we weren't done with Titans. For most of the TITANS run, George and I lived only a few blocks from each other, and we got together at a local diner to work out the details of every issue. But by 1986 I was living in California, and George was living in New York. I don't remember exactly how the notion of a Titans graphic novel came to be, but I remember flying to New York to meet with George and then-editor Barbara Randall. I didn't have much of an idea, but the notion of the Gamesmaster and his Game Players was there from the beginning. I remember the three of us working out rough details of the story. At the time, because of personal reasons, I was going through a pretty bad writer's block, so George typed up the plot based on what we discussed as well as including ideas of his own so he could begin drawing right away.

As I remember it, some time later George sent me the first draft of the plot; it was hitting the story's broad strokes but wasn't overly detailed. But that was fine because during the last few years of our Titans run together I'd usually come in with the basic idea for the story, then we'd talk the plot out and George would draw it and I'd finish it with the dialogue. This was pretty much the same but with a little less involvement by me because of the writer's block.

Pages started to come in, and I was blown away by them. George had decided to draw the book on paper much larger than the normal original art size. He wanted to go wild with the book and draw scenes that could never have been done on the smaller art pages. Each page was more incredible than the preceding one.

Rather than write a page here or there, go on to other projects, wait for more art and then go back to writing GAMES, I decided to wait for all the art to be finished so I could dialogue them without interruptions. I wanted the story to read like a novel, and I wanted to make certain my writing was consistent over so many pages. But as each page came in I was champing at the bit waiting to start the dialogue.

George drew 70 or so pages of the story before Titans fatigue set in. I'm sure he will talk about it in his Afterword, but at any rate George stopped working on GAMES, I think intending to come back at some point, but not right away. But he started writing and drawing other titles, and I was busy writing not only comics but animation and other media, and we never got back to GAMES. The full-sized Xeroxes of George's 70 magnificent pages sat in my closet for years. Every so often I'd look at them and just wish there was a way to complete the story, but DC's thought, much to my chagrin, was that this book had to be pencilled only by George and written only by me. It was to be our Titans swan song, and either it was going to be done right or not done at all. Ultimately, as much as I wanted to see the work in print, I could not argue with that.

Anyway, time passed to 2004 and I was with friends at the Los Angeles County Fair when I got a phone call from George asking if I would still be interested in finishing GAMES.

I said yes.

No. I *shouted* yes.

Plans were made, and the book was announced to the fan press.

I'm honestly not sure what happened after that, but somehow the project got derailed again. I'm also not sure what happened after that, but I do remember visiting New York and mentioning to now-DC co-publisher Dan DiDio that the 30th anniversary of George and my Titans was coming up in 2010 and if GAMES was ever to be done, now was the best time. A month or so later, GAMES was started up again. And that leads us to this book.

But things had changed. We had never worked out the ending of the original 1987 graphic novel story. After page 70 or so we only had scattered ideas and no real conclusion; that would have of course happened, but it just didn't make it into the initial plot and would have been worked out had the book proceeded back in '88. Also, George and I, as well as the rest of the world, had drastically changed in the interim. The story, as we originally imagined it, wouldn't have the punch today that it would have had in 1988, not only because of world events but also because the style of storytelling itself had changed.

So we went back to rethinking everything we'd done. New motivations were given to characters. New villains were created. The entire story, from page one on, frankly got more than a rethink; it got a brand new emission, new body construction and a major league paint job. In short, a brand-new story was built on the bones of all the art that had preexisted. We threw out a few scenes that no longer worked, rethought others, and added new ones to set up where we were going with this brand-new plot. My writer's block being over for decades, I typed up the new ideas and George culled them as he worked on the last art pages. So today we have a story that was originally plotted and half drawn in 1988, and replotted with the other half-a-book's-worth of art completed in 2010.

Longest. Titans. Deadline. Ever.

It is my hope that this story has the very best of what people remember George and my Titans to be as well as a solid and surprising story for today's audience. We've been thrilled with the changes made, and if anything we wish the book could have been much longer in order to explore some of the new ideas we came up with.

Before I close, a quick story. George and I got together a few months ago at Megacon in Orlando, Florida, for a breakfast where we'd talk about the book and toss out some ideas. This was to be our first new get-together on this project. GAMES inker (and great artist in his own right) Mike Perkins joined as George and I batted ideas back and forth, each coming up with concepts, tossing out others, anticipating what the other was going to say, and putting together this story that had been gestating for so long. George and I came out of it thinking from the moment we sat down that it was exactly like it was in the old days when we worked together. Mike said that being there was like a fan dream because he felt that connection between us was still there, strong as ever.

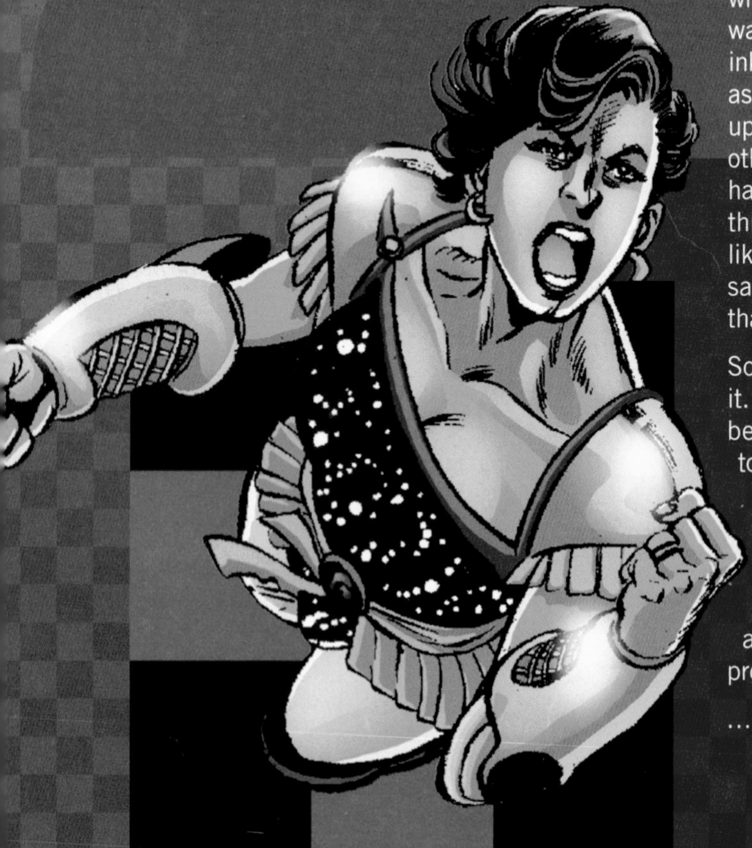

So there you have it. The genesis of GAMES, as I remember it. It's been a long time coming—23 years!—and I sincerely believe it was worth the wait. The story we're giving you today is much stronger than the one we had originally come up with nearly a quarter century ago. We hope you will all agree.

Over the years I've said time and again in interviews that George was the greatest partner I've had as well as a great friend. I am just so pleased that doing this book proved once again...

...some things never change.

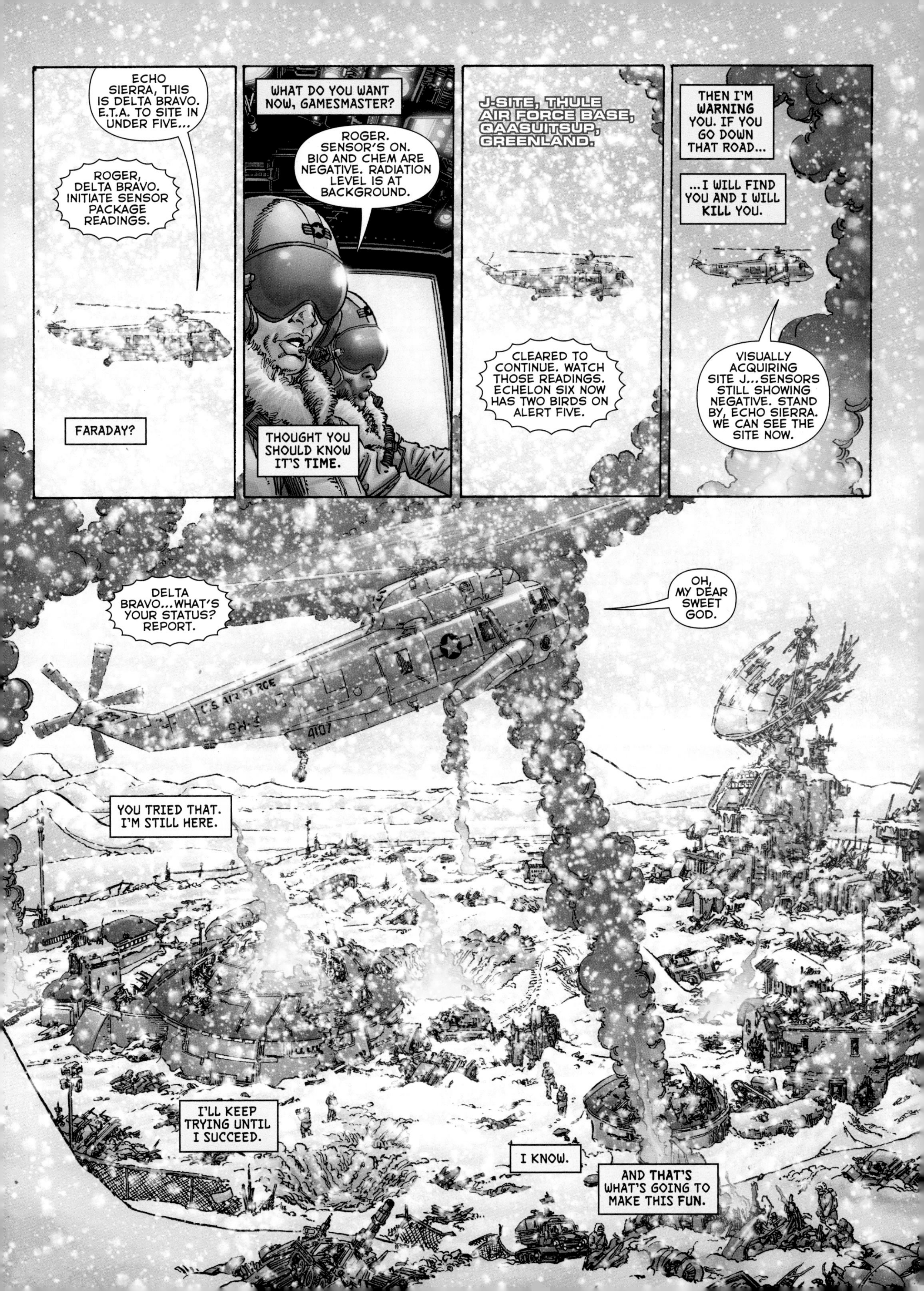
ECHO SIERRA, THIS IS DELTA BRAVO. E.T.A. TO SITE IN UNDER FIVE...
ROGER, DELTA BRAVO. INITIATE SENSOR PACKAGE READINGS.
FARADAY?
WHAT DO YOU WANT NOW, GAMESMASTER?
ROGER. SENSOR'S ON. BIO AND CHEM ARE NEGATIVE. RADIATION LEVEL IS AT BACKGROUND.
THOUGHT YOU SHOULD KNOW IT'S TIME.
J-SITE, THULE AIR FORCE BASE, QAASUITSUP, GREENLAND.
CLEARED TO CONTINUE. WATCH THOSE READINGS. ECHELON SIX NOW HAS TWO BIRDS ON ALERT FIVE.
THEN I'M WARNING YOU. IF YOU GO DOWN THAT ROAD...
...I WILL FIND YOU AND I WILL KILL YOU.
VISUALLY ACQUIRING SITE J...SENSORS STILL SHOWING NEGATIVE. STAND BY, ECHO SIERRA. WE CAN SEE THE SITE NOW.
DELTA BRAVO...WHAT'S YOUR STATUS? REPORT.
OH, MY DEAR SWEET GOD.
U.S. AIR FORCE
SH-3
4107
YOU TRIED THAT. I'M STILL HERE.
I'LL KEEP TRYING UNTIL I SUCCEED.
I KNOW.
AND THAT'S WHAT'S GOING TO MAKE THIS FUN.

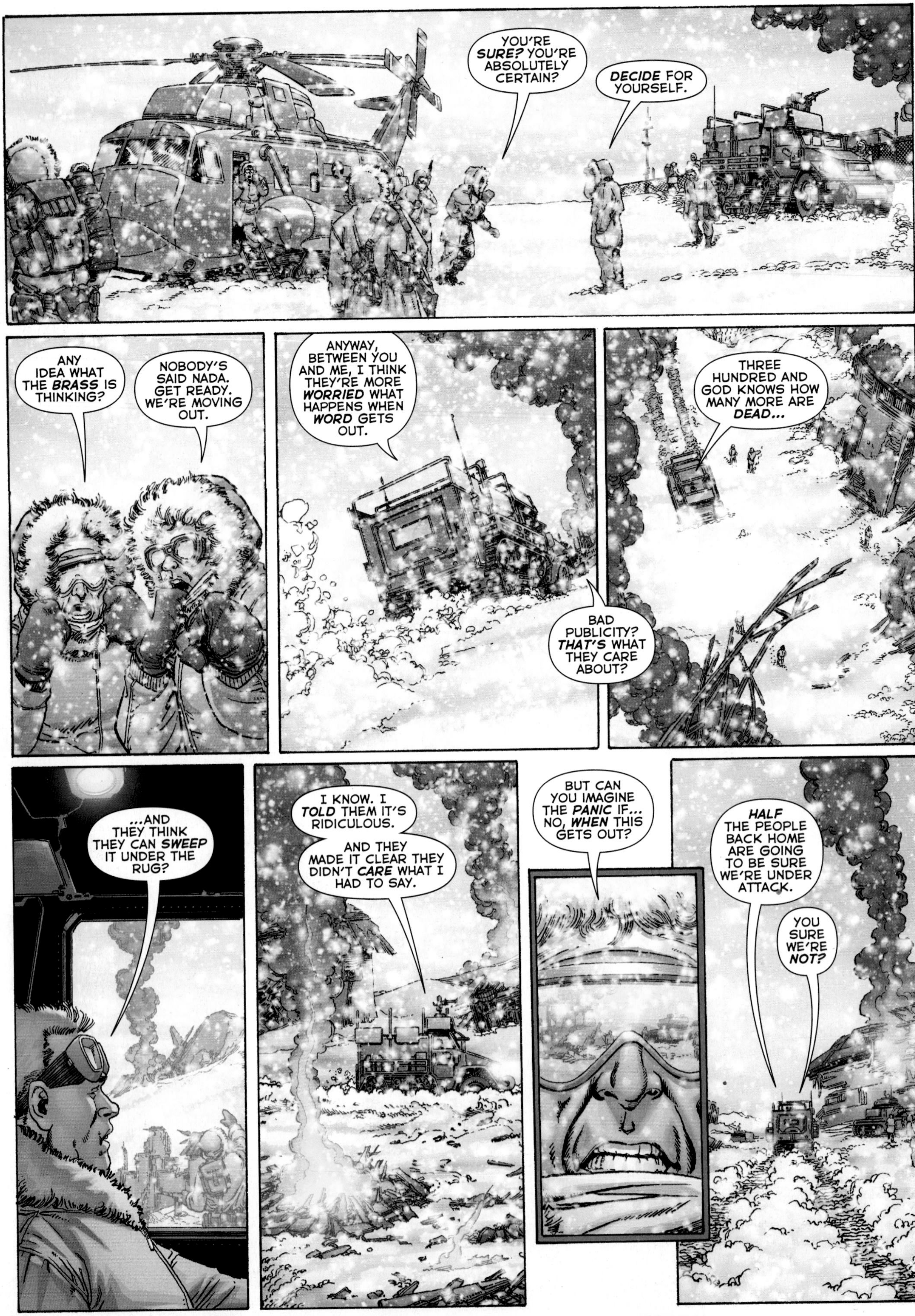
YOU'RE SURE? YOU'RE ABSOLUTELY CERTAIN?
DECIDE FOR YOURSELF.
ANY IDEA WHAT THE BRASS IS THINKING?
NOBODY'S SAID NADA. GET READY. WE'RE MOVING OUT.
ANYWAY, BETWEEN YOU AND ME, I THINK THEY'RE MORE WORRIED WHAT HAPPENS WHEN WORD GETS OUT.
BAD PUBLICITY? THAT'S WHAT THEY CARE ABOUT?
THREE HUNDRED AND GOD KNOWS HOW MANY MORE ARE DEAD...
...AND THEY THINK THEY CAN SWEEP IT UNDER THE RUG?
I KNOW. I TOLD THEM IT'S RIDICULOUS.
AND THEY MADE IT CLEAR THEY DIDN'T CARE WHAT I HAD TO SAY.
BUT CAN YOU IMAGINE THE PANIC IF... NO, WHEN THIS GETS OUT?
HALF THE PEOPLE BACK HOME ARE GOING TO BE SURE WE'RE UNDER ATTACK.
YOU SURE WE'RE NOT?

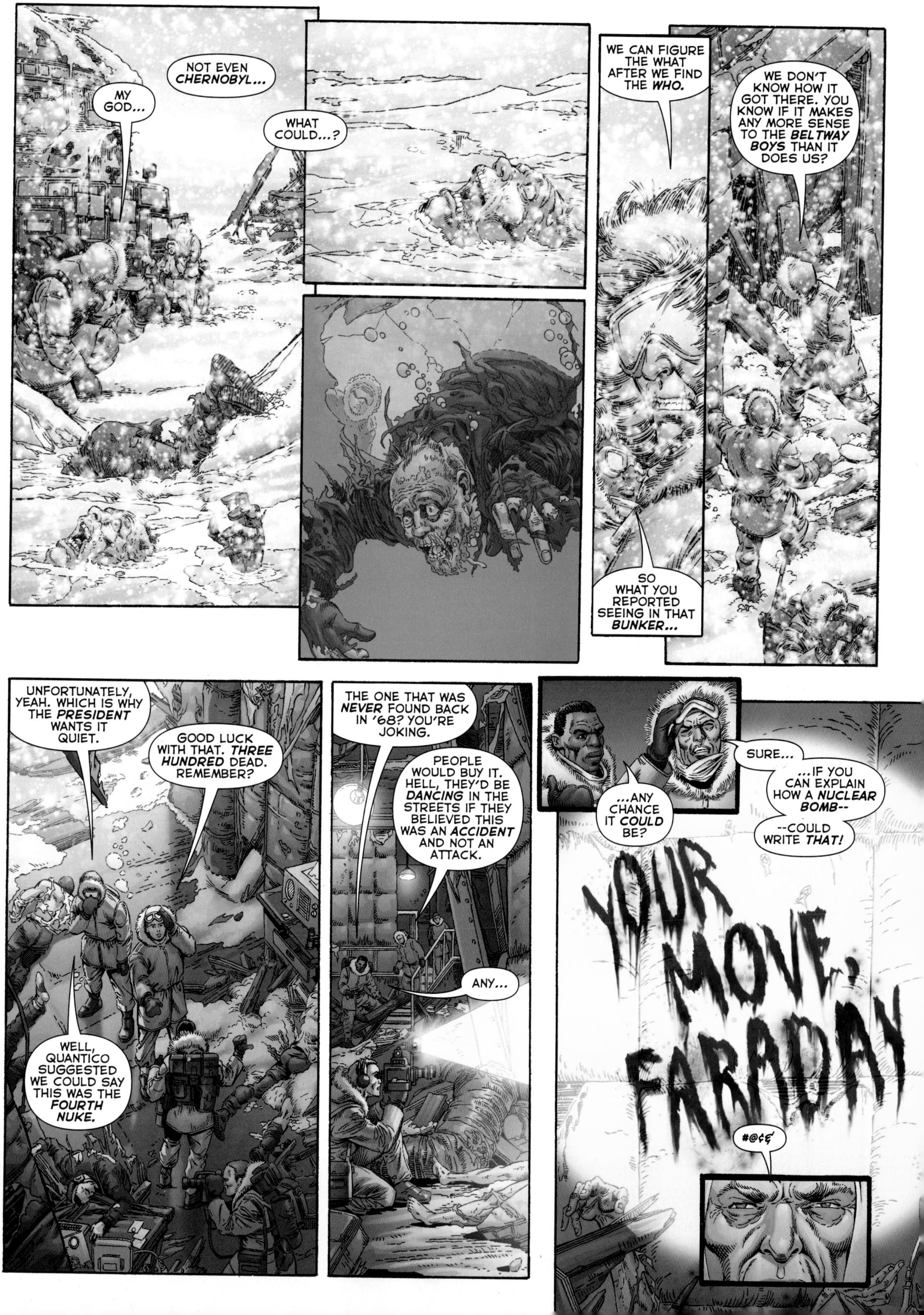
NOT EVEN CHERNOBYL...
MY GOD...
WHAT COULD...?
WE CAN FIGURE THE WHAT AFTER WE FIND THE WHO.
WE DON'T KNOW HOW IT GOT THERE. YOU KNOW IF IT MAKES ANY MORE SENSE TO THE BELTWAY BOYS THAN IT DOES US?
SO WHAT YOU REPORTED SEEING IN THAT BUNKER...
UNFORTUNATELY, YEAH. WHICH IS WHY THE PRESIDENT WANTS IT QUIET.
GOOD LUCK WITH THAT. THREE HUNDRED DEAD. REMEMBER?
WELL, QUANTICO SUGGESTED WE COULD SAY THIS WAS THE FOURTH NUKE.
THE ONE THAT WAS NEVER FOUND BACK IN '68? YOU'RE JOKING.
PEOPLE WOULD BUY IT. HELL, THEY'D BE DANCING IN THE STREETS IF THEY BELIEVED THIS WAS AN ACCIDENT AND NOT AN ATTACK.
ANY...
...ANY CHANCE IT COULD BE?
SURE...
...IF YOU CAN EXPLAIN HOW A NUCLEAR BOMB--
--COULD WRITE THAT!
YOUR MOVE, FARADAY
#@¢€

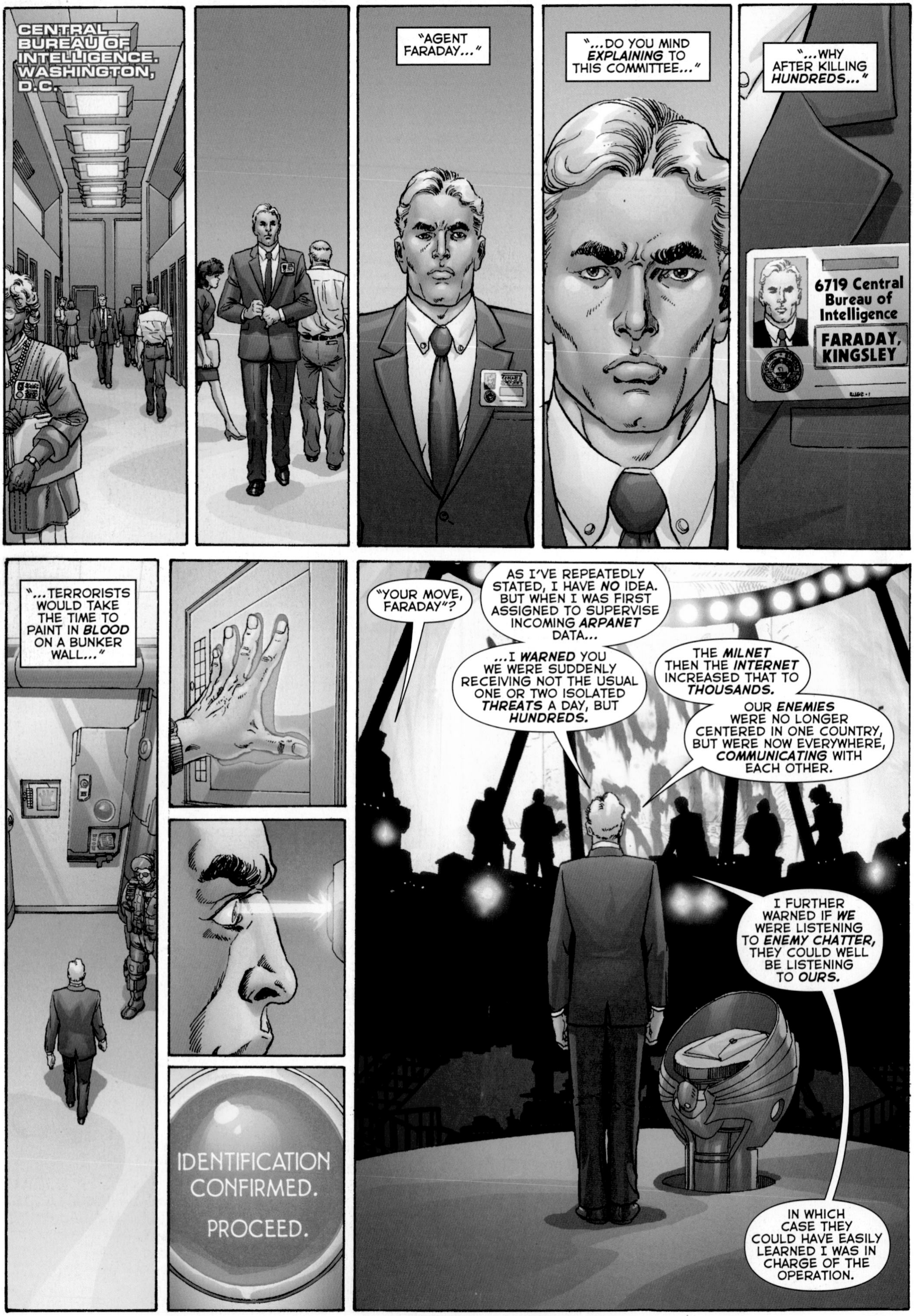

CENTRAL BUREAU OF INTELLIGENCE. WASHINGTON, D.C.
"AGENT FARADAY..."
"...DO YOU MIND EXPLAINING TO THIS COMMITTEE..."
"...WHY AFTER KILLING HUNDREDS..."
6719 Central Bureau of Intelligence
FARADAY, KINGSLEY
"...TERRORISTS WOULD TAKE THE TIME TO PAINT IN BLOOD ON A BUNKER WALL..."
IDENTIFICATION CONFIRMED.
PROCEED.
"YOUR MOVE, FARADAY"?
AS I'VE REPEATEDLY STATED, I HAVE NO IDEA. BUT WHEN I WAS FIRST ASSIGNED TO SUPERVISE INCOMING ARPANET DATA...
...I WARNED YOU WE WERE SUDDENLY RECEIVING NOT THE USUAL ONE OR TWO ISOLATED THREATS A DAY, BUT HUNDREDS.
THE MILNET THEN THE INTERNET INCREASED THAT TO THOUSANDS.
OUR ENEMIES WERE NO LONGER CENTERED IN ONE COUNTRY, BUT WERE NOW EVERYWHERE, COMMUNICATING WITH EACH OTHER.
I FURTHER WARNED IF WE WERE LISTENING TO ENEMY CHATTER, THEY COULD WELL BE LISTENING TO OURS.
IN WHICH CASE THEY COULD HAVE EASILY LEARNED I WAS IN CHARGE OF THE OPERATION.

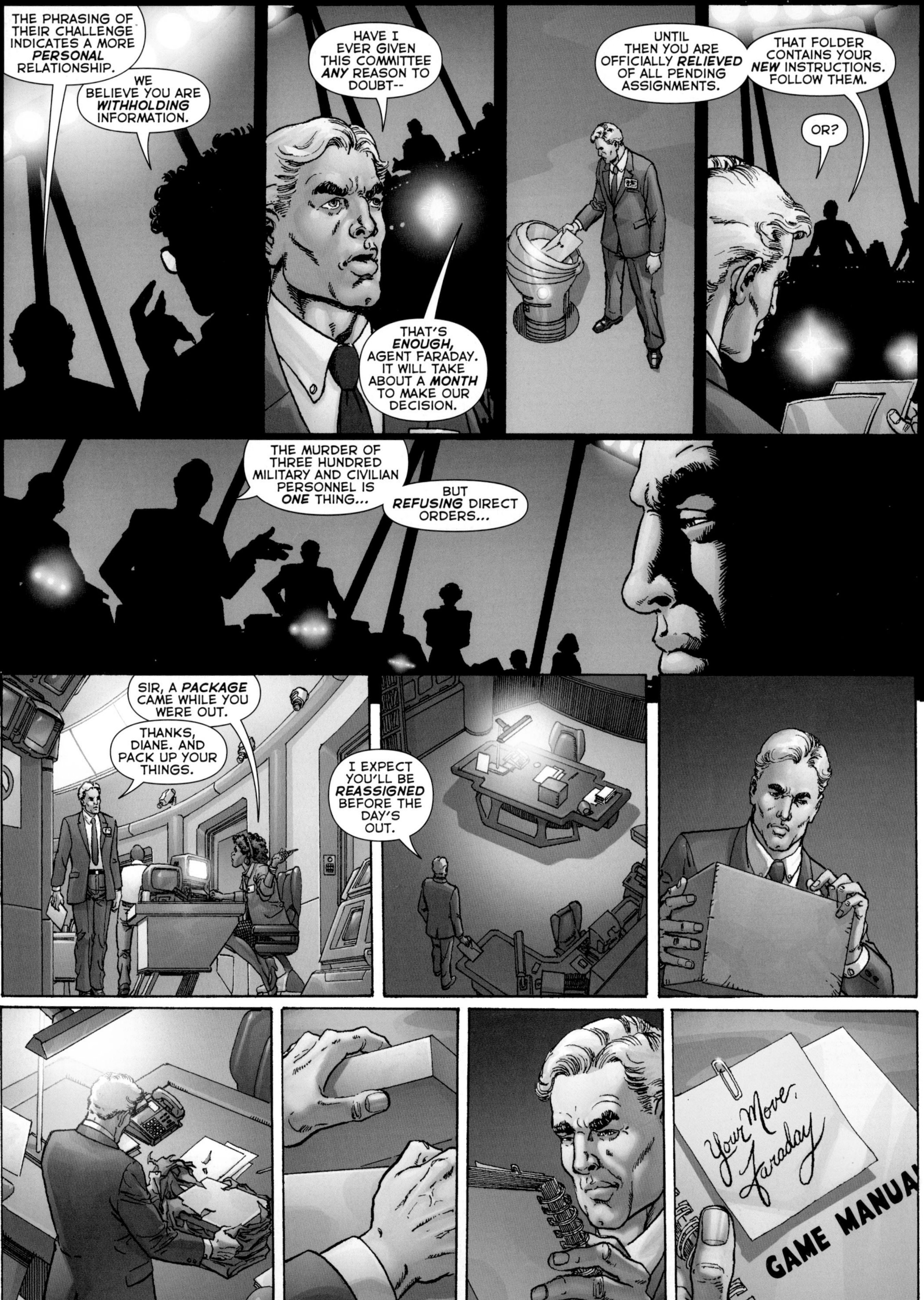
THE PHRASING OF THEIR CHALLENGE INDICATES A MORE PERSONAL RELATIONSHIP.
WE BELIEVE YOU ARE WITHHOLDING INFORMATION.
HAVE I EVER GIVEN THIS COMMITTEE ANY REASON TO DOUBT--
THAT'S ENOUGH, AGENT FARADAY. IT WILL TAKE ABOUT A MONTH TO MAKE OUR DECISION.
UNTIL THEN YOU ARE OFFICIALLY RELIEVED OF ALL PENDING ASSIGNMENTS.
THAT FOLDER CONTAINS YOUR NEW INSTRUCTIONS. FOLLOW THEM.
OR?
THE MURDER OF THREE HUNDRED MILITARY AND CIVILIAN PERSONNEL IS ONE THING...
BUT REFUSING DIRECT ORDERS...
SIR, A PACKAGE CAME WHILE YOU WERE OUT.
THANKS, DIANE. AND PACK UP YOUR THINGS.
I EXPECT YOU'LL BE REASSIGNED BEFORE THE DAY'S OUT.
Your Move, Faraday
GAME MANUA

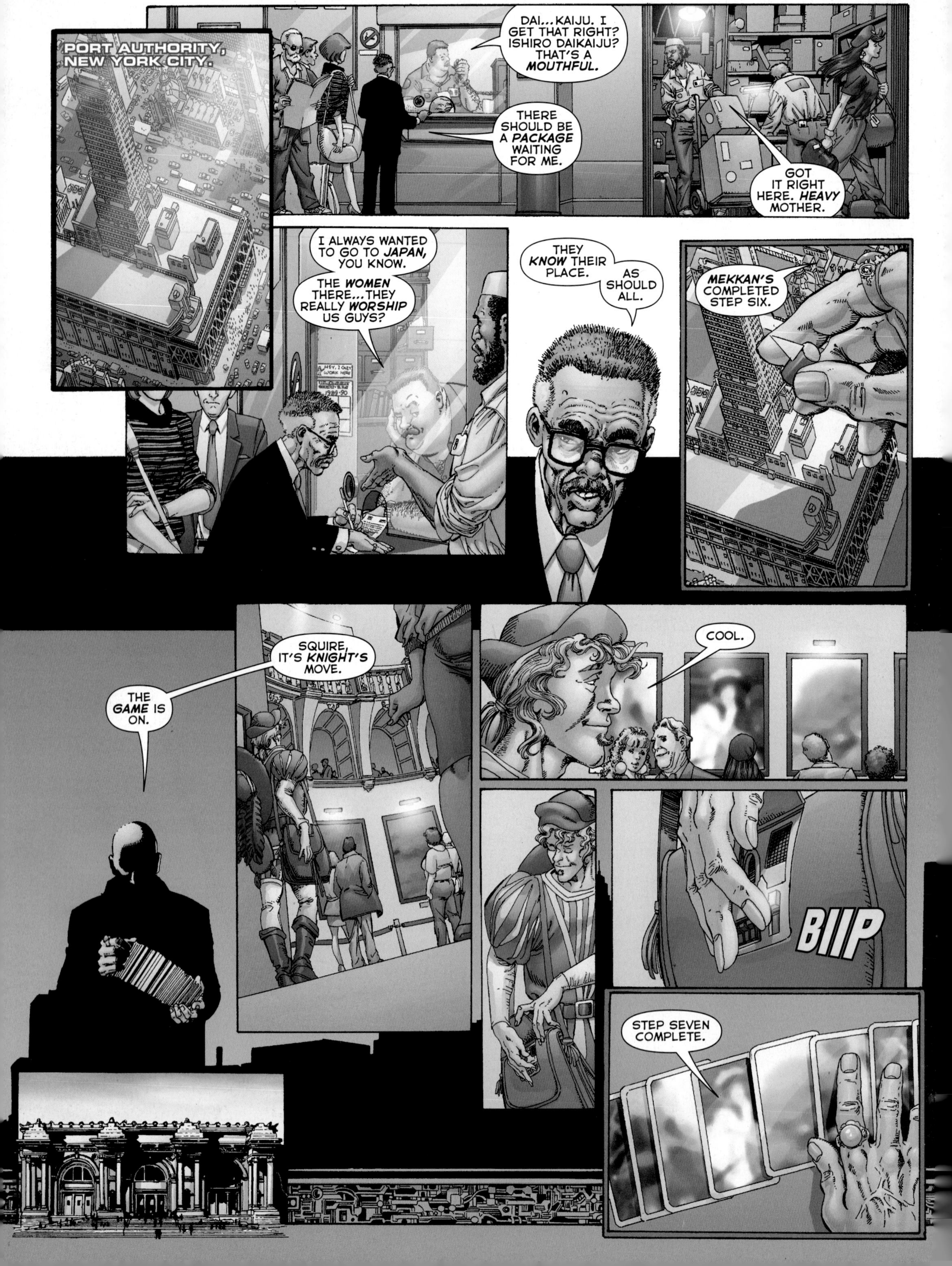
PORT AUTHORITY, NEW YORK CITY.
DAI...KAIJU. I GET THAT RIGHT? ISHIRO DAIKAIJU? THAT'S A MOUTHFUL.
THERE SHOULD BE A PACKAGE WAITING FOR ME.
GOT IT RIGHT HERE. HEAVY MOTHER.
I ALWAYS WANTED TO GO TO JAPAN, YOU KNOW.
THE WOMEN THERE...THEY REALLY WORSHIP US GUYS?
THEY KNOW THEIR PLACE.
AS SHOULD ALL.
MEKKAN'S COMPLETED STEP SIX.
THE GAME IS ON.
SQUIRE, IT'S KNIGHT'S MOVE.
COOL.
BIIP
STEP SEVEN COMPLETE.

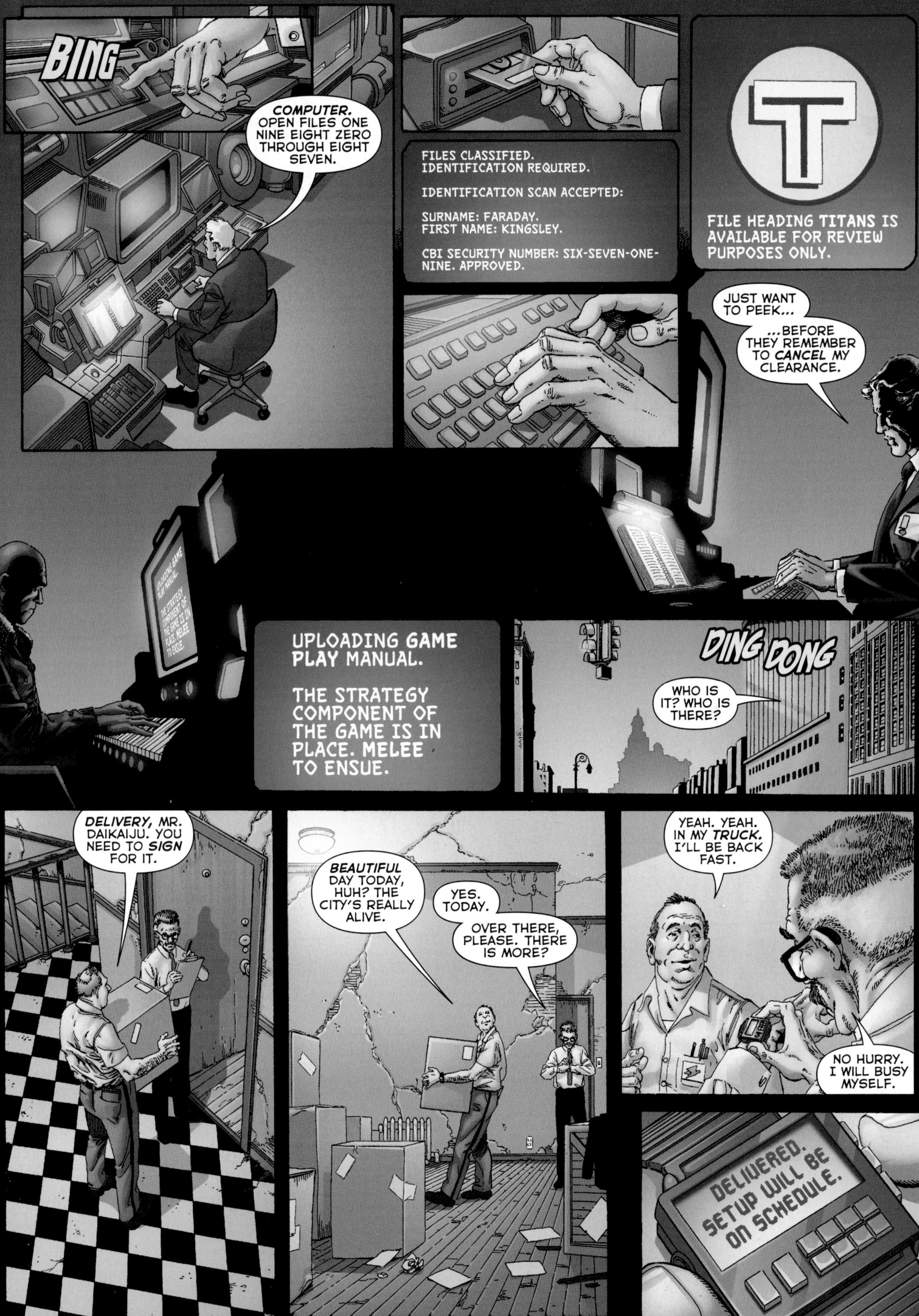
BING
COMPUTER. OPEN FILES ONE NINE EIGHT ZERO THROUGH EIGHT SEVEN.
FILES CLASSIFIED. IDENTIFICATION REQUIRED.
IDENTIFICATION SCAN ACCEPTED:
SURNAME: FARADAY. FIRST NAME: KINGSLEY.
CBI SECURITY NUMBER: SIX-SEVEN-ONE-NINE. APPROVED.
FILE HEADING TITANS IS AVAILABLE FOR REVIEW PURPOSES ONLY.
JUST WANT TO PEEK...
...BEFORE THEY REMEMBER TO CANCEL MY CLEARANCE.
UPLOADING GAME PLAY MANUAL.
THE STRATEGY COMPONENT OF THE GAME IS IN PLACE. MELEE TO ENSUE.
DING DONG
WHO IS IT? WHO IS THERE?
DELIVERY, MR. DAIKAIJU. YOU NEED TO SIGN FOR IT.
BEAUTIFUL DAY TODAY, HUH? THE CITY'S REALLY ALIVE.
YES. TODAY.
OVER THERE, PLEASE. THERE IS MORE?
YEAH. YEAH. IN MY TRUCK. I'LL BE BACK FAST.
NO HURRY. I WILL BUSY MYSELF.
DELIVERED. SETUP WILL BE ON SCHEDULE.

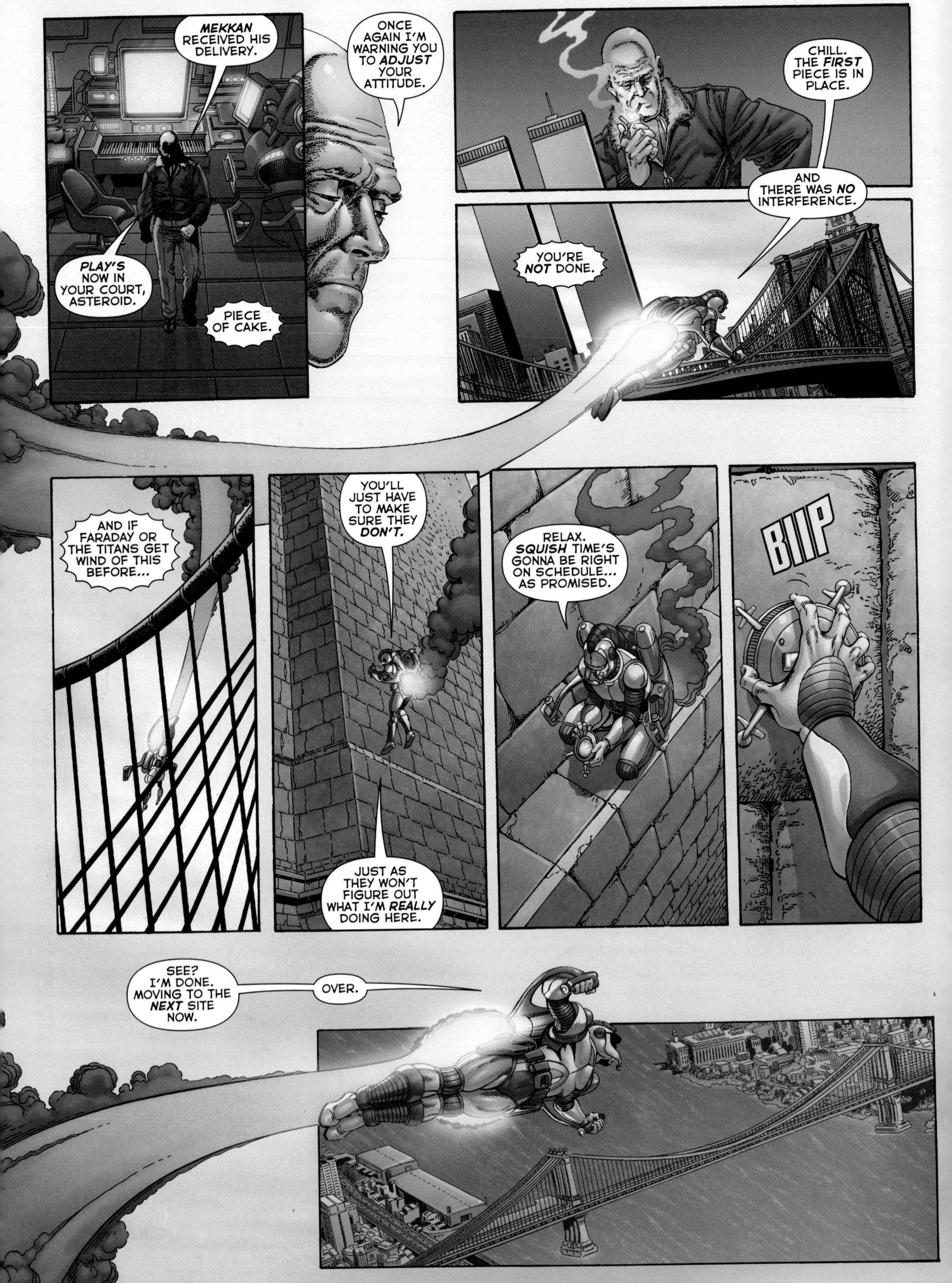

MEKKAN RECEIVED HIS DELIVERY.
PLAY'S NOW IN YOUR COURT, ASTEROID.
PIECE OF CAKE.
ONCE AGAIN I'M WARNING YOU TO ADJUST YOUR ATTITUDE.
CHILL. THE FIRST PIECE IS IN PLACE.
AND THERE WAS NO INTERFERENCE.
YOU'RE NOT DONE.
AND IF FARADAY OR THE TITANS GET WIND OF THIS BEFORE...
YOU'LL JUST HAVE TO MAKE SURE THEY DON'T.
JUST AS THEY WON'T FIGURE OUT WHAT I'M REALLY DOING HERE.
RELAX. SQUISH TIME'S GONNA BE RIGHT ON SCHEDULE... AS PROMISED.
BIIP
SEE? I'M DONE. MOVING TO THE NEXT SITE NOW.
OVER.

WEST SIDE SCHOOL FOR THE HANDICAPPED.

AGENT FARADAY, YEAH, I JUST GOT HERE.

NO. I DON'T SEE ANY *LURKERS*.

DOESN'T LOOK LIKE SHE'S A *TARGET*.

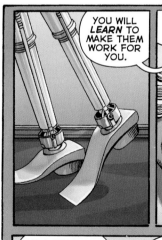

BUT DON'T WORRY. I'LL KEEP ON HER LIKE A *SHADOW*.

MISS SIMMS, I *DON'T* THINK I CAN DO THIS. IT HURTS A LOT.

MAYBE I NEED *MORE* TIME?

VICKI, REMEMBER, BECAUSE YOU'RE NOT *ACCUSTOMED* TO THE NEW PROSTHETICS...

...IT WILL *HURT*, BUT I PROMISE, ONLY FOR A WHILE.

YOU WILL *LEARN* TO MAKE THEM WORK FOR YOU.

IT'S A MATTER OF PATIENCE AND *PERSEVERANCE*.

YEAH. YOU JUST GOTTA *BALANCE* YOURSELF.

YOU CAN DO IT. WE ALL DID.

SEE?

YOU *STOPPED* THINKING ABOUT IT...

...AND NOW YOU'RE *STANDING* AND WALKING.

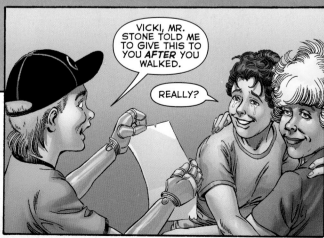

VICKI, MR. STONE TOLD ME TO GIVE THIS TO YOU *AFTER* YOU WALKED.

REALLY?

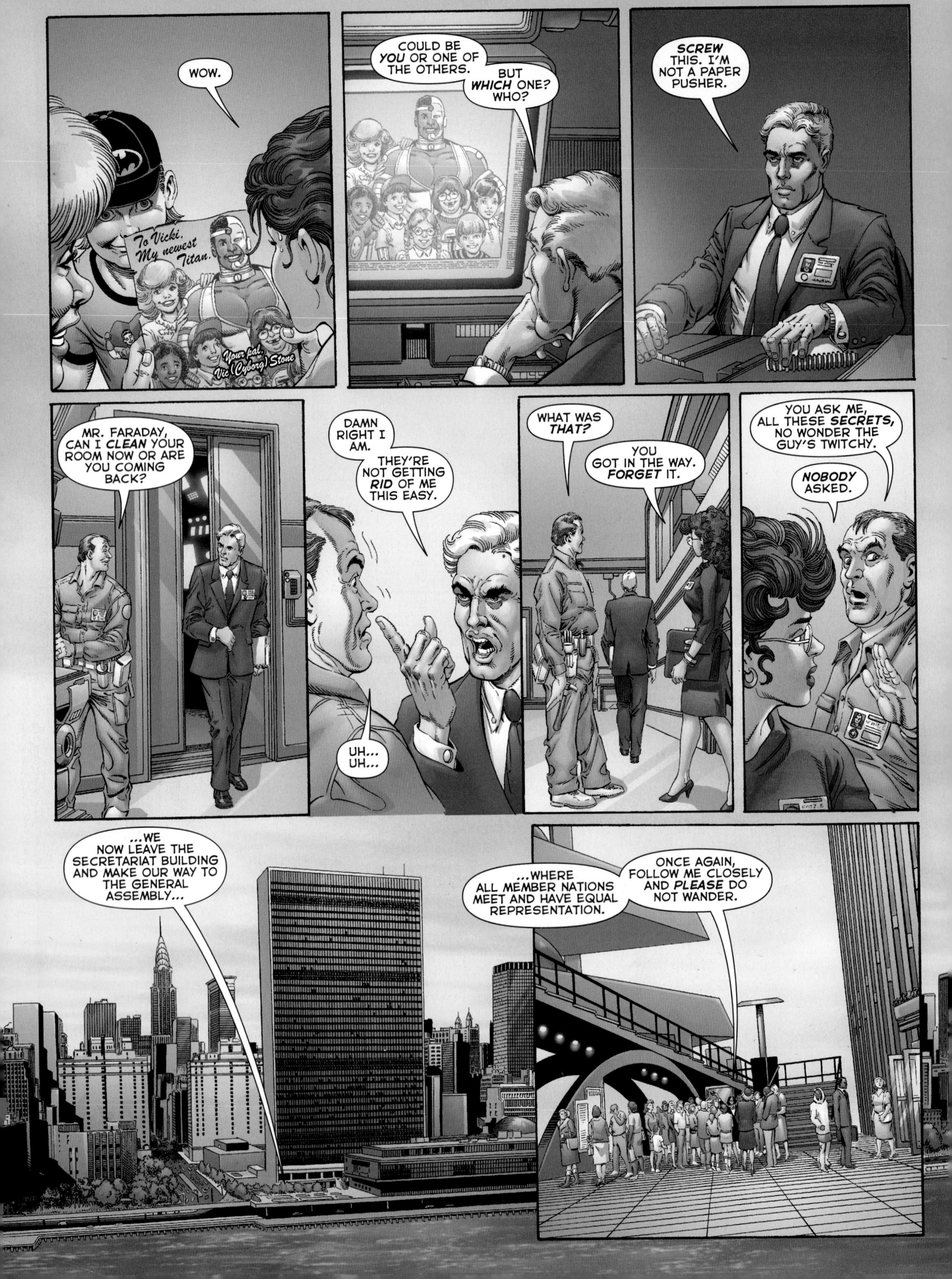
WOW.
To Vicki, My newest Titan.
Your pal, Vic (Cyborg) Stone
COULD BE YOU OR ONE OF THE OTHERS.
BUT WHICH ONE? WHO?
SCREW THIS. I'M NOT A PAPER PUSHER.
MR. FARADAY, CAN I CLEAN YOUR ROOM NOW OR ARE YOU COMING BACK?
DAMN RIGHT I AM.
THEY'RE NOT GETTING RID OF ME THIS EASY.
UH... UH...
WHAT WAS THAT?
YOU GOT IN THE WAY. FORGET IT.
YOU ASK ME, ALL THESE SECRETS, NO WONDER THE GUY'S TWITCHY.
NOBODY ASKED.
...WE NOW LEAVE THE SECRETARIAT BUILDING AND MAKE OUR WAY TO THE GENERAL ASSEMBLY...
...WHERE ALL MEMBER NATIONS MEET AND HAVE EQUAL REPRESENTATION.
ONCE AGAIN, FOLLOW ME CLOSELY AND PLEASE DO NOT WANDER.

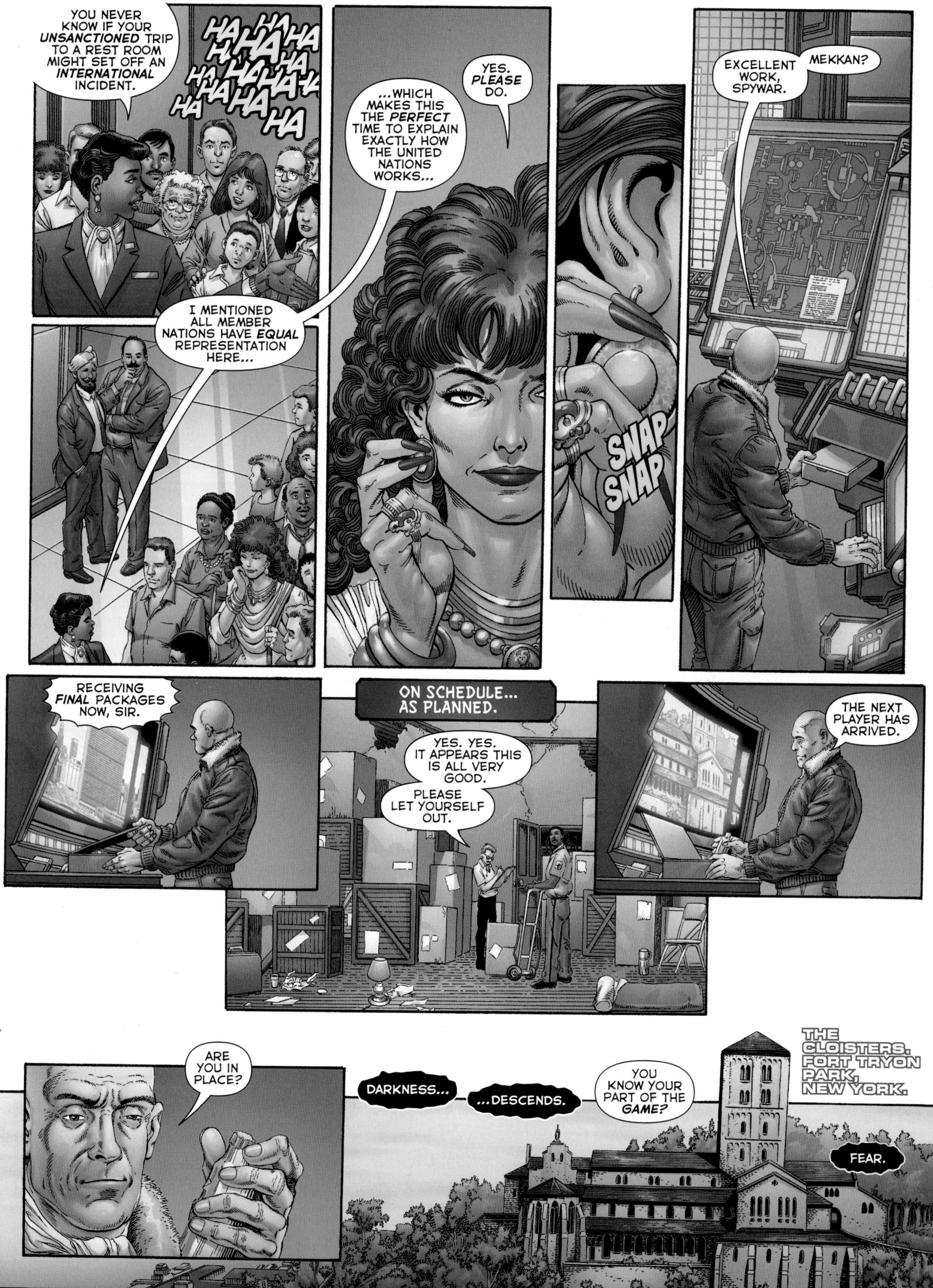

YOU NEVER KNOW IF YOUR UNSANCTIONED TRIP TO A REST ROOM MIGHT SET OFF AN INTERNATIONAL INCIDENT.
HA HA HA HA HA HA HA HA HA HA HA HA HA HA HA
I MENTIONED ALL MEMBER NATIONS HAVE EQUAL REPRESENTATION HERE...
...WHICH MAKES THIS THE PERFECT TIME TO EXPLAIN EXACTLY HOW THE UNITED NATIONS WORKS...
YES. PLEASE DO.
SNAP SNAP
EXCELLENT WORK, SPYWAR.
MEKKAN?
RECEIVING FINAL PACKAGES NOW, SIR.
ON SCHEDULE... AS PLANNED.
YES. YES. IT APPEARS THIS IS ALL VERY GOOD.
PLEASE LET YOURSELF OUT.
THE NEXT PLAYER HAS ARRIVED.
ARE YOU IN PLACE?
DARKNESS...
...DESCENDS.
YOU KNOW YOUR PART OF THE GAME?
THE CLOISTERS. FORT TRYON PARK, NEW YORK.
FEAR.

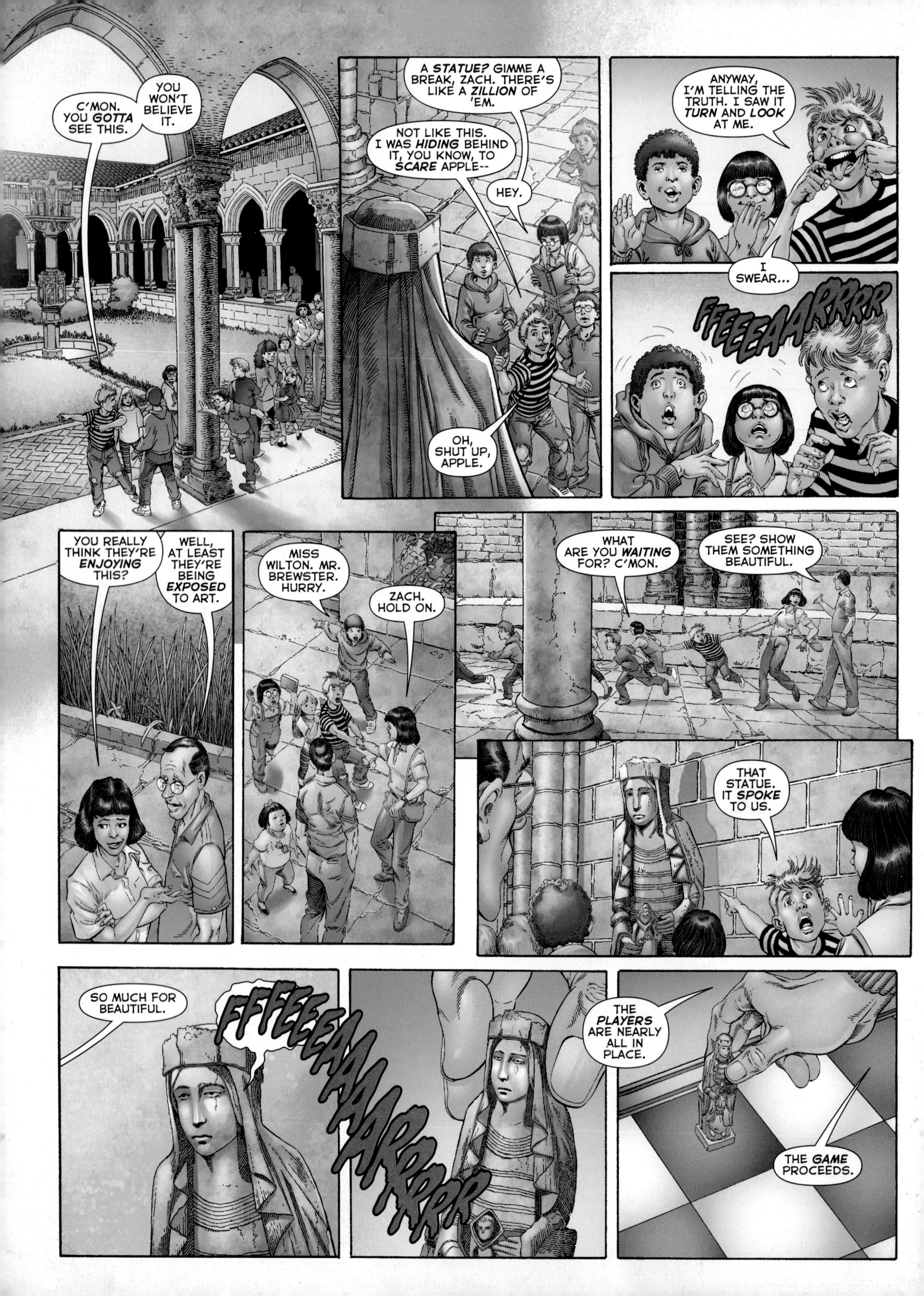
C'MON. YOU GOTTA SEE THIS.
YOU WON'T BELIEVE IT.
A STATUE? GIMME A BREAK, ZACH. THERE'S LIKE A ZILLION OF 'EM.
NOT LIKE THIS. I WAS HIDING BEHIND IT, YOU KNOW, TO SCARE APPLE--
HEY.
OH, SHUT UP, APPLE.
ANYWAY, I'M TELLING THE TRUTH. I SAW IT TURN AND LOOK AT ME.
I SWEAR...
FFEEEAARRRR
YOU REALLY THINK THEY'RE ENJOYING THIS?
WELL, AT LEAST THEY'RE BEING EXPOSED TO ART.
MISS WILTON. MR. BREWSTER. HURRY.
ZACH. HOLD ON.
WHAT ARE YOU WAITING FOR? C'MON.
SEE? SHOW THEM SOMETHING BEAUTIFUL.
THAT STATUE. IT SPOKE TO US.
SO MUCH FOR BEAUTIFUL.
FFFEEEAAAARRRRR
THE PLAYERS ARE NEARLY ALL IN PLACE.
THE GAME PROCEEDS.

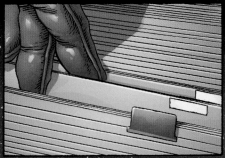

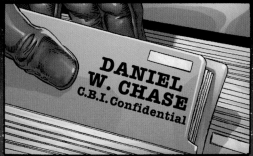

DANIEL W. CHASE
C.B.I. Confidential

YES, SIR. HE'S STILL INSIDE HIS *OFFICE.*

HE'S BEEN ON THE PHONE WITH HIS *WIFE* FOR THE PAST HALF HOUR...

THEY'RE CURRENTLY IMMERSED IN A HEATED DISCUSSION OVER WHAT *MOVIE* TO SEE TONIGHT.

YEAH. THAT'S ABOUT AS MUCH AS THOSE TWO *EVER* ARGUE.

WANT ME TO LET YOU KNOW WHAT MOVIE THEY PICK?

NEARING *WAYNE MANOR.* RUNNING SILENT.

NO SIGN OF THE *PRINCIPALS.*

BUT THE *BUTLER* IS GOING ABOUT HIS WORK.

PRETTY SPRY FOR AN *OLDER GUY.*

ROGER THAT. I'LL STAY IN POSITION.

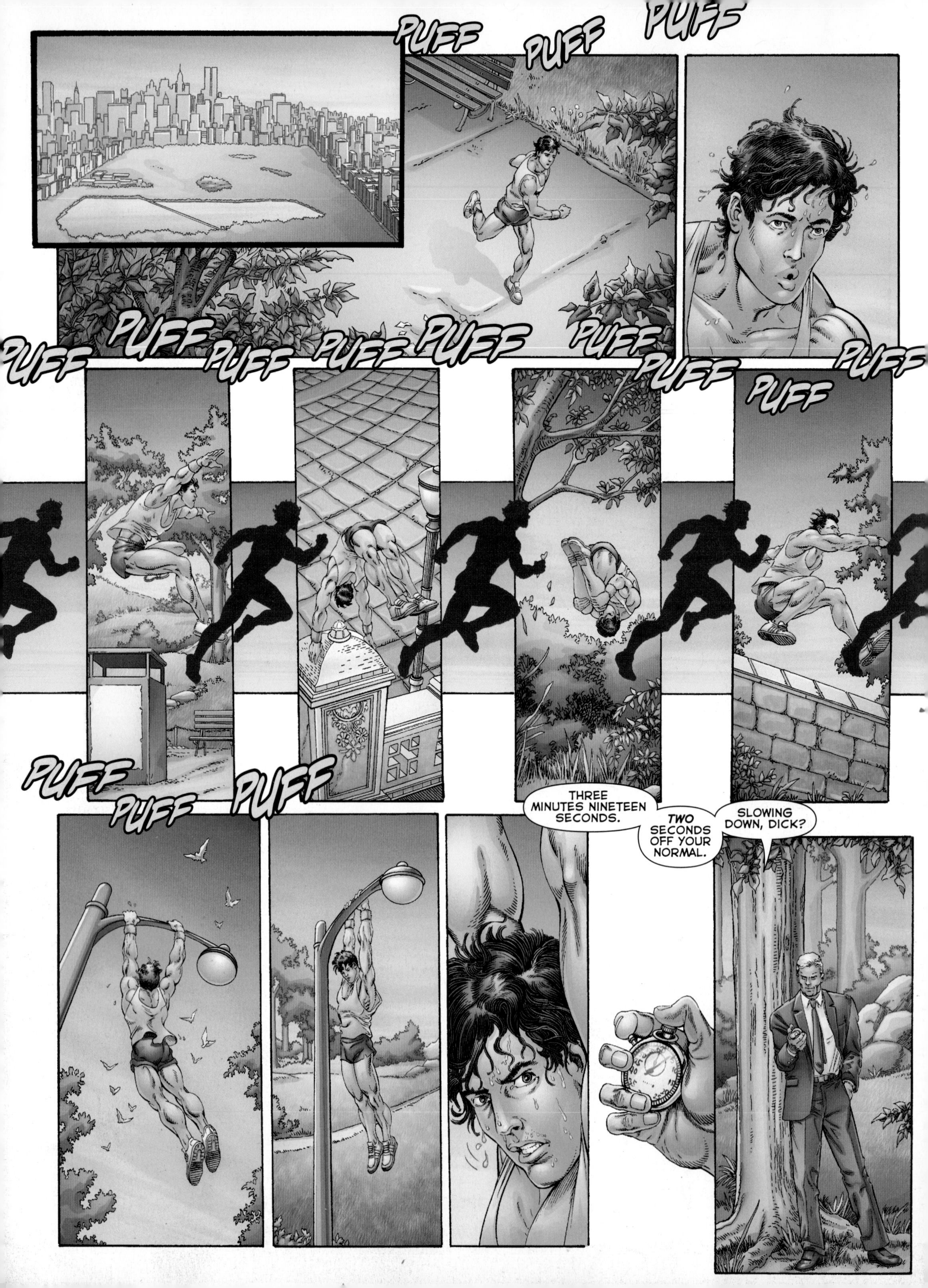
PUFF
PUFF
PUFF
PUFF
PUFF
PUFF
PUFF
PUFF
PUFF
PUFF
PUFF
PUFF
PUFF
PUFF
PUFF
THREE MINUTES NINETEEN SECONDS.
TWO SECONDS OFF YOUR NORMAL.
SLOWING DOWN, DICK?

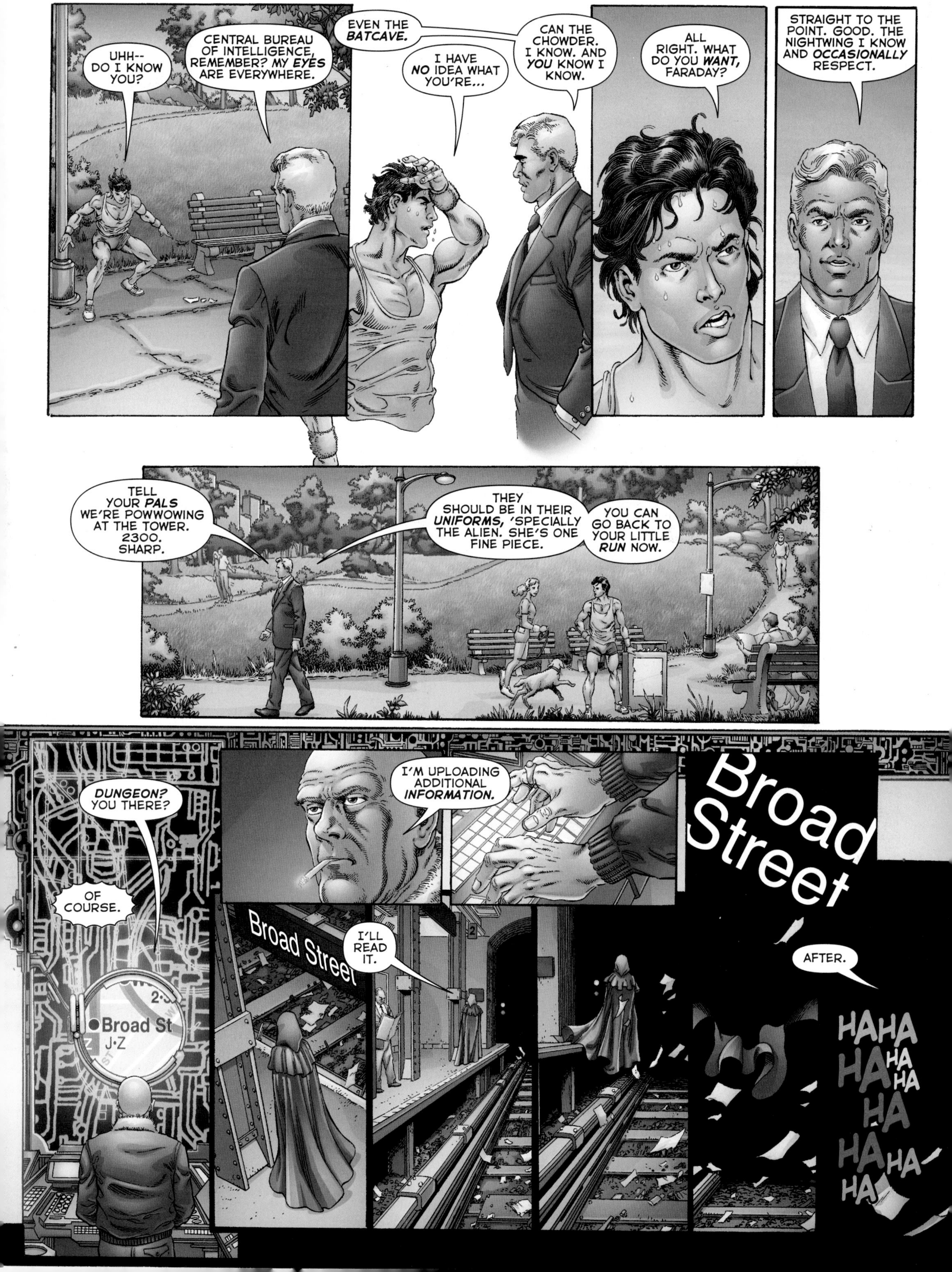
UHH-- DO I KNOW YOU?
CENTRAL BUREAU OF INTELLIGENCE, REMEMBER? MY EYES ARE EVERYWHERE.
EVEN THE BATCAVE.
I HAVE NO IDEA WHAT YOU'RE...
CAN THE CHOWDER. I KNOW. AND YOU KNOW I KNOW.
ALL RIGHT. WHAT DO YOU WANT, FARADAY?
STRAIGHT TO THE POINT. GOOD. THE NIGHTWING I KNOW AND OCCASIONALLY RESPECT.
TELL YOUR PALS WE'RE POWWOWING AT THE TOWER. 2300. SHARP.
THEY SHOULD BE IN THEIR UNIFORMS, 'SPECIALLY THE ALIEN. SHE'S ONE FINE PIECE.
YOU CAN GO BACK TO YOUR LITTLE RUN NOW.
DUNGEON? YOU THERE?
OF COURSE.
I'M UPLOADING ADDITIONAL INFORMATION.
Broad Street
Broad St
J·Z
Broad Street
I'LL READ IT.
AFTER.
HAHA HAHA HAHA HA HAHA HA- HA

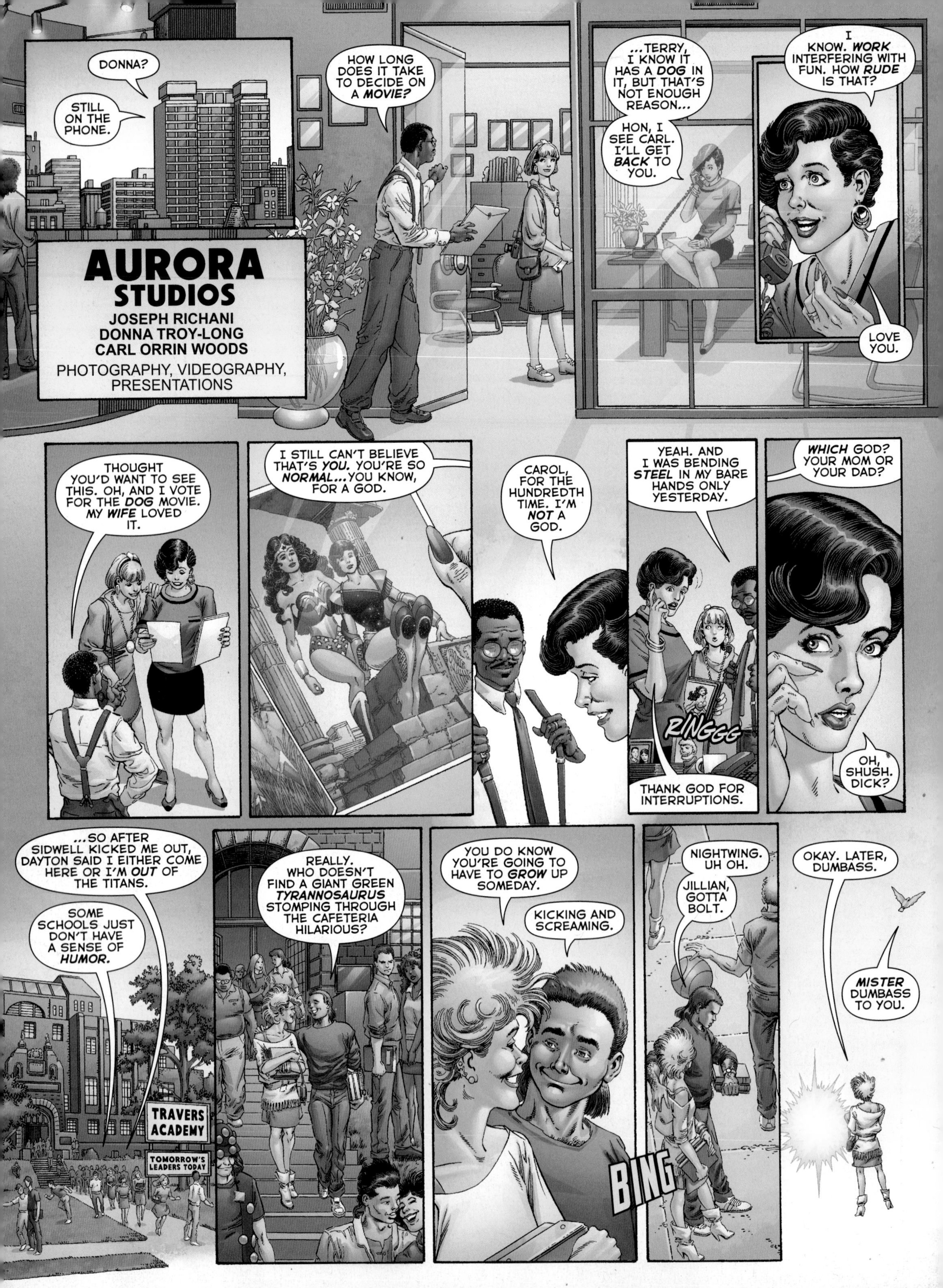
DONNA?
STILL ON THE PHONE.
AURORA STUDIOS
JOSEPH RICHANI
DONNA TROY-LONG
CARL ORRIN WOODS
PHOTOGRAPHY, VIDEOGRAPHY, PRESENTATIONS
HOW LONG DOES IT TAKE TO DECIDE ON A MOVIE?
...TERRY, I KNOW IT HAS A DOG IN IT, BUT THAT'S NOT ENOUGH REASON...
HON, I SEE CARL. I'LL GET BACK TO YOU.
I KNOW. WORK INTERFERING WITH FUN. HOW RUDE IS THAT?
LOVE YOU.
THOUGHT YOU'D WANT TO SEE THIS. OH, AND I VOTE FOR THE DOG MOVIE. MY WIFE LOVED IT.
I STILL CAN'T BELIEVE THAT'S YOU. YOU'RE SO NORMAL...YOU KNOW, FOR A GOD.
CAROL, FOR THE HUNDREDTH TIME. I'M NOT A GOD.
YEAH. AND I WAS BENDING STEEL IN MY BARE HANDS ONLY YESTERDAY.
RINGGG
THANK GOD FOR INTERRUPTIONS.
WHICH GOD? YOUR MOM OR YOUR DAD?
OH, SHUSH. DICK?
...SO AFTER SIDWELL KICKED ME OUT, DAYTON SAID I EITHER COME HERE OR I'M OUT OF THE TITANS.
SOME SCHOOLS JUST DON'T HAVE A SENSE OF HUMOR.
TRAVERS ACADEMY
TOMORROW'S LEADERS TODAY
REALLY. WHO DOESN'T FIND A GIANT GREEN TYRANNOSAURUS STOMPING THROUGH THE CAFETERIA HILARIOUS?
YOU DO KNOW YOU'RE GOING TO HAVE TO GROW UP SOMEDAY.
KICKING AND SCREAMING.
BING
NIGHTWING. UH OH.
JILLIAN, GOTTA BOLT.
OKAY. LATER, DUMBASS.
MISTER DUMBASS TO YOU.

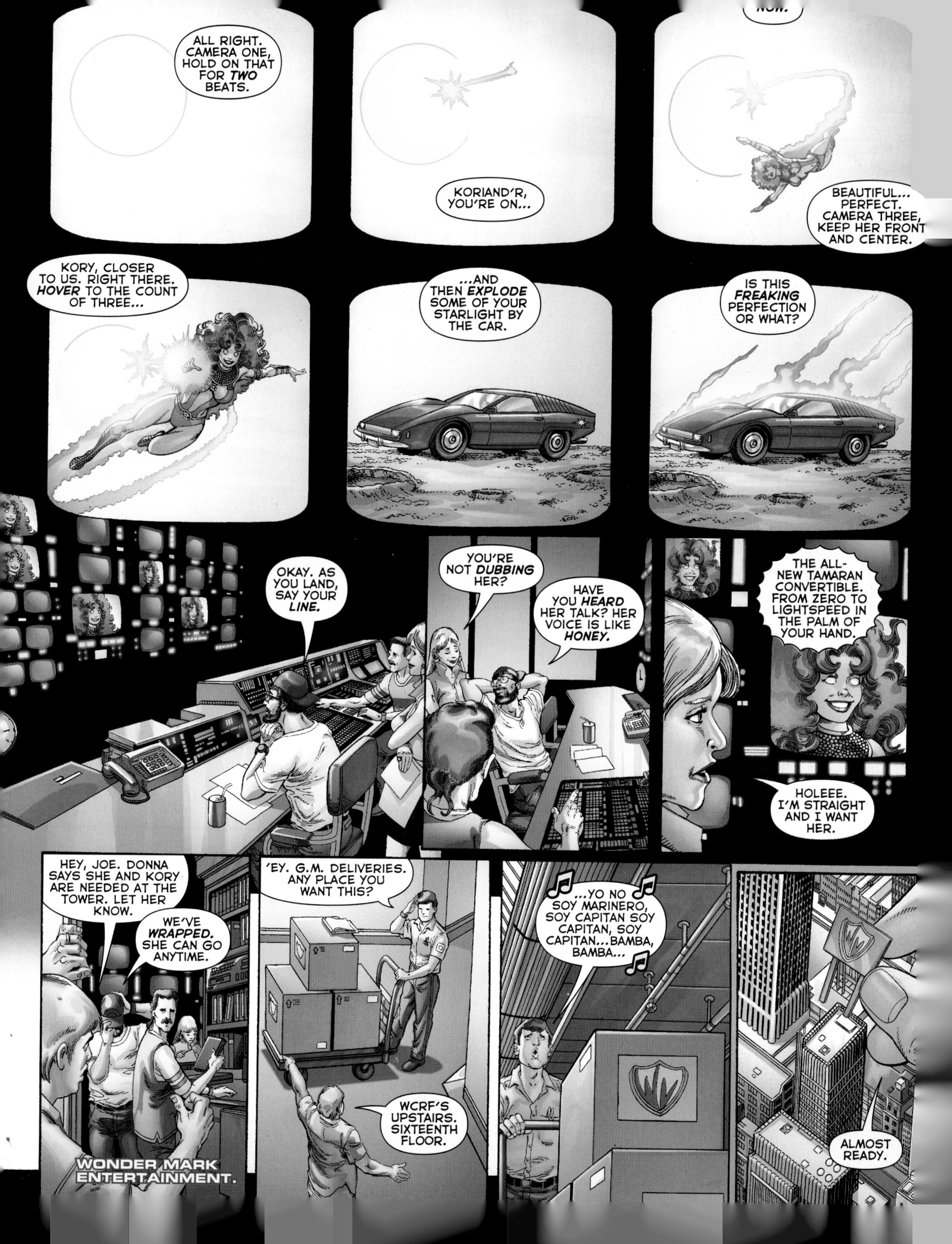
ALL RIGHT. CAMERA ONE, HOLD ON THAT FOR TWO BEATS.
KORIAND'R, YOU'RE ON...
BEAUTIFUL... PERFECT. CAMERA THREE, KEEP HER FRONT AND CENTER.
KORY, CLOSER TO US. RIGHT THERE. HOVER TO THE COUNT OF THREE...
...AND THEN EXPLODE SOME OF YOUR STARLIGHT BY THE CAR.
IS THIS FREAKING PERFECTION OR WHAT?
OKAY. AS YOU LAND, SAY YOUR LINE.
YOU'RE NOT DUBBING HER?
HAVE YOU HEARD HER TALK? HER VOICE IS LIKE HONEY.
THE ALL-NEW TAMARAN CONVERTIBLE. FROM ZERO TO LIGHTSPEED IN THE PALM OF YOUR HAND.
HOLEEE. I'M STRAIGHT AND I WANT HER.
HEY, JOE. DONNA SAYS SHE AND KORY ARE NEEDED AT THE TOWER. LET HER KNOW.
WE'VE WRAPPED. SHE CAN GO ANYTIME.
WONDER MARK ENTERTAINMENT.
'EY. G.M. DELIVERIES. ANY PLACE YOU WANT THIS?
WCRF'S UPSTAIRS. SIXTEENTH FLOOR.
...YO NO SOY MARINERO, SOY CAPITAN SOY CAPITAN, SOY CAPITAN...BAMBA, BAMBA...
ALMOST READY.

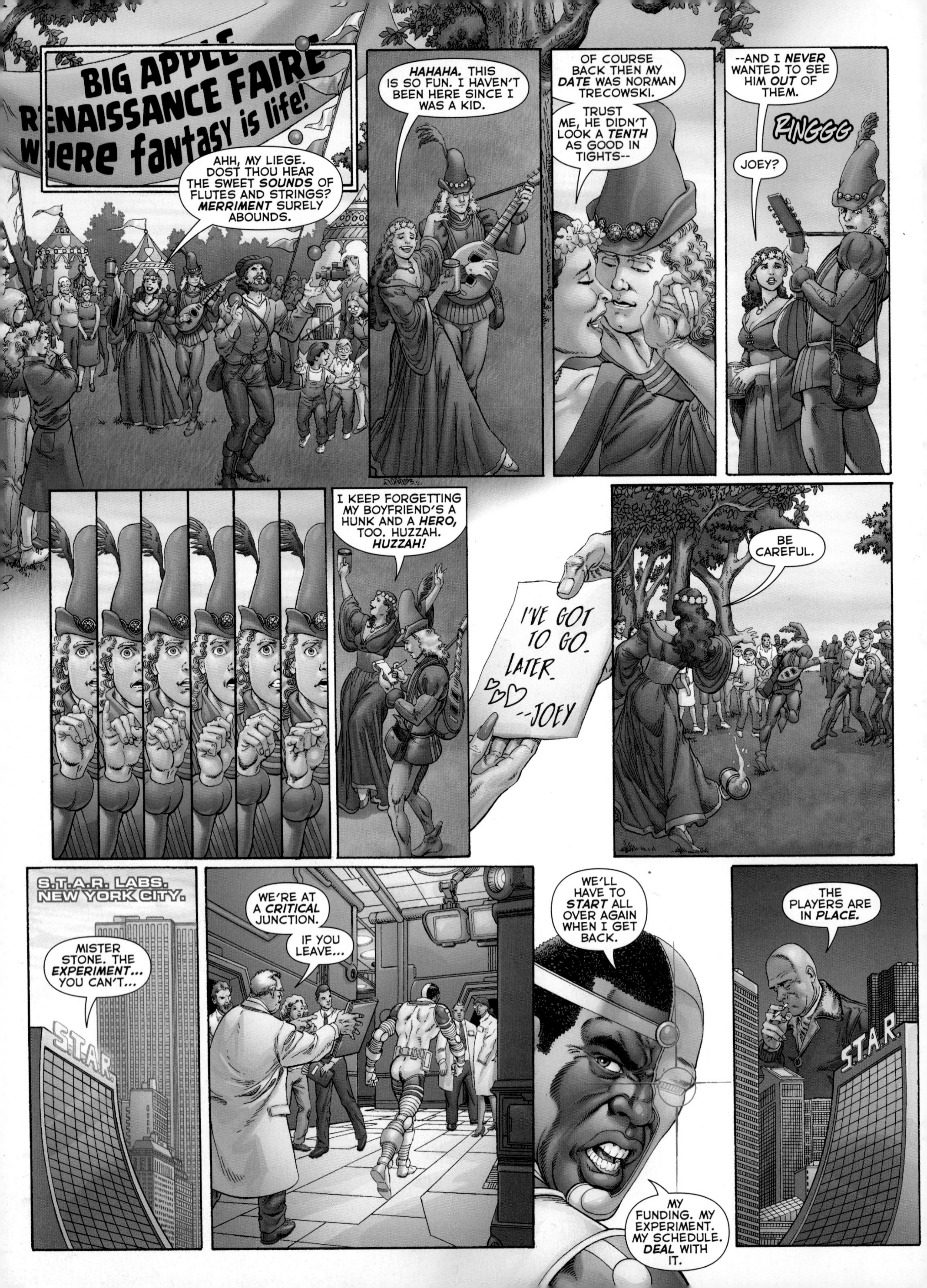
BIG APPLE RENAISSANCE FAIRE where fantasy is life!
AHH, MY LIEGE. DOST THOU HEAR THE SWEET SOUNDS OF FLUTES AND STRINGS? MERRIMENT SURELY ABOUNDS.
HAHAHA. THIS IS SO FUN. I HAVEN'T BEEN HERE SINCE I WAS A KID.
OF COURSE BACK THEN MY DATE WAS NORMAN TRECOWSKI.
TRUST ME, HE DIDN'T LOOK A TENTH AS GOOD IN TIGHTS--
--AND I NEVER WANTED TO SEE HIM OUT OF THEM.
RINGGG
JOEY?
I KEEP FORGETTING MY BOYFRIEND'S A HUNK AND A HERO, TOO. HUZZAH. HUZZAH!
I'VE GOT TO GO. LATER. --JOEY
BE CAREFUL.
S.T.A.R. LABS. NEW YORK CITY.
MISTER STONE. THE EXPERIMENT... YOU CAN'T...
WE'RE AT A CRITICAL JUNCTION.
IF YOU LEAVE...
WE'LL HAVE TO START ALL OVER AGAIN WHEN I GET BACK.
MY FUNDING. MY EXPERIMENT. MY SCHEDULE. DEAL WITH IT.
THE PLAYERS ARE IN PLACE.

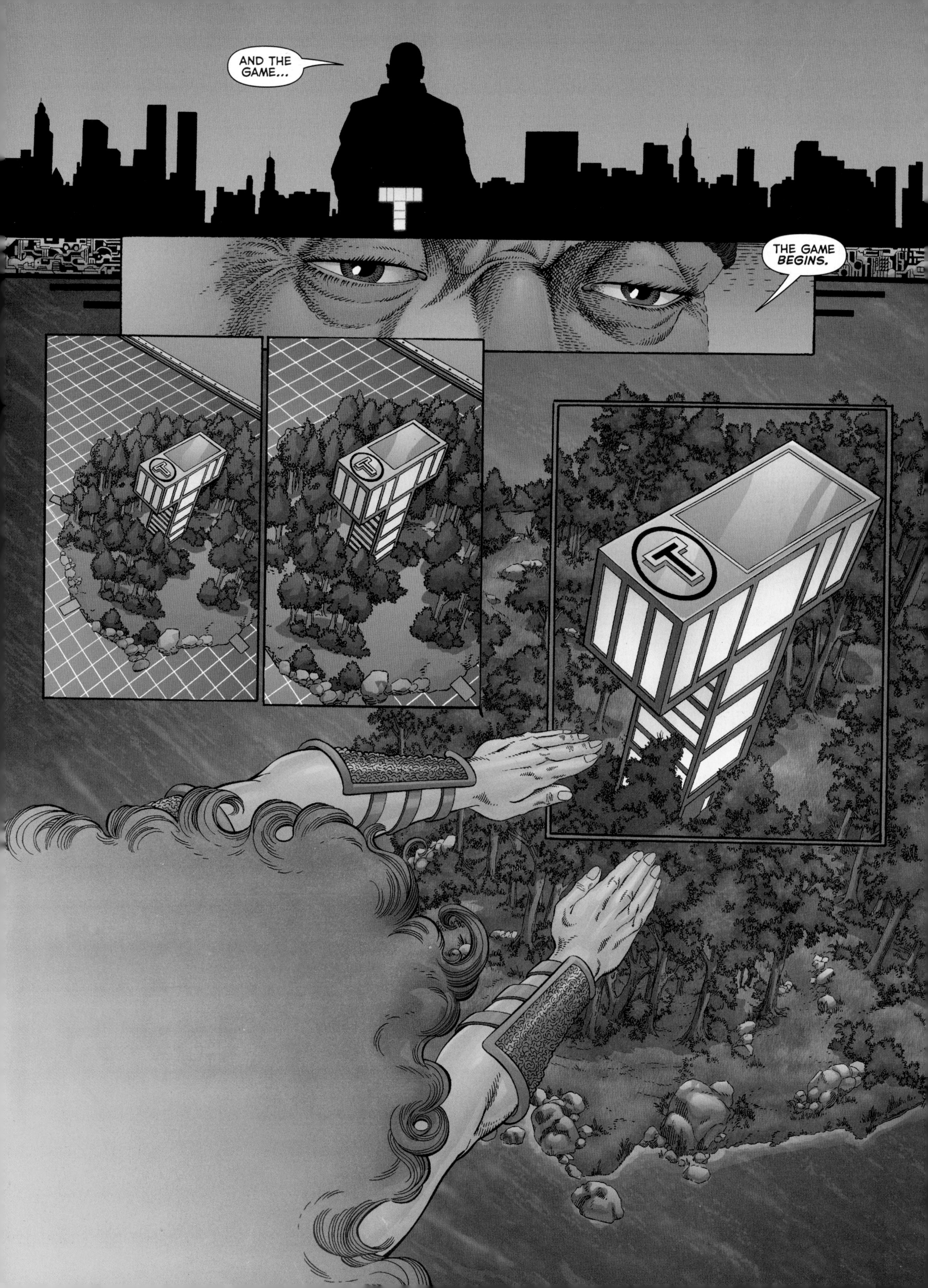
AND THE GAME...
THE GAME BEGINS.

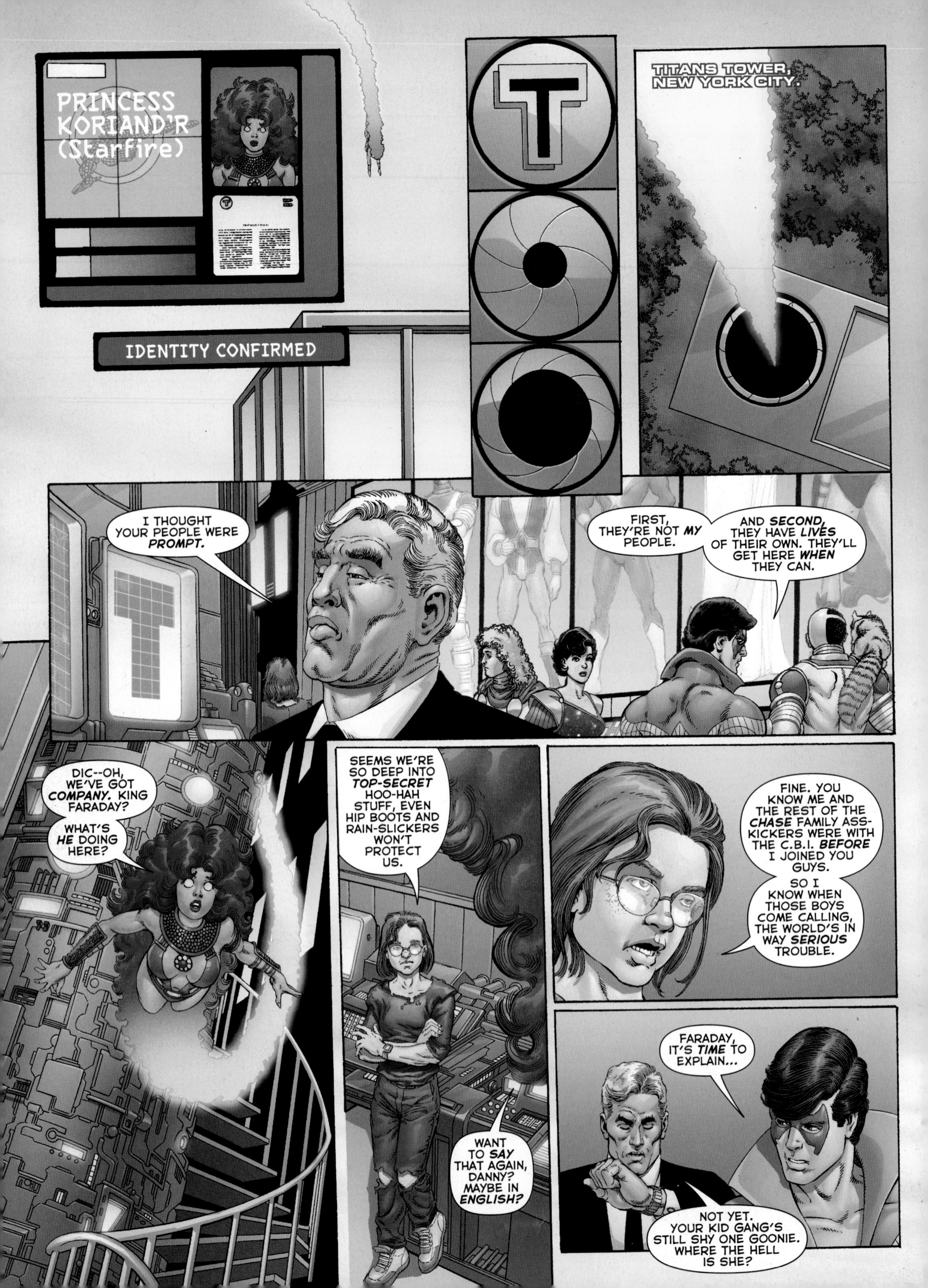
PRINCESS KORIAND'R (Starfire)
IDENTITY CONFIRMED
TITANS TOWER, NEW YORK CITY.
I THOUGHT YOUR PEOPLE WERE *PROMPT.*
FIRST, THEY'RE NOT *MY* PEOPLE.
AND *SECOND,* THEY HAVE *LIVES* OF THEIR OWN. THEY'LL GET HERE *WHEN* THEY CAN.
DIC--OH, WE'VE GOT *COMPANY.* KING FARADAY?
WHAT'S *HE* DOING HERE?
SEEMS WE'RE SO DEEP INTO *TOP-SECRET* HOO-HAH STUFF, EVEN HIP BOOTS AND RAIN-SLICKERS WON'T PROTECT US.
WANT TO *SAY* THAT AGAIN, DANNY? MAYBE IN *ENGLISH?*
FINE. YOU KNOW ME AND THE REST OF THE *CHASE* FAMILY ASS-KICKERS WERE WITH THE C.B.I. *BEFORE* I JOINED YOU GUYS.
SO I KNOW WHEN THOSE BOYS COME CALLING, THE WORLD'S IN WAY *SERIOUS* TROUBLE.
FARADAY, IT'S *TIME* TO EXPLAIN...
NOT YET. YOUR KID GANG'S STILL SHY ONE GOONIE. WHERE THE HELL IS SHE?

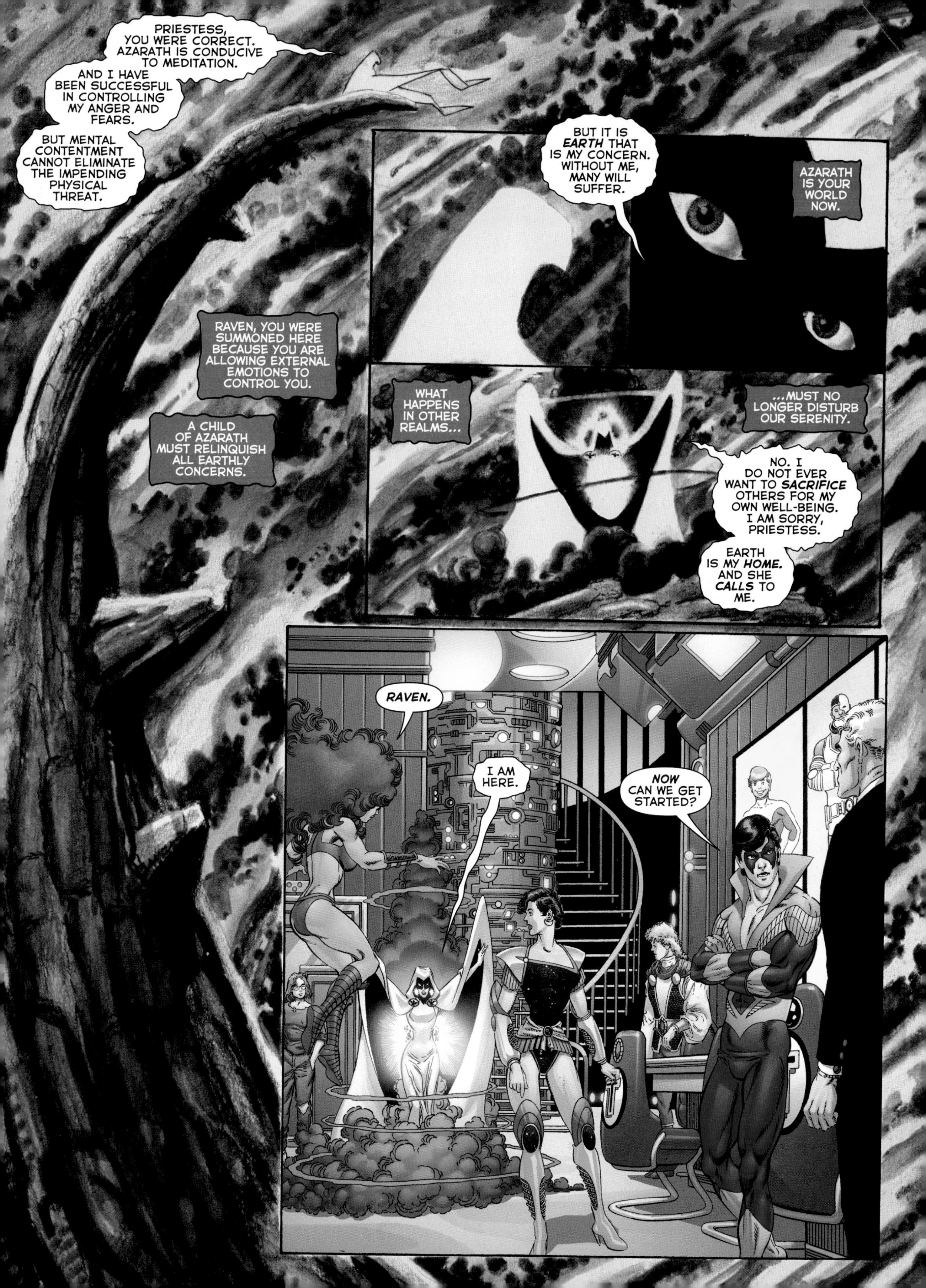
PRIESTESS, YOU WERE CORRECT. AZARATH IS CONDUCIVE TO MEDITATION.
AND I HAVE BEEN SUCCESSFUL IN CONTROLLING MY ANGER AND FEARS.
BUT MENTAL CONTENTMENT CANNOT ELIMINATE THE IMPENDING PHYSICAL THREAT.
BUT IT IS EARTH THAT IS MY CONCERN. WITHOUT ME, MANY WILL SUFFER.
AZARATH IS YOUR WORLD NOW.
RAVEN, YOU WERE SUMMONED HERE BECAUSE YOU ARE ALLOWING EXTERNAL EMOTIONS TO CONTROL YOU.
A CHILD OF AZARATH MUST RELINQUISH ALL EARTHLY CONCERNS.
WHAT HAPPENS IN OTHER REALMS...
...MUST NO LONGER DISTURB OUR SERENITY.
NO. I DO NOT EVER WANT TO SACRIFICE OTHERS FOR MY OWN WELL-BEING. I AM SORRY, PRIESTESS.
EARTH IS MY HOME. AND SHE CALLS TO ME.
RAVEN.
I AM HERE.
NOW CAN WE GET STARTED?

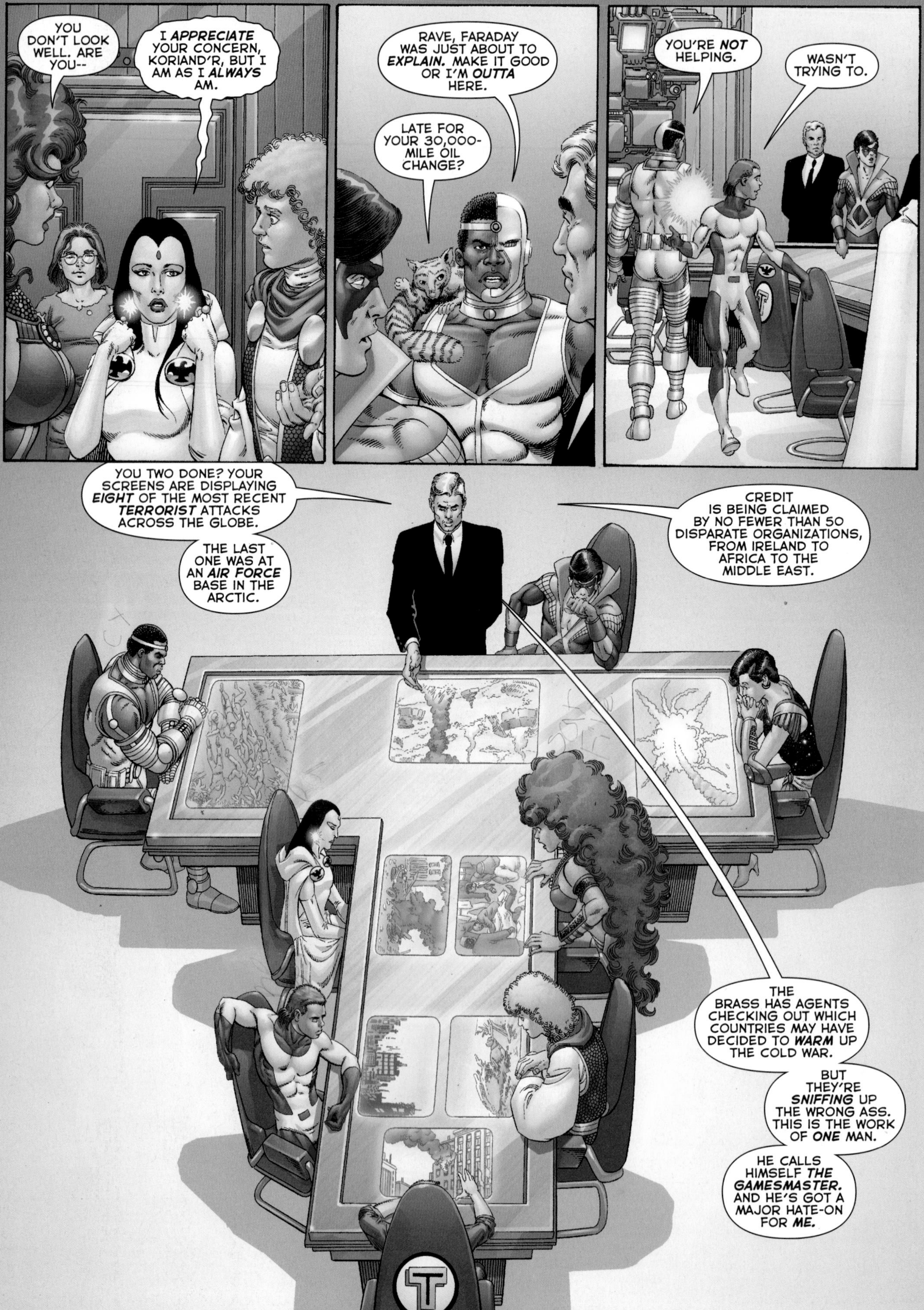

YOU DON'T LOOK WELL. ARE YOU--
I APPRECIATE YOUR CONCERN, KORIAND'R, BUT I AM AS I ALWAYS AM.
RAVE, FARADAY WAS JUST ABOUT TO EXPLAIN. MAKE IT GOOD OR I'M OUTTA HERE.
LATE FOR YOUR 30,000-MILE OIL CHANGE?
YOU'RE NOT HELPING.
WASN'T TRYING TO.
YOU TWO DONE? YOUR SCREENS ARE DISPLAYING EIGHT OF THE MOST RECENT TERRORIST ATTACKS ACROSS THE GLOBE.
THE LAST ONE WAS AT AN AIR FORCE BASE IN THE ARCTIC.
CREDIT IS BEING CLAIMED BY NO FEWER THAN 50 DISPARATE ORGANIZATIONS, FROM IRELAND TO AFRICA TO THE MIDDLE EAST.
THE BRASS HAS AGENTS CHECKING OUT WHICH COUNTRIES MAY HAVE DECIDED TO WARM UP THE COLD WAR.
BUT THEY'RE SNIFFING UP THE WRONG ASS. THIS IS THE WORK OF ONE MAN.
HE CALLS HIMSELF THE GAMESMASTER. AND HE'S GOT A MAJOR HATE-ON FOR ME.

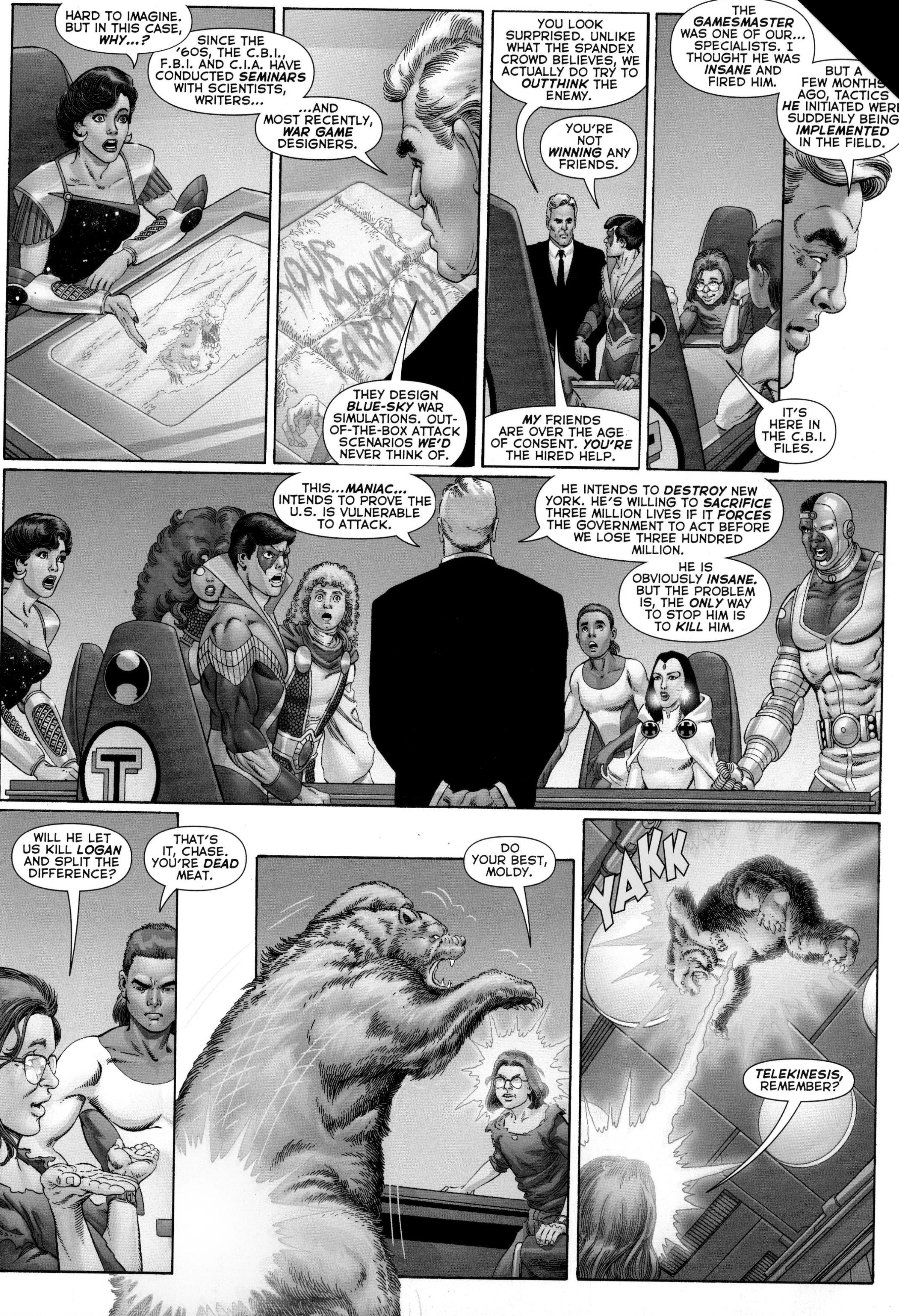
HARD TO IMAGINE. BUT IN THIS CASE, WHY...?
SINCE THE '60S, THE C.B.I., F.B.I. AND C.I.A. HAVE CONDUCTED SEMINARS WITH SCIENTISTS, WRITERS...
...AND MOST RECENTLY, WAR GAME DESIGNERS.
THEY DESIGN BLUE-SKY WAR SIMULATIONS. OUT-OF-THE-BOX ATTACK SCENARIOS WE'D NEVER THINK OF.
YOU LOOK SURPRISED. UNLIKE WHAT THE SPANDEX CROWD BELIEVES, WE ACTUALLY DO TRY TO OUTTHINK THE ENEMY.
YOU'RE NOT WINNING ANY FRIENDS.
MY FRIENDS ARE OVER THE AGE OF CONSENT. YOU'RE THE HIRED HELP.
THE GAMESMASTER WAS ONE OF OUR... SPECIALISTS. I THOUGHT HE WAS INSANE AND FIRED HIM.
BUT A FEW MONTHS AGO, TACTICS HE INITIATED WERE SUDDENLY BEING IMPLEMENTED IN THE FIELD.
IT'S HERE IN THE C.B.I. FILES.
THIS...MANIAC... INTENDS TO PROVE THE U.S. IS VULNERABLE TO ATTACK.
HE INTENDS TO DESTROY NEW YORK. HE'S WILLING TO SACRIFICE THREE MILLION LIVES IF IT FORCES THE GOVERNMENT TO ACT BEFORE WE LOSE THREE HUNDRED MILLION.
HE IS OBVIOUSLY INSANE. BUT THE PROBLEM IS, THE ONLY WAY TO STOP HIM IS TO KILL HIM.
WILL HE LET US KILL LOGAN AND SPLIT THE DIFFERENCE?
THAT'S IT, CHASE. YOU'RE DEAD MEAT.
DO YOUR BEST, MOLDY.
YAKK
TELEKINESIS, REMEMBER?

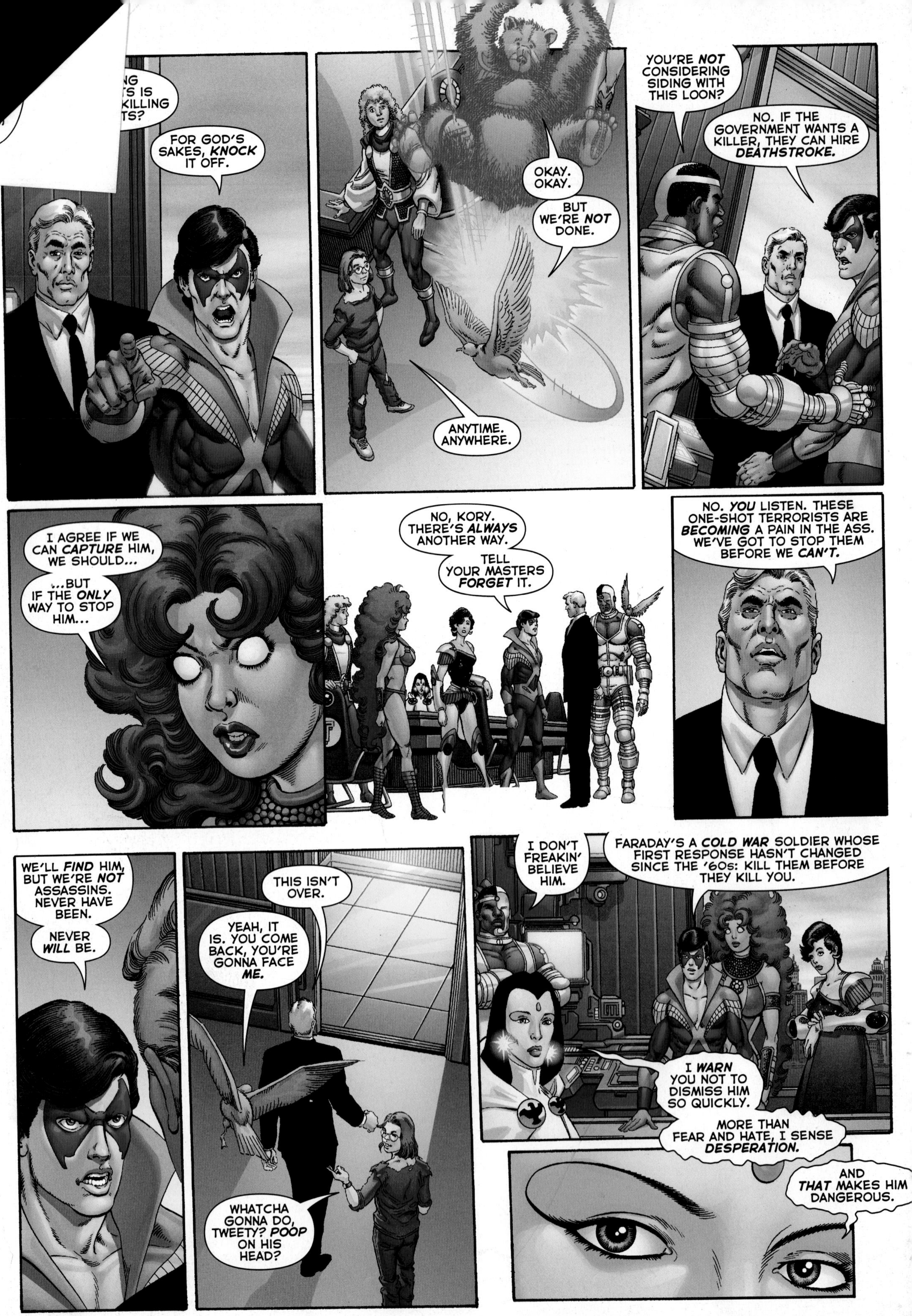
FOR GOD'S SAKES, KNOCK IT OFF.
OKAY. OKAY.
BUT WE'RE NOT DONE.
ANYTIME. ANYWHERE.
YOU'RE NOT CONSIDERING SIDING WITH THIS LOON?
NO. IF THE GOVERNMENT WANTS A KILLER, THEY CAN HIRE DEATHSTROKE.
I AGREE IF WE CAN CAPTURE HIM, WE SHOULD...
...BUT IF THE ONLY WAY TO STOP HIM...
NO, KORY. THERE'S ALWAYS ANOTHER WAY.
TELL YOUR MASTERS FORGET IT.
NO. YOU LISTEN. THESE ONE-SHOT TERRORISTS ARE BECOMING A PAIN IN THE ASS. WE'VE GOT TO STOP THEM BEFORE WE CAN'T.
WE'LL FIND HIM, BUT WE'RE NOT ASSASSINS. NEVER HAVE BEEN.
NEVER WILL BE.
THIS ISN'T OVER.
YEAH, IT IS. YOU COME BACK, YOU'RE GONNA FACE ME.
WHATCHA GONNA DO, TWEETY? POOP ON HIS HEAD?
I DON'T FREAKIN' BELIEVE HIM.
FARADAY'S A COLD WAR SOLDIER WHOSE FIRST RESPONSE HASN'T CHANGED SINCE THE '60s: KILL THEM BEFORE THEY KILL YOU.
I WARN YOU NOT TO DISMISS HIM SO QUICKLY.
MORE THAN FEAR AND HATE, I SENSE DESPERATION.
AND THAT MAKES HIM DANGEROUS.

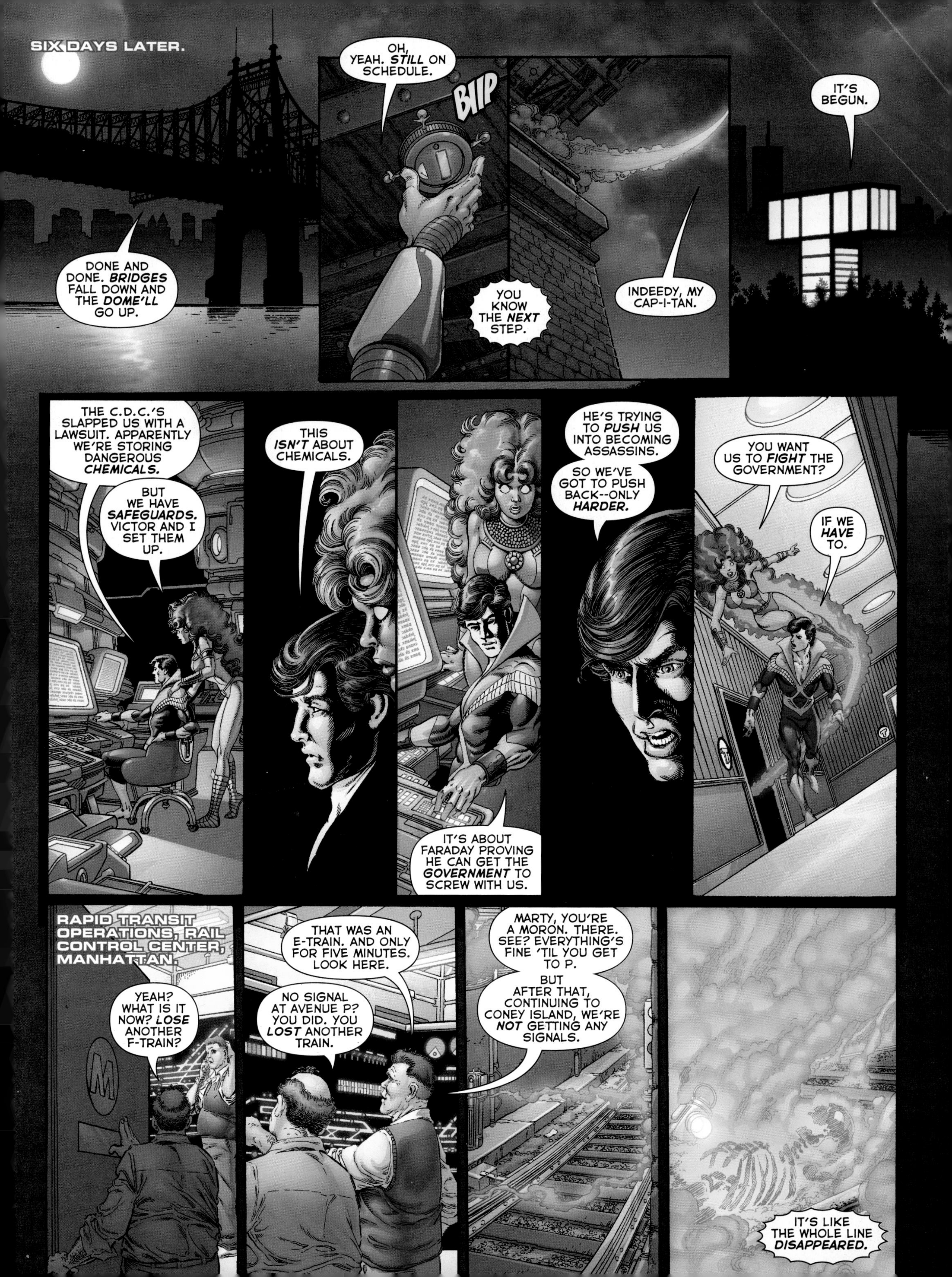
SIX DAYS LATER.
DONE AND DONE. BRIDGES FALL DOWN AND THE DOME'LL GO UP.
OH, YEAH. STILL ON SCHEDULE.
BIIP
YOU KNOW THE NEXT STEP.
INDEEDY, MY CAP-I-TAN.
IT'S BEGUN.
THE C.D.C.'S SLAPPED US WITH A LAWSUIT. APPARENTLY WE'RE STORING DANGEROUS CHEMICALS.
BUT WE HAVE SAFEGUARDS. VICTOR AND I SET THEM UP.
THIS ISN'T ABOUT CHEMICALS.
IT'S ABOUT FARADAY PROVING HE CAN GET THE GOVERNMENT TO SCREW WITH US.
HE'S TRYING TO PUSH US INTO BECOMING ASSASSINS.
SO WE'VE GOT TO PUSH BACK--ONLY HARDER.
YOU WANT US TO FIGHT THE GOVERNMENT?
IF WE HAVE TO.
RAPID TRANSIT OPERATIONS, RAIL CONTROL CENTER, MANHATTAN.
YEAH? WHAT IS IT NOW? LOSE ANOTHER F-TRAIN?
THAT WAS AN E-TRAIN. AND ONLY FOR FIVE MINUTES. LOOK HERE.
NO SIGNAL AT AVENUE P? YOU DID. YOU LOST ANOTHER TRAIN.
MARTY, YOU'RE A MORON. THERE. SEE? EVERYTHING'S FINE 'TIL YOU GET TO P.
BUT AFTER THAT, CONTINUING TO CONEY ISLAND, WE'RE NOT GETTING ANY SIGNALS.
IT'S LIKE THE WHOLE LINE DISAPPEARED.

S.T.A.R. LABS

NO, NO. I DON'T CARE WHAT THEY WANT. WE'RE *NOT* SHUTTING DOWN STONE'S PROJECT.

AMY...

THIS *ISN'T* MY FAULT, DR. CHARLES.

NEW YORK NEWS

DEATH IN SUBWAY accident or murder?

IS THIS YOUR *SIGNATURE?* IT'S IN YOUR HANDWRITING.

THEY *FORCED* ME.

WHO?

THE C.B.I. DID. AN AGENT NAMED FARADAY *THREATENED* TO ELIMINATE GOVERNMENT FUNDING TO OUR *OTHER* RESEARCH UNITS IF I DIDN'T.

I HAVEN'T SEEN DAYTON THIS MAD SINCE THE *LAST* THING I DID THAT MADE HIM THIS MAD.

SIR, I'M SURE YOUR *ACCOUNTING* TEAM...

QUESTOR, THE GOVERNMENT'S NOT AUDITING MY ACCOUNTING TEAM. THEY'RE AUDITING *ME* FOR THE MISTAKES THOSE IDIOTS MADE.

I WANT THEM *FIRED.* I WANT *EVERYONE* FIRED. AND ONE MORE WORD OUT OF YOU, I'LL HAVE YOU FIRE YOURSELF.

I'VE GOT A *BAD* FEELING ABOUT THIS, JILLIAN. AND IT'S SPELLED F-A-R-A-D-A-Y.

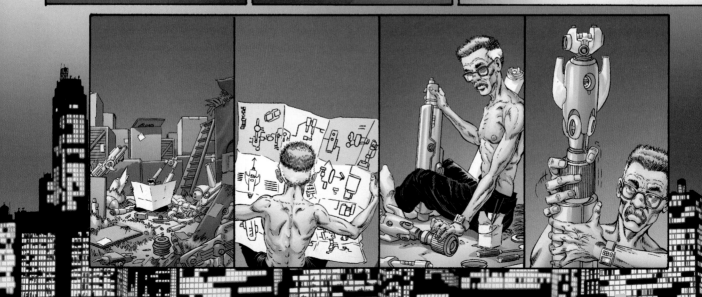

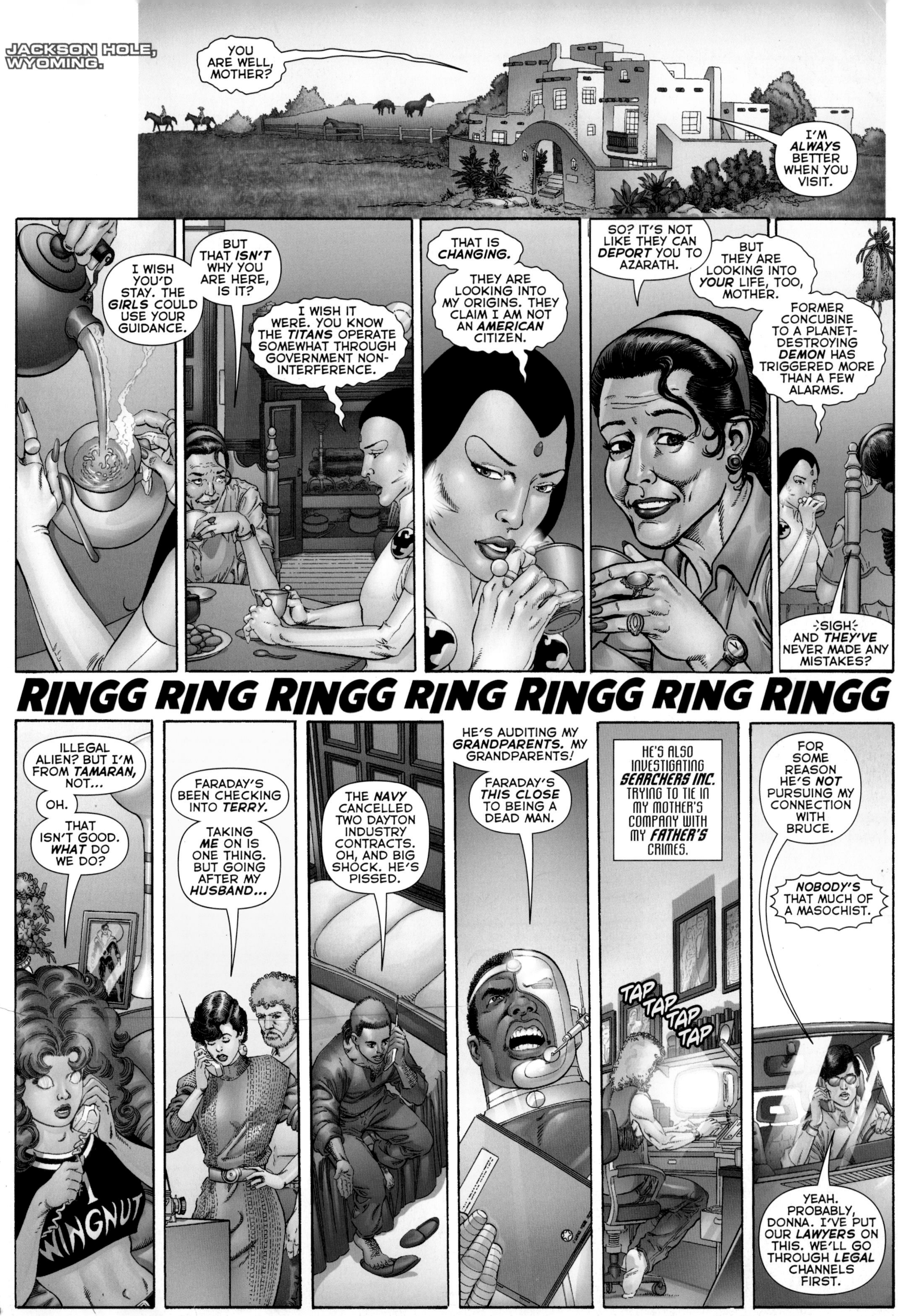
JACKSON HOLE, WYOMING.
YOU ARE WELL, MOTHER?
I'M ALWAYS BETTER WHEN YOU VISIT.
I WISH YOU'D STAY. THE GIRLS COULD USE YOUR GUIDANCE.
BUT THAT ISN'T WHY YOU ARE HERE, IS IT?
I WISH IT WERE. YOU KNOW THE TITANS OPERATE SOMEWHAT THROUGH GOVERNMENT NON-INTERFERENCE.
THAT IS CHANGING.
THEY ARE LOOKING INTO MY ORIGINS. THEY CLAIM I AM NOT AN AMERICAN CITIZEN.
SO? IT'S NOT LIKE THEY CAN DEPORT YOU TO AZARATH.
BUT THEY ARE LOOKING INTO YOUR LIFE, TOO, MOTHER.
FORMER CONCUBINE TO A PLANET-DESTROYING DEMON HAS TRIGGERED MORE THAN A FEW ALARMS.
SIGH AND THEY'VE NEVER MADE ANY MISTAKES?
RINGG RING RINGG RING RINGG RING RINGG
ILLEGAL ALIEN? BUT I'M FROM TAMARAN, NOT...
OH.
THAT ISN'T GOOD. WHAT DO WE DO?
WINGNUT
FARADAY'S BEEN CHECKING INTO TERRY.
TAKING ME ON IS ONE THING. BUT GOING AFTER MY HUSBAND...
THE NAVY CANCELLED TWO DAYTON INDUSTRY CONTRACTS. OH, AND BIG SHOCK. HE'S PISSED.
HE'S AUDITING MY GRANDPARENTS. MY GRANDPARENTS!
FARADAY'S THIS CLOSE TO BEING A DEAD MAN.
HE'S ALSO INVESTIGATING SEARCHERS INC. TRYING TO TIE IN MY MOTHER'S COMPANY WITH MY FATHER'S CRIMES.
TAP TAP TAP TAP
FOR SOME REASON HE'S NOT PURSUING MY CONNECTION WITH BRUCE.
NOBODY'S THAT MUCH OF A MASOCHIST.
YEAH. PROBABLY, DONNA. I'VE PUT OUR LAWYERS ON THIS. WE'LL GO THROUGH LEGAL CHANNELS FIRST.

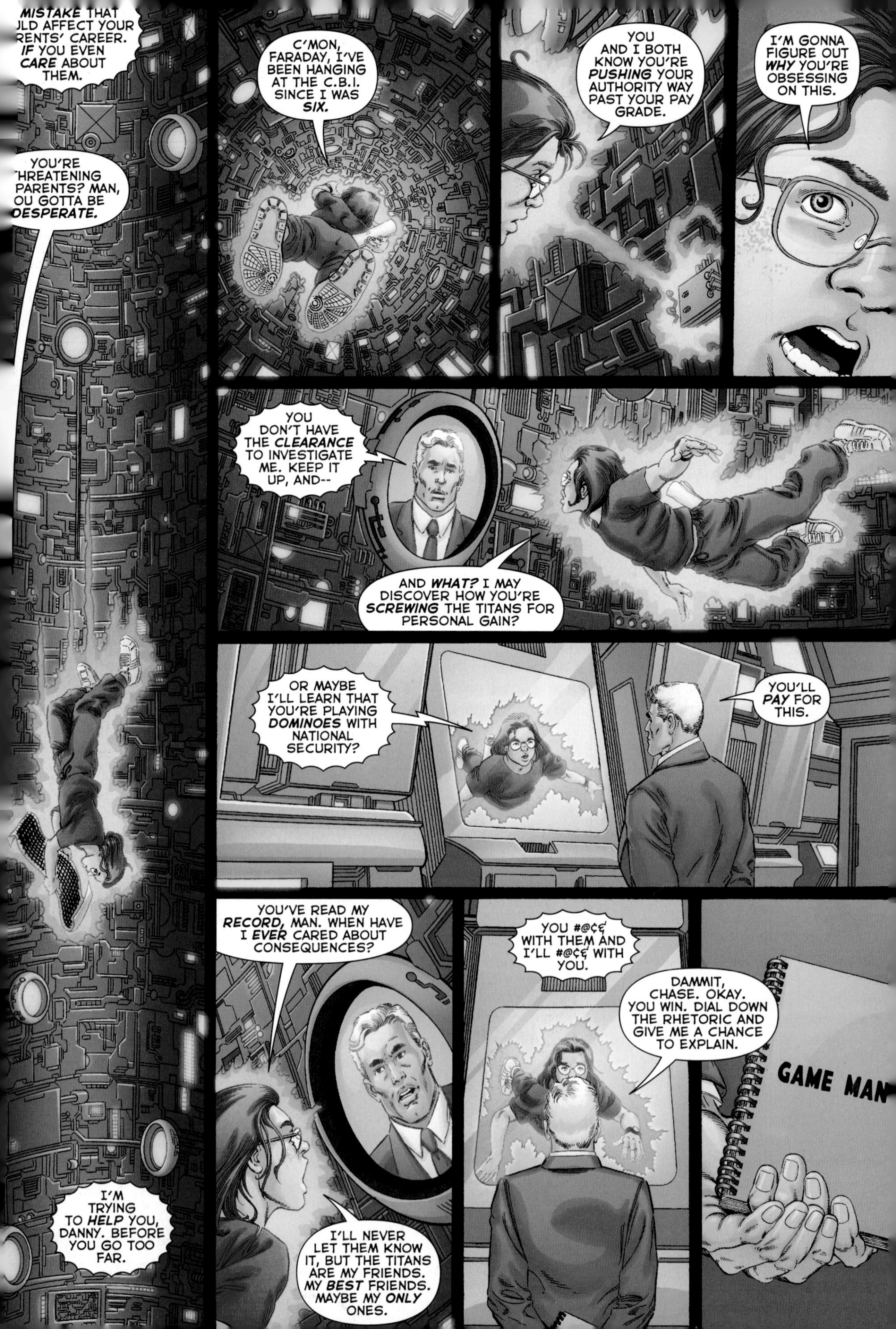

MISTAKE THAT
ULD AFFECT YOUR
RENTS' CAREER.
IF YOU EVEN
CARE ABOUT
THEM.
YOU'RE
THREATENING
PARENTS? MAN,
OU GOTTA BE
DESPERATE.
C'MON, FARADAY, I'VE BEEN HANGING AT THE C.B.I. SINCE I WAS SIX.
YOU AND I BOTH KNOW YOU'RE PUSHING YOUR AUTHORITY WAY PAST YOUR PAY GRADE.
I'M GONNA FIGURE OUT WHY YOU'RE OBSESSING ON THIS.
YOU DON'T HAVE THE CLEARANCE TO INVESTIGATE ME. KEEP IT UP, AND--
AND WHAT? I MAY DISCOVER HOW YOU'RE SCREWING THE TITANS FOR PERSONAL GAIN?
OR MAYBE I'LL LEARN THAT YOU'RE PLAYING DOMINOES WITH NATIONAL SECURITY?
YOU'LL PAY FOR THIS.
I'M TRYING TO HELP YOU, DANNY. BEFORE YOU GO TOO FAR.
YOU'VE READ MY RECORD, MAN. WHEN HAVE I EVER CARED ABOUT CONSEQUENCES?
I'LL NEVER LET THEM KNOW IT, BUT THE TITANS ARE MY FRIENDS. MY BEST FRIENDS. MAYBE MY ONLY ONES.
YOU #@¢$ WITH THEM AND I'LL #@¢$ WITH YOU.
DAMMIT, CHASE. OKAY. YOU WIN. DIAL DOWN THE RHETORIC AND GIVE ME A CHANCE TO EXPLAIN.
GAME MAN

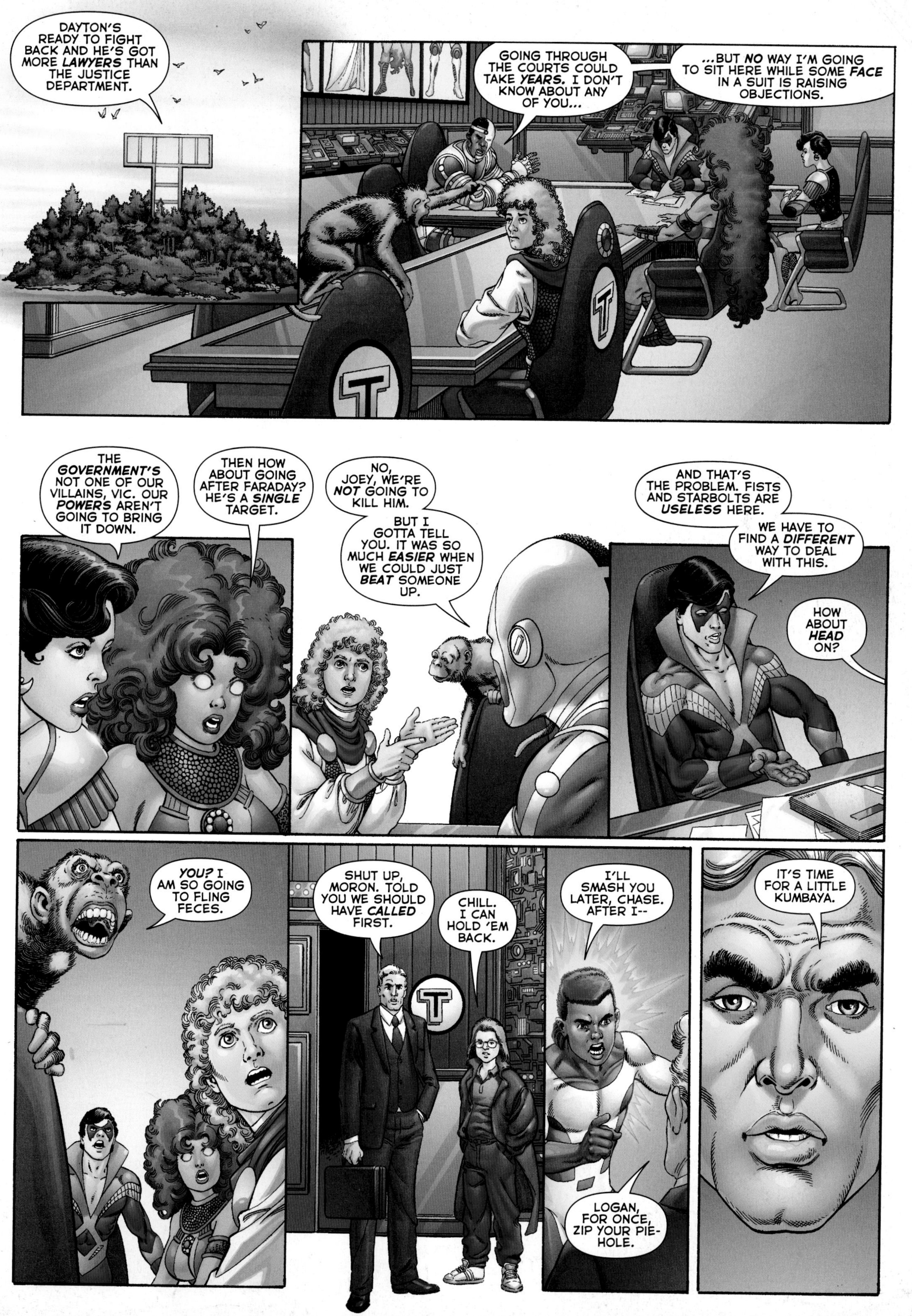
DAYTON'S READY TO FIGHT BACK AND HE'S GOT MORE LAWYERS THAN THE JUSTICE DEPARTMENT.
GOING THROUGH THE COURTS COULD TAKE YEARS. I DON'T KNOW ABOUT ANY OF YOU...
...BUT NO WAY I'M GOING TO SIT HERE WHILE SOME FACE IN A SUIT IS RAISING OBJECTIONS.
THE GOVERNMENT'S NOT ONE OF OUR VILLAINS, VIC. OUR POWERS AREN'T GOING TO BRING IT DOWN.
THEN HOW ABOUT GOING AFTER FARADAY? HE'S A SINGLE TARGET.
NO, JOEY, WE'RE NOT GOING TO KILL HIM.
BUT I GOTTA TELL YOU. IT WAS SO MUCH EASIER WHEN WE COULD JUST BEAT SOMEONE UP.
AND THAT'S THE PROBLEM. FISTS AND STARBOLTS ARE USELESS HERE.
WE HAVE TO FIND A DIFFERENT WAY TO DEAL WITH THIS.
HOW ABOUT HEAD ON?
YOU? I AM SO GOING TO FLING FECES.
SHUT UP, MORON. TOLD YOU WE SHOULD HAVE CALLED FIRST.
CHILL. I CAN HOLD 'EM BACK.
I'LL SMASH YOU LATER, CHASE. AFTER I--
LOGAN, FOR ONCE, ZIP YOUR PIE-HOLE.
IT'S TIME FOR A LITTLE KUMBAYA.

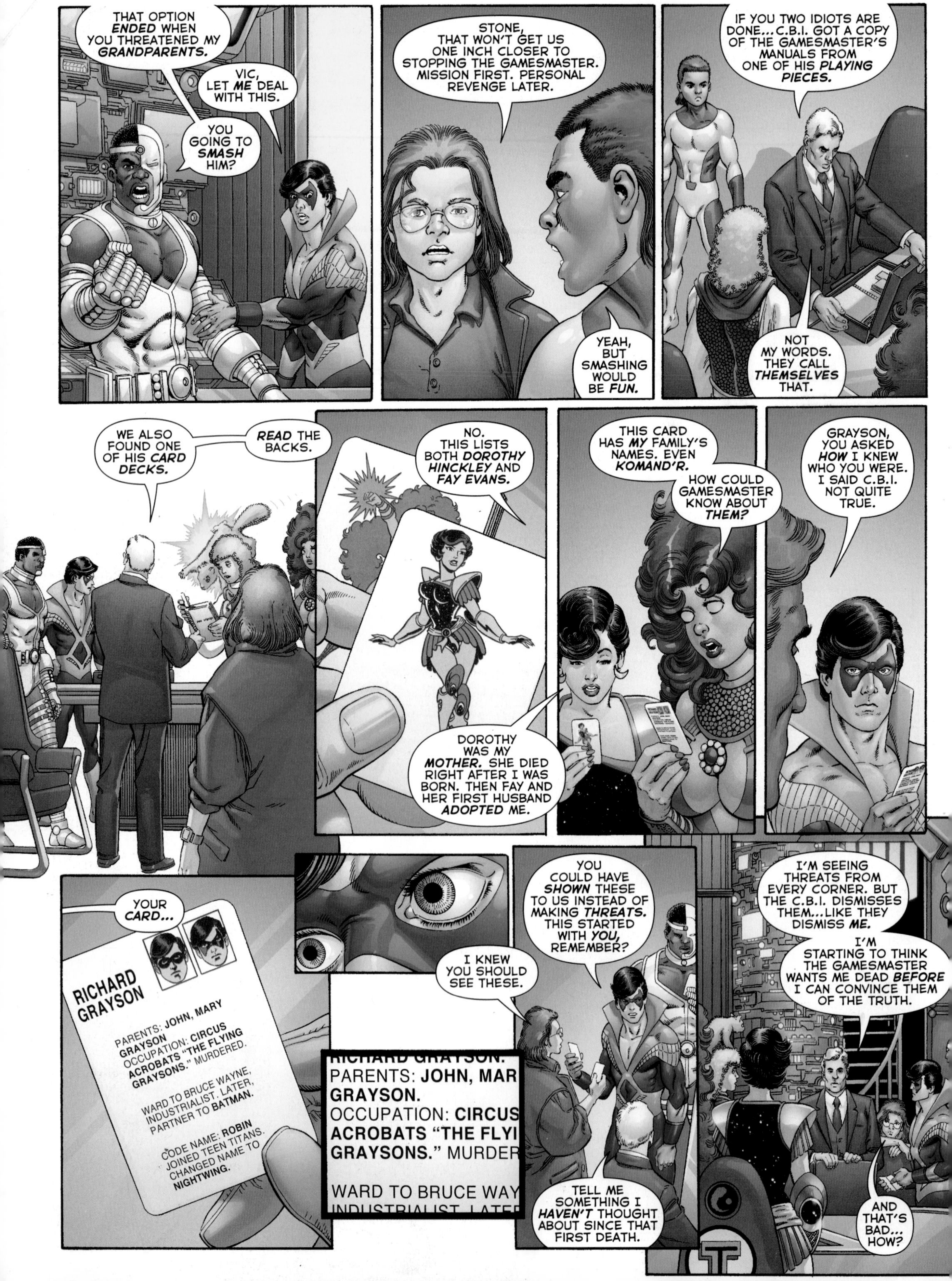
THAT OPTION ENDED WHEN YOU THREATENED MY GRANDPARENTS.
VIC, LET ME DEAL WITH THIS.
YOU GOING TO SMASH HIM?
STONE, THAT WON'T GET US ONE INCH CLOSER TO STOPPING THE GAMESMASTER. MISSION FIRST. PERSONAL REVENGE LATER.
YEAH, BUT SMASHING WOULD BE FUN.
IF YOU TWO IDIOTS ARE DONE... C.B.I. GOT A COPY OF THE GAMESMASTER'S MANUALS FROM ONE OF HIS PLAYING PIECES.
NOT MY WORDS. THEY CALL THEMSELVES THAT.
WE ALSO FOUND ONE OF HIS CARD DECKS.
READ THE BACKS.
NO. THIS LISTS BOTH DOROTHY HINCKLEY AND FAY EVANS.
DOROTHY WAS MY MOTHER. SHE DIED RIGHT AFTER I WAS BORN. THEN FAY AND HER FIRST HUSBAND ADOPTED ME.
THIS CARD HAS MY FAMILY'S NAMES. EVEN KOMAND'R.
HOW COULD GAMESMASTER KNOW ABOUT THEM?
GRAYSON, YOU ASKED HOW I KNEW WHO YOU WERE. I SAID C.B.I. NOT QUITE TRUE.
YOUR CARD...
RICHARD GRAYSON
PARENTS: JOHN, MARY GRAYSON
OCCUPATION: CIRCUS ACROBATS "THE FLYING GRAYSONS." MURDERED.
WARD TO BRUCE WAYNE, INDUSTRIALIST. LATER, PARTNER TO BATMAN.
CODE NAME: ROBIN
JOINED TEEN TITANS. CHANGED NAME TO NIGHTWING.
PARENTS: JOHN, MAR
GRAYSON.
OCCUPATION: CIRCUS
ACROBATS "THE FLYI
GRAYSONS." MURDER
WARD TO BRUCE WAY
I KNEW YOU SHOULD SEE THESE.
YOU COULD HAVE SHOWN THESE TO US INSTEAD OF MAKING THREATS. THIS STARTED WITH YOU, REMEMBER?
TELL ME SOMETHING I HAVEN'T THOUGHT ABOUT SINCE THAT FIRST DEATH.
I'M SEEING THREATS FROM EVERY CORNER. BUT THE C.B.I. DISMISSES THEM... LIKE THEY DISMISS ME.
I'M STARTING TO THINK THE GAMESMASTER WANTS ME DEAD BEFORE I CAN CONVINCE THEM OF THE TRUTH.
AND THAT'S BAD... HOW?

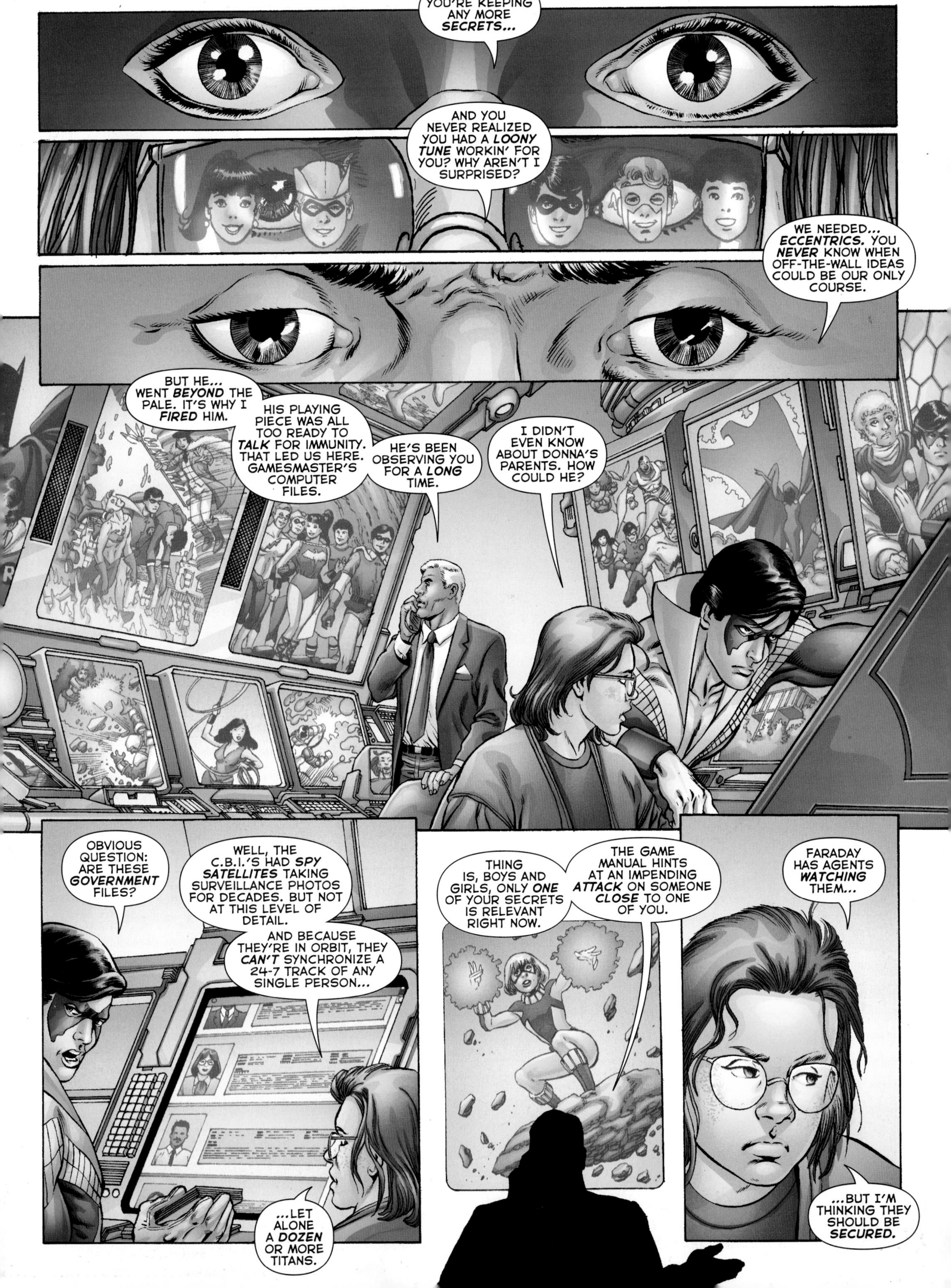

FARADAY, IF YOU'RE KEEPING ANY MORE SECRETS...
AND YOU NEVER REALIZED YOU HAD A LOONY TUNE WORKIN' FOR YOU? WHY AREN'T I SURPRISED?
WE NEEDED... ECCENTRICS. YOU NEVER KNOW WHEN OFF-THE-WALL IDEAS COULD BE OUR ONLY COURSE.
BUT HE... WENT BEYOND THE PALE. IT'S WHY I FIRED HIM.
HIS PLAYING PIECE WAS ALL TOO READY TO TALK FOR IMMUNITY. THAT LED US HERE. GAMESMASTER'S COMPUTER FILES.
HE'S BEEN OBSERVING YOU FOR A LONG TIME.
I DIDN'T EVEN KNOW ABOUT DONNA'S PARENTS. HOW COULD HE?
OBVIOUS QUESTION: ARE THESE GOVERNMENT FILES?
WELL, THE C.B.I.'S HAD SPY SATELLITES TAKING SURVEILLANCE PHOTOS FOR DECADES. BUT NOT AT THIS LEVEL OF DETAIL.
AND BECAUSE THEY'RE IN ORBIT, THEY CAN'T SYNCHRONIZE A 24-7 TRACK OF ANY SINGLE PERSON...
...LET ALONE A DOZEN OR MORE TITANS.
THING IS, BOYS AND GIRLS, ONLY ONE OF YOUR SECRETS IS RELEVANT RIGHT NOW.
THE GAME MANUAL HINTS AT AN IMPENDING ATTACK ON SOMEONE CLOSE TO ONE OF YOU.
FARADAY HAS AGENTS WATCHING THEM...
...BUT I'M THINKING THEY SHOULD BE SECURED.

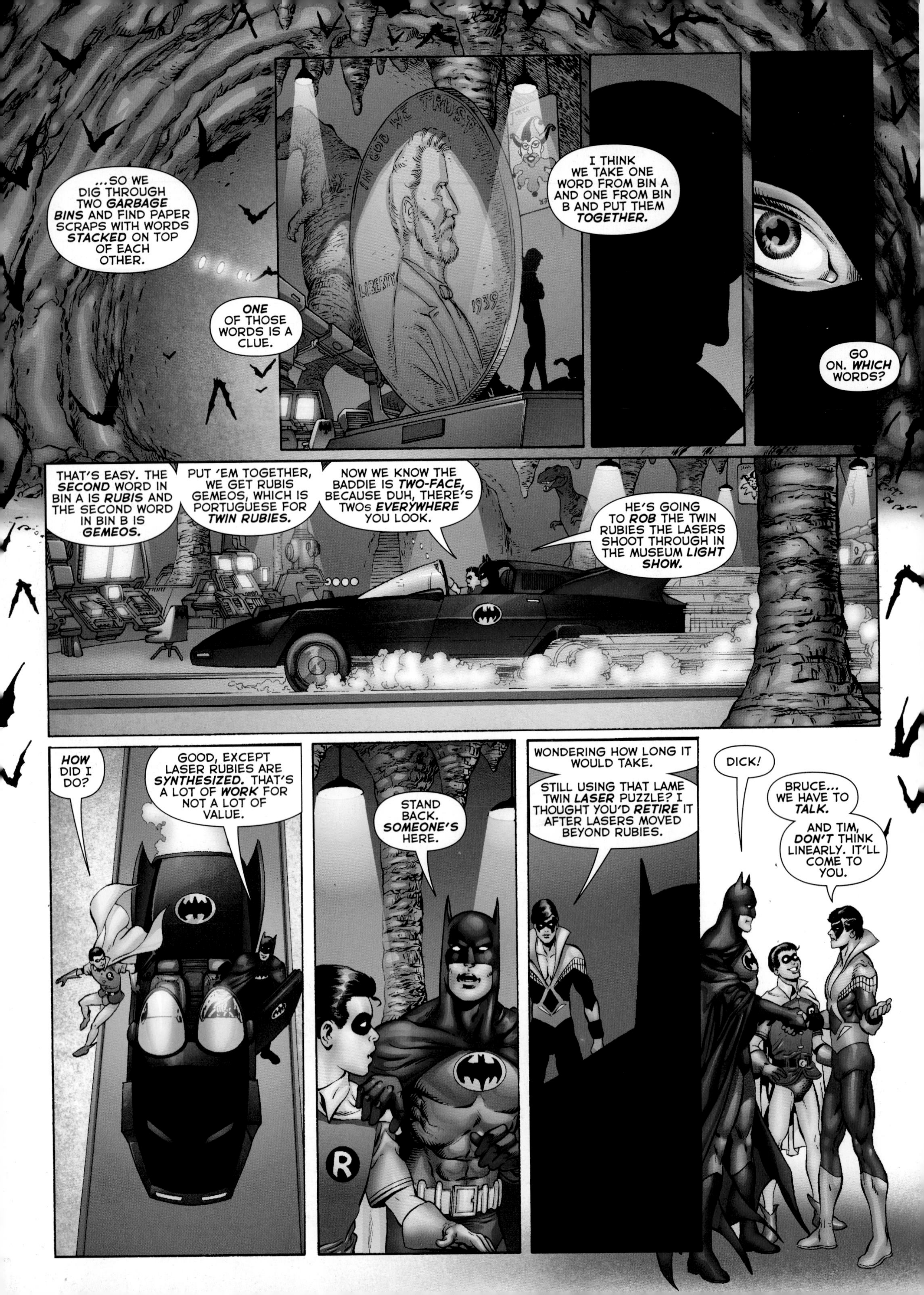

...SO WE DIG THROUGH TWO *GARBAGE BINS* AND FIND PAPER SCRAPS WITH WORDS *STACKED* ON TOP OF EACH OTHER.
ONE OF THOSE WORDS IS A CLUE.
IN GOD WE TRUST
LIBERTY
1939
I THINK WE TAKE ONE WORD FROM BIN A AND ONE FROM BIN B AND PUT THEM *TOGETHER.*
GO ON. *WHICH* WORDS?
THAT'S EASY. THE *SECOND* WORD IN BIN A IS *RUBIS* AND THE SECOND WORD IN BIN B IS *GEMEOS.*
PUT 'EM TOGETHER, WE GET RUBIS GEMEOS, WHICH IS PORTUGUESE FOR *TWIN RUBIES.*
NOW WE KNOW THE BADDIE IS *TWO-FACE,* BECAUSE DUH, THERE'S TWOs *EVERYWHERE* YOU LOOK.
HE'S GOING TO *ROB* THE TWIN RUBIES THE LASERS SHOOT THROUGH IN THE MUSEUM *LIGHT SHOW.*
HOW DID I DO?
GOOD, EXCEPT LASER RUBIES ARE *SYNTHESIZED.* THAT'S A LOT OF *WORK* FOR NOT A LOT OF VALUE.
STAND BACK. *SOMEONE'S* HERE.
WONDERING HOW LONG IT WOULD TAKE.
STILL USING THAT LAME TWIN *LASER* PUZZLE? I THOUGHT YOU'D *RETIRE* IT AFTER LASERS MOVED BEYOND RUBIES.
DICK!
BRUCE... WE HAVE TO *TALK.*
AND TIM, *DON'T* THINK LINEARLY. IT'LL COME TO YOU.

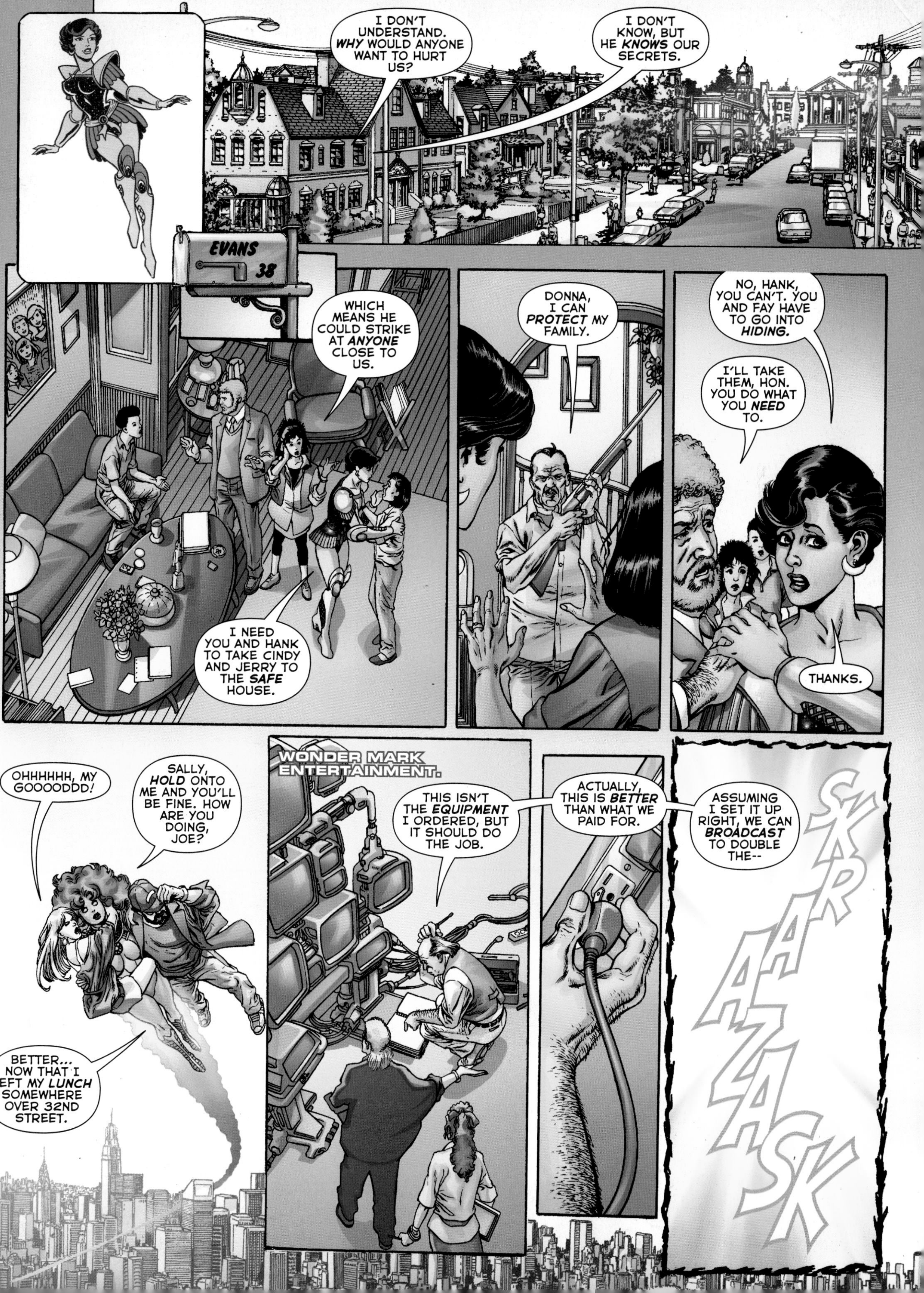
I DON'T UNDERSTAND. WHY WOULD ANYONE WANT TO HURT US?
I DON'T KNOW, BUT HE KNOWS OUR SECRETS.
EVANS
38
WHICH MEANS HE COULD STRIKE AT ANYONE CLOSE TO US.
I NEED YOU AND HANK TO TAKE CINDY AND JERRY TO THE SAFE HOUSE.
DONNA, I CAN PROTECT MY FAMILY.
NO, HANK, YOU CAN'T. YOU AND FAY HAVE TO GO INTO HIDING.
I'LL TAKE THEM, HON. YOU DO WHAT YOU NEED TO.
THANKS.
OHHHHHH, MY GOOOODDD!
SALLY, HOLD ONTO ME AND YOU'LL BE FINE. HOW ARE YOU DOING, JOE?
BETTER... NOW THAT I LEFT MY LUNCH SOMEWHERE OVER 32ND STREET.
WONDER MARK ENTERTAINMENT.
THIS ISN'T THE EQUIPMENT I ORDERED, BUT IT SHOULD DO THE JOB.
ACTUALLY, THIS IS BETTER THAN WHAT WE PAID FOR.
ASSUMING I SET IT UP RIGHT, WE CAN BROADCAST TO DOUBLE THE--
SKRAAAZAASK

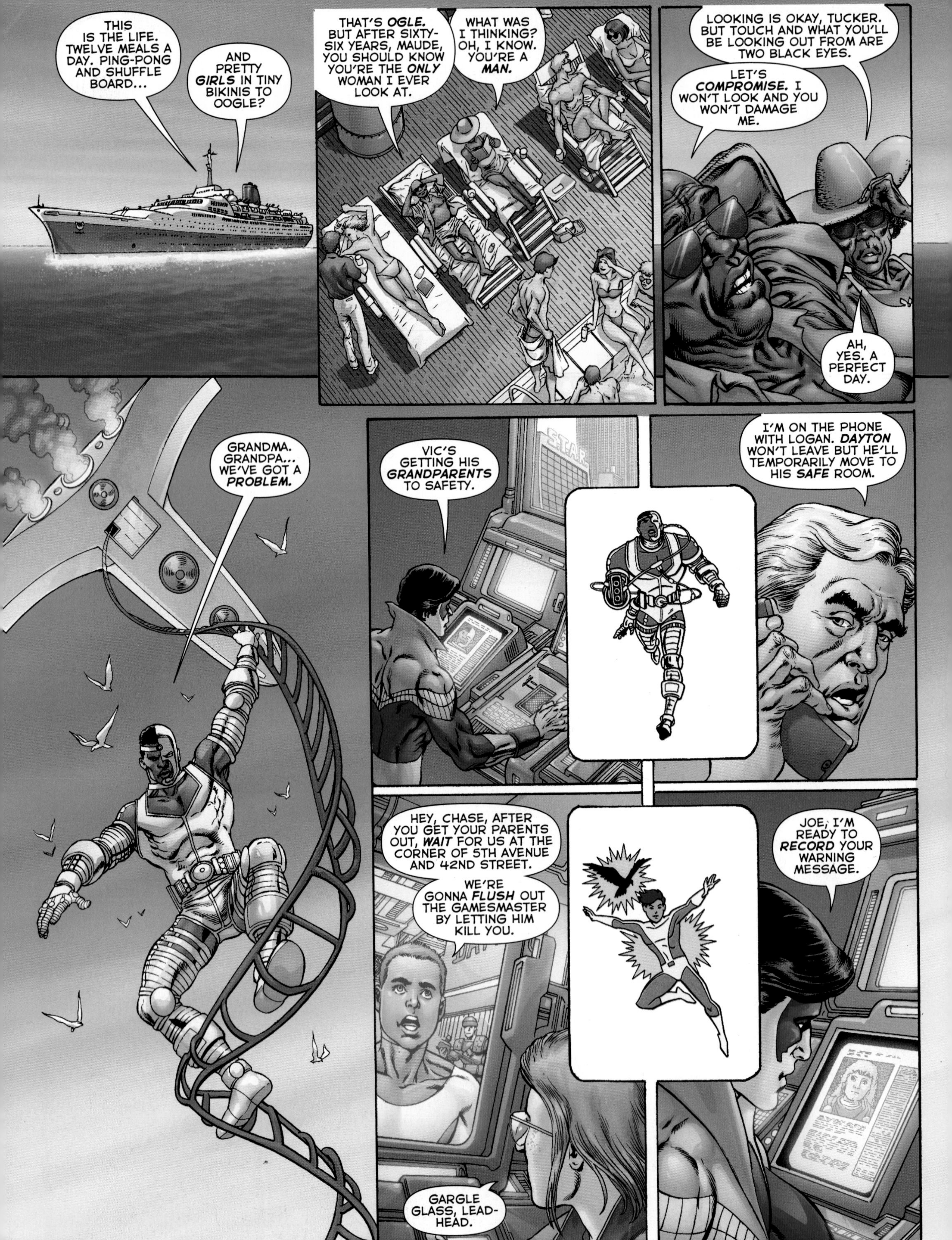
THIS IS THE LIFE. TWELVE MEALS A DAY. PING-PONG AND SHUFFLE BOARD...
AND PRETTY GIRLS IN TINY BIKINIS TO OOGLE?
THAT'S OGLE. BUT AFTER SIXTY-SIX YEARS, MAUDE, YOU SHOULD KNOW YOU'RE THE ONLY WOMAN I EVER LOOK AT.
WHAT WAS I THINKING? OH, I KNOW. YOU'RE A MAN.
LOOKING IS OKAY, TUCKER. BUT TOUCH AND WHAT YOU'LL BE LOOKING OUT FROM ARE TWO BLACK EYES.
LET'S COMPROMISE. I WON'T LOOK AND YOU WON'T DAMAGE ME.
AH, YES. A PERFECT DAY.
GRANDMA. GRANDPA... WE'VE GOT A PROBLEM.
VIC'S GETTING HIS GRANDPARENTS TO SAFETY.
I'M ON THE PHONE WITH LOGAN. DAYTON WON'T LEAVE BUT HE'LL TEMPORARILY MOVE TO HIS SAFE ROOM.
HEY, CHASE, AFTER YOU GET YOUR PARENTS OUT, WAIT FOR US AT THE CORNER OF 5TH AVENUE AND 42ND STREET.
WE'RE GONNA FLUSH OUT THE GAMESMASTER BY LETTING HIM KILL YOU.
GARGLE GLASS, LEAD-HEAD.
JOE, I'M READY TO RECORD YOUR WARNING MESSAGE.

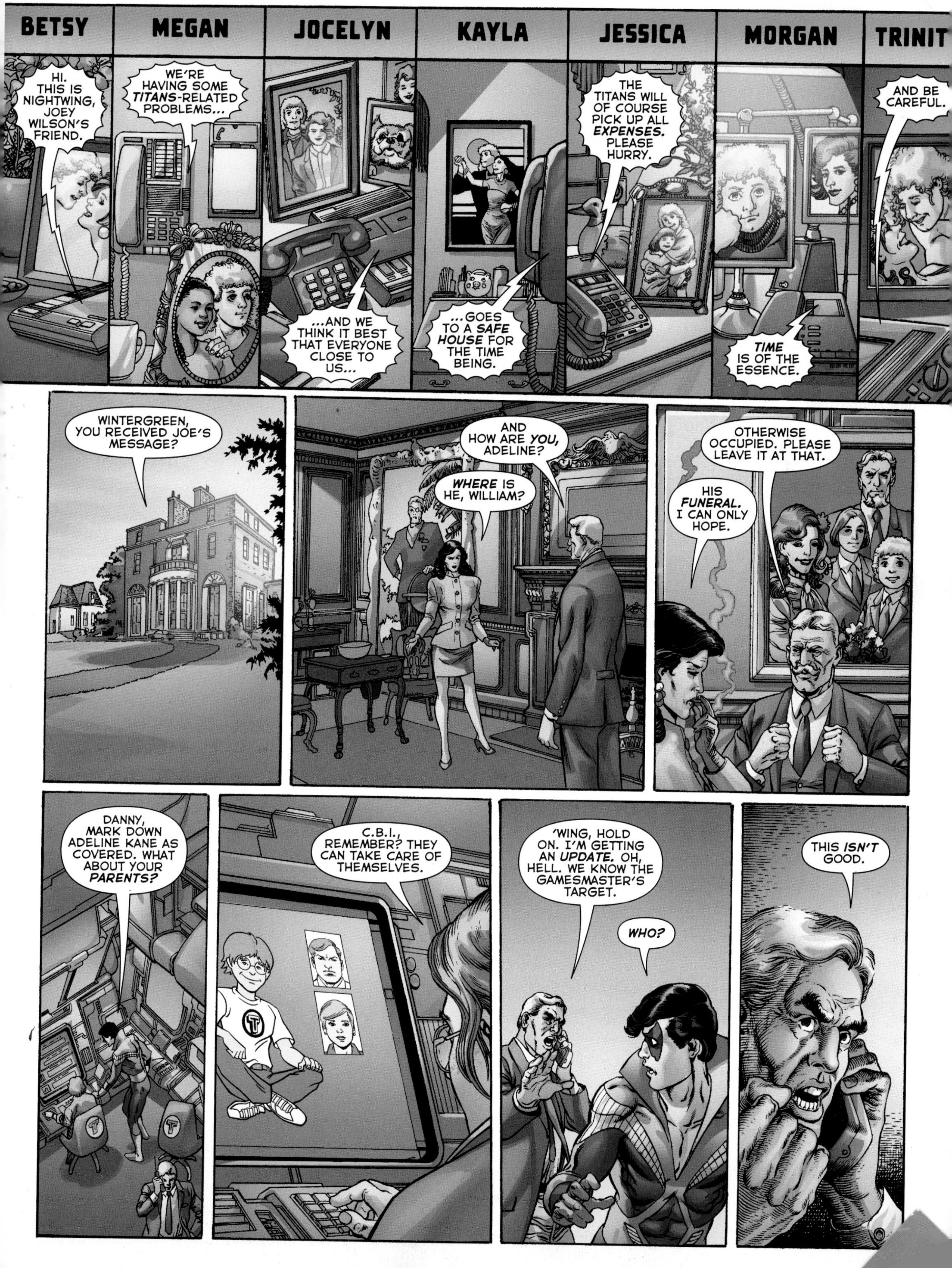
BETSY
HI. THIS IS NIGHTWING, JOEY WILSON'S FRIEND.
MEGAN
WE'RE HAVING SOME TITANS-RELATED PROBLEMS...
JOCELYN
...AND WE THINK IT BEST THAT EVERYONE CLOSE TO US...
KAYLA
...GOES TO A SAFE HOUSE FOR THE TIME BEING.
JESSICA
THE TITANS WILL OF COURSE PICK UP ALL EXPENSES. PLEASE HURRY.
MORGAN
TIME IS OF THE ESSENCE.
TRINIT
AND BE CAREFUL.
WINTERGREEN, YOU RECEIVED JOE'S MESSAGE?
AND HOW ARE YOU, ADELINE?
WHERE IS HE, WILLIAM?
OTHERWISE OCCUPIED. PLEASE LEAVE IT AT THAT.
HIS FUNERAL. I CAN ONLY HOPE.
DANNY, MARK DOWN ADELINE KANE AS COVERED. WHAT ABOUT YOUR PARENTS?
C.B.I., REMEMBER? THEY CAN TAKE CARE OF THEMSELVES.
'WING, HOLD ON. I'M GETTING AN UPDATE. OH, HELL. WE KNOW THE GAMESMASTER'S TARGET.
WHO?
THIS ISN'T GOOD.

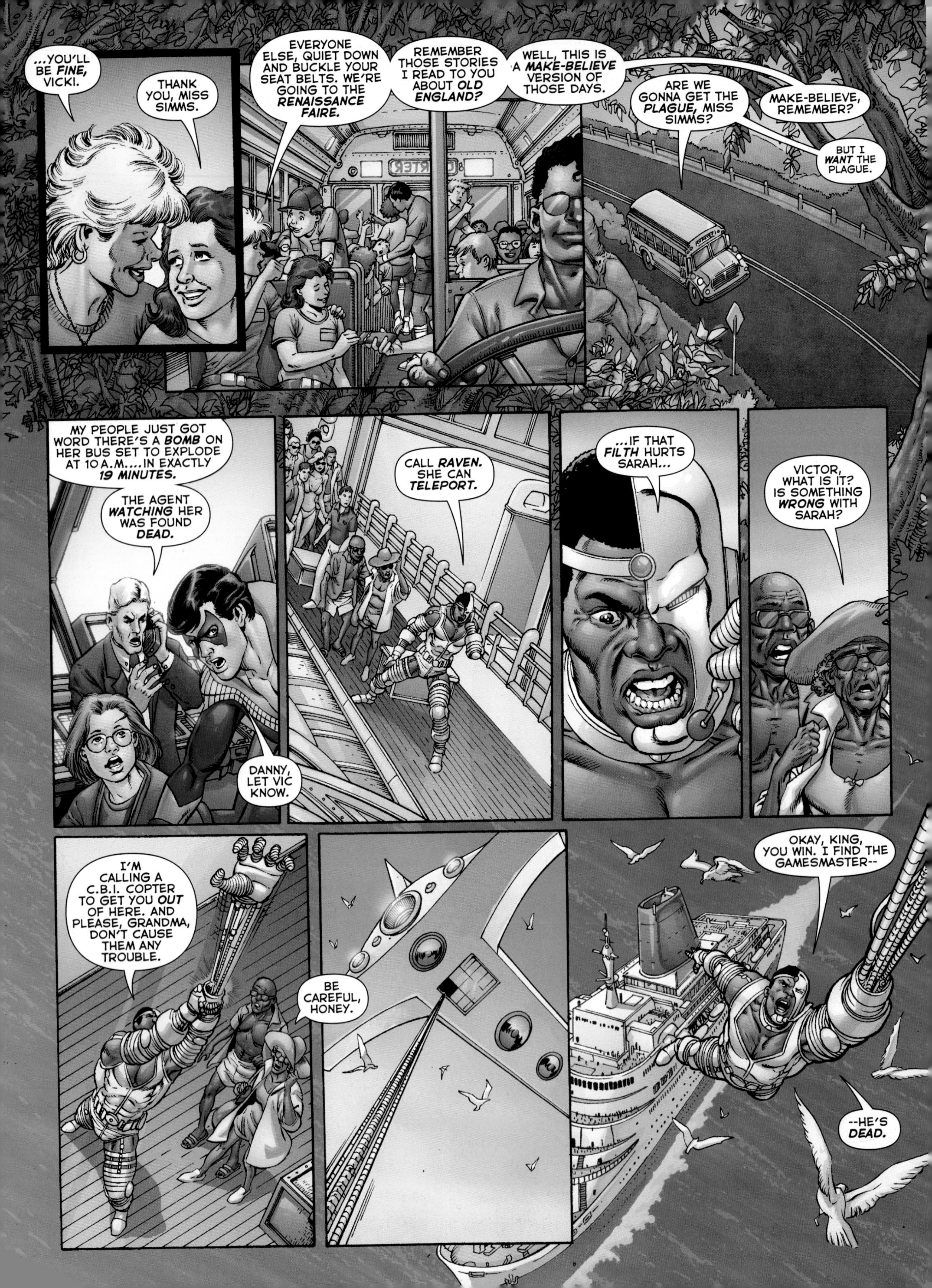
...YOU'LL BE FINE, VICKI.
THANK YOU, MISS SIMMS.
EVERYONE ELSE, QUIET DOWN AND BUCKLE YOUR SEAT BELTS. WE'RE GOING TO THE RENAISSANCE FAIRE.
REMEMBER THOSE STORIES I READ TO YOU ABOUT OLD ENGLAND?
WELL, THIS IS A MAKE-BELIEVE VERSION OF THOSE DAYS.
ARE WE GONNA GET THE PLAGUE, MISS SIMMS?
MAKE-BELIEVE, REMEMBER?
BUT I WANT THE PLAGUE.
MY PEOPLE JUST GOT WORD THERE'S A BOMB ON HER BUS SET TO EXPLODE AT 10 A.M.... IN EXACTLY 19 MINUTES.
THE AGENT WATCHING HER WAS FOUND DEAD.
DANNY, LET VIC KNOW.
CALL RAVEN. SHE CAN TELEPORT.
...IF THAT FILTH HURTS SARAH...
VICTOR, WHAT IS IT? IS SOMETHING WRONG WITH SARAH?
I'M CALLING A C.B.I. COPTER TO GET YOU OUT OF HERE. AND PLEASE, GRANDMA, DON'T CAUSE THEM ANY TROUBLE.
BE CAREFUL, HONEY.
OKAY, KING, YOU WIN. I FIND THE GAMESMASTER--
--HE'S DEAD.

A *BOMB?* ARE YOU SURE?

NO WAY OF KNOWING FROM HERE.

BUT YOU GOTTA GET THE *KIDS* OFF THE BUS.

OKAY. OKAY, LUIS, PULL OVER.

BUT...

DO IT.

IT'S GOING TO TAKE TIME. MANY OF THOSE KIDS HAVE LEG OR FOOT *PROSTHESES.*

I'VE GOT *COPTERS* ON THE WAY WITH PERSONNEL TO HELP MOVE THEM.

TRY RAVEN AGAIN. SHE'S THE *BEST* HOPE WE HAVE.

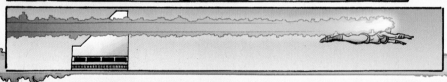

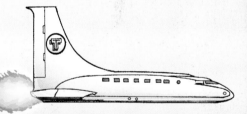

...THIS HAS BEEN *WONDERFUL.*

I CAN UNDERSTAND WHY YOU OPENED YOUR *RANCH* HERE.

IT'S PEACEFUL, LIKE *AZARATH...*

...ONLY WITHOUT THOSE PESKY *DEMON* THINGS HANGING OVER OUR HEADS.

WE *SADDLE* UP EVERY EVENING, HEAD OUT INTO THE SETTING SUN...

...AND ENJOY THE *WONDERS* OF NATURE...

... WITHOUT A SINGLE *CARE* IN THE WORLD.

BEEP BEEP BEEP BEEP BEEP BEEP

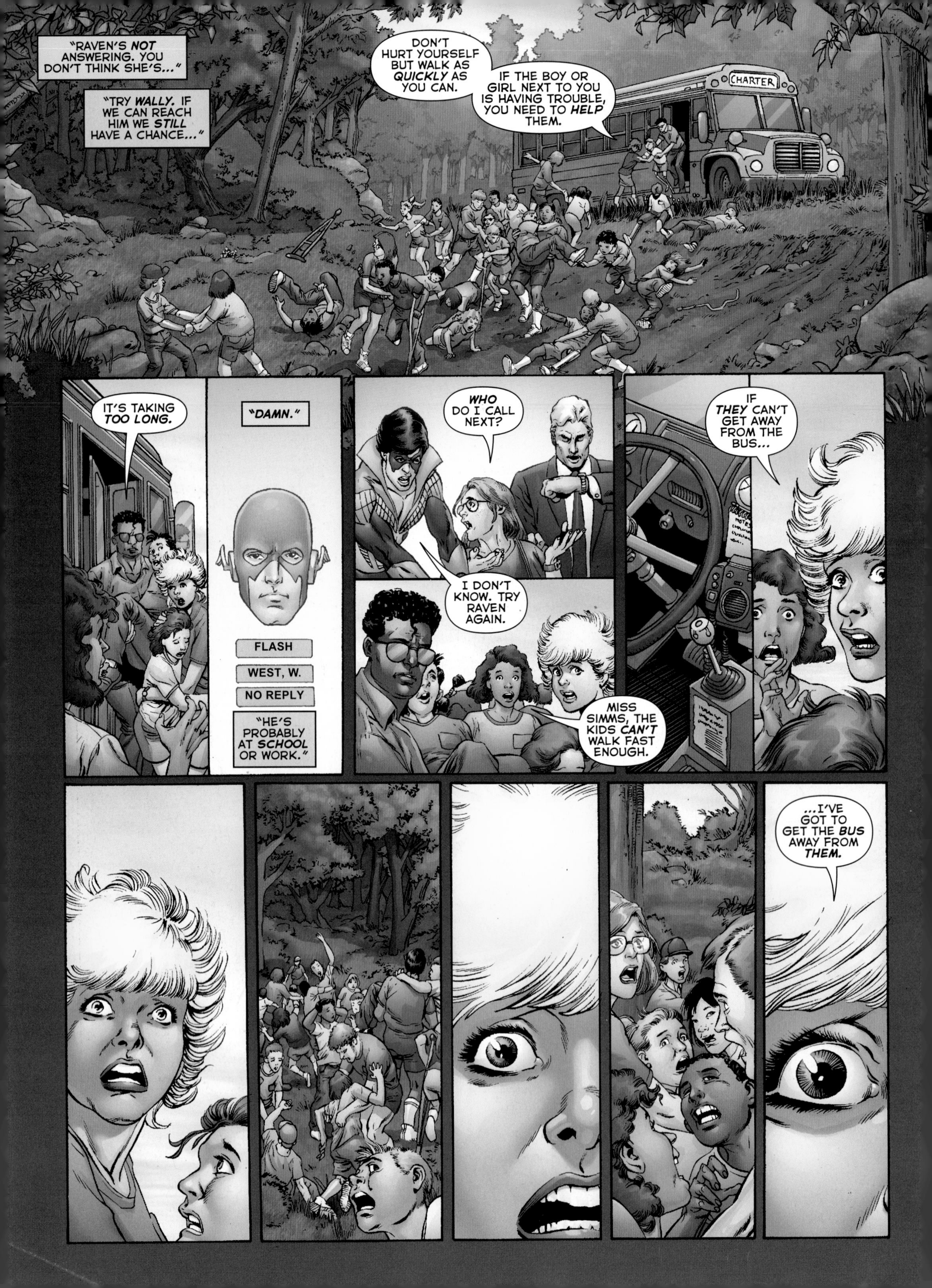
"RAVEN'S NOT ANSWERING. YOU DON'T THINK SHE'S..."
"TRY WALLY. IF WE CAN REACH HIM WE STILL HAVE A CHANCE..."
DON'T HURT YOURSELF BUT WALK AS QUICKLY AS YOU CAN.
IF THE BOY OR GIRL NEXT TO YOU IS HAVING TROUBLE, YOU NEED TO HELP THEM.
CHARTER
IT'S TAKING TOO LONG.
"DAMN."
FLASH
WEST, W.
NO REPLY
"HE'S PROBABLY AT SCHOOL OR WORK."
WHO DO I CALL NEXT?
I DON'T KNOW. TRY RAVEN AGAIN.
MISS SIMMS, THE KIDS CAN'T WALK FAST ENOUGH.
IF THEY CAN'T GET AWAY FROM THE BUS...
...I'VE GOT TO GET THE BUS AWAY FROM THEM.

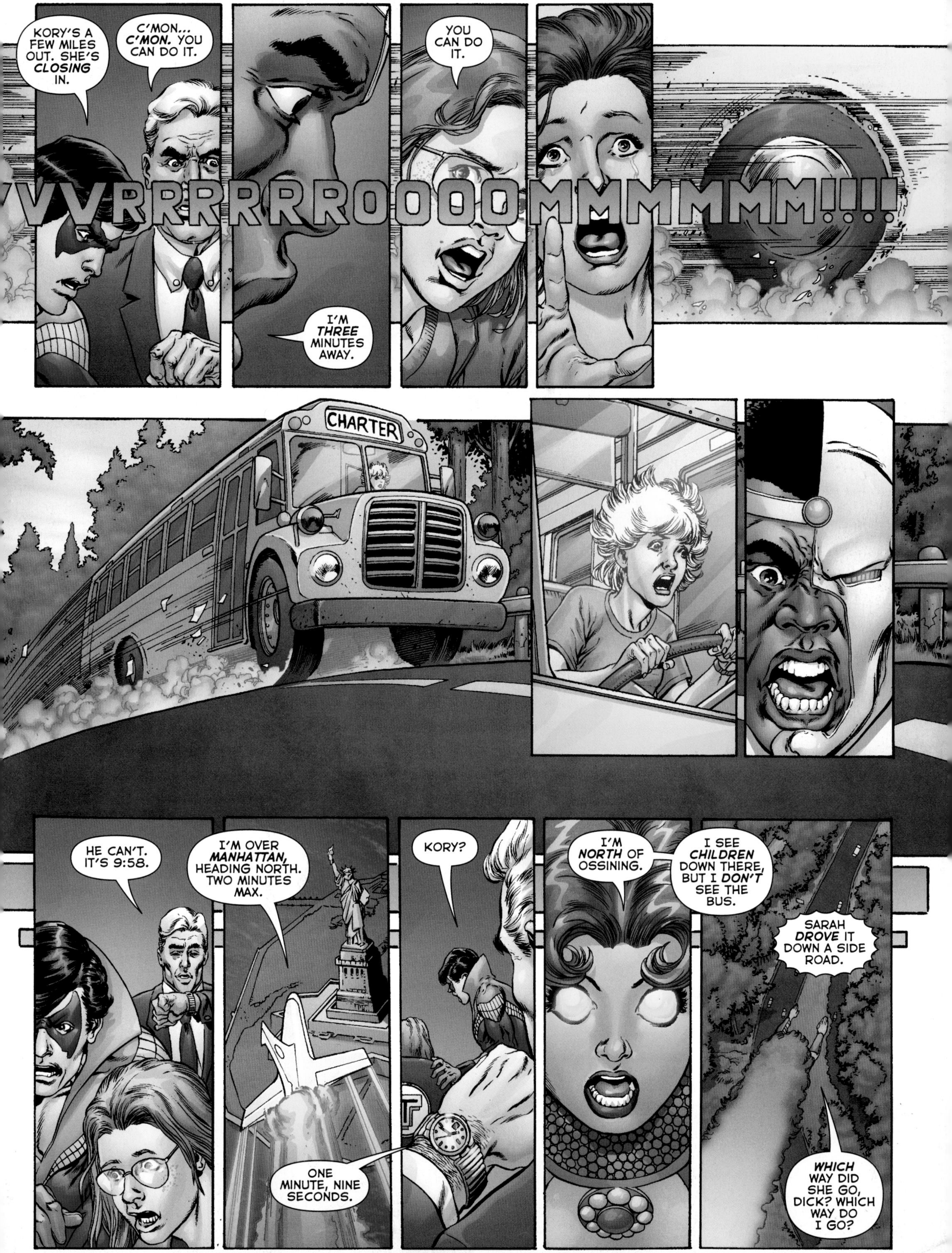
KORY'S A FEW MILES OUT. SHE'S CLOSING IN.
C'MON... C'MON. YOU CAN DO IT.
I'M THREE MINUTES AWAY.
YOU CAN DO IT.
VVVRRRRRROOOOOMMMMMMM!!!!
CHARTER
HE CAN'T. IT'S 9:58.
I'M OVER MANHATTAN, HEADING NORTH. TWO MINUTES MAX.
KORY?
ONE MINUTE, NINE SECONDS.
I'M NORTH OF OSSINING.
I SEE CHILDREN DOWN THERE, BUT I DON'T SEE THE BUS.
SARAH DROVE IT DOWN A SIDE ROAD.
WHICH WAY DID SHE GO, DICK? WHICH WAY DO I GO?

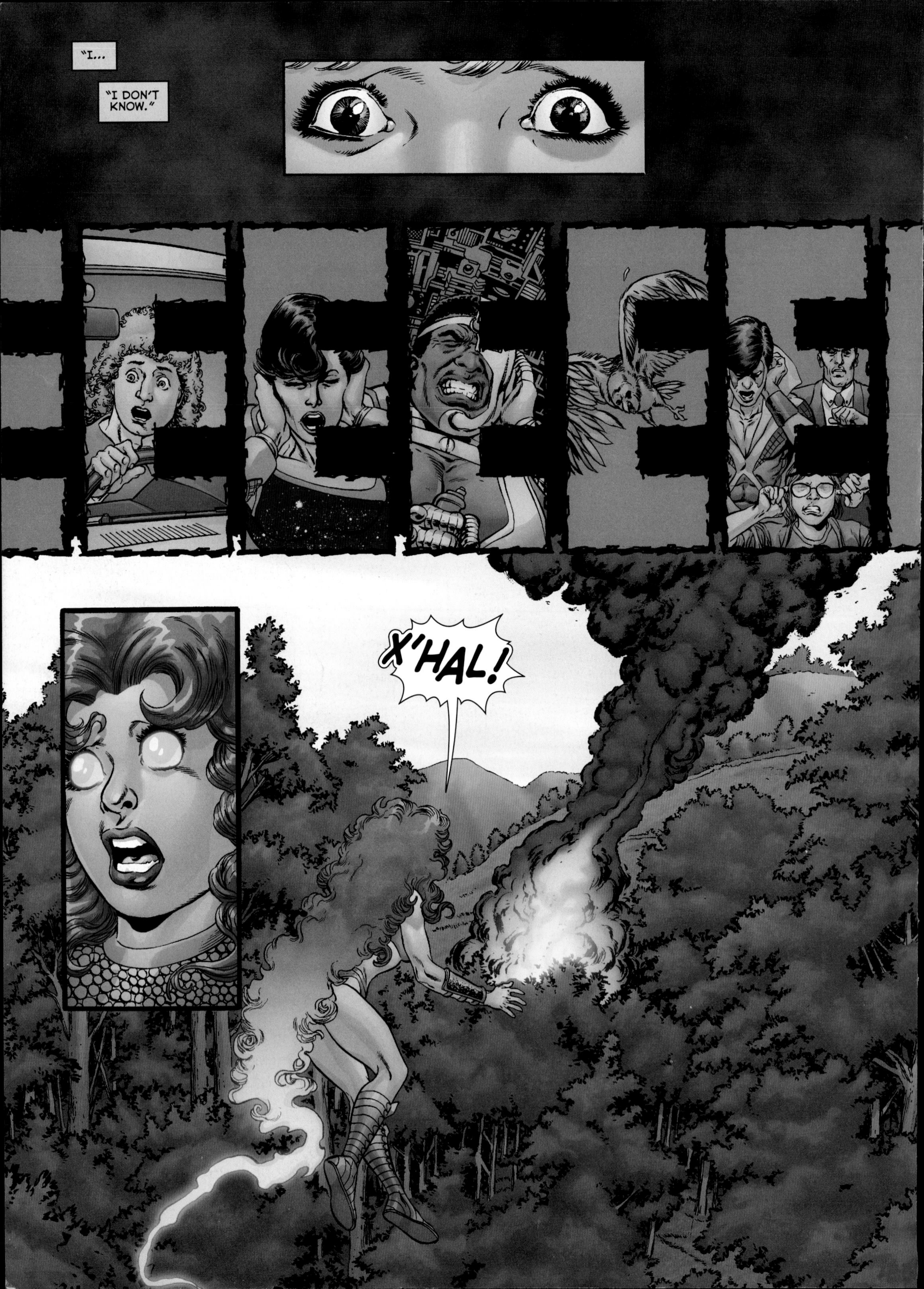
"I...
"I DON'T KNOW."
X'HAL!

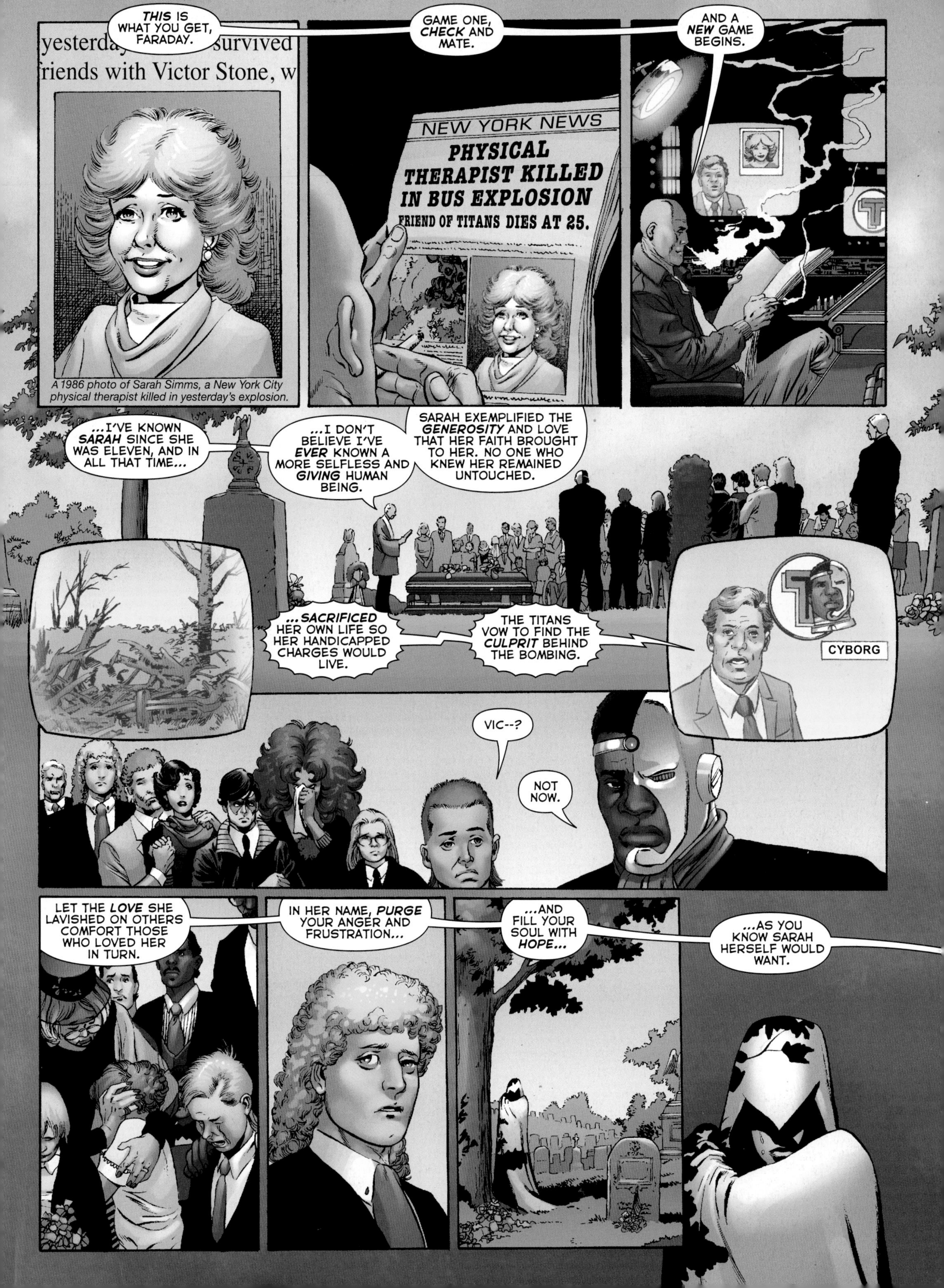

THIS IS WHAT YOU GET, FARADAY.
yesterday ... survived
friends with Victor Stone, w
A 1986 photo of Sarah Simms, a New York City physical therapist killed in yesterday's explosion.
GAME ONE, CHECK AND MATE.
NEW YORK NEWS
PHYSICAL THERAPIST KILLED IN BUS EXPLOSION
FRIEND OF TITANS DIES AT 25.
AND A NEW GAME BEGINS.
...I'VE KNOWN SARAH SINCE SHE WAS ELEVEN, AND IN ALL THAT TIME...
...I DON'T BELIEVE I'VE EVER KNOWN A MORE SELFLESS AND GIVING HUMAN BEING.
SARAH EXEMPLIFIED THE GENEROSITY AND LOVE THAT HER FAITH BROUGHT TO HER. NO ONE WHO KNEW HER REMAINED UNTOUCHED.
...SACRIFICED HER OWN LIFE SO HER HANDICAPPED CHARGES WOULD LIVE.
THE TITANS VOW TO FIND THE CULPRIT BEHIND THE BOMBING.
CYBORG
VIC--?
NOT NOW.
LET THE LOVE SHE LAVISHED ON OTHERS COMFORT THOSE WHO LOVED HER IN TURN.
IN HER NAME, PURGE YOUR ANGER AND FRUSTRATION...
...AND FILL YOUR SOUL WITH HOPE...
...AS YOU KNOW SARAH HERSELF WOULD WANT.

DON'T TRY TO STOP ME.

VIC, I'M GOING THROUGH THE WRECKAGE.

IF THERE'S ANY EVIDENCE I'LL FIND IT.

AND WHEN I DO, I'LL COME TO YOU FIRST. TRUST ME.

RIGHT NOW THE ONLY ONE I TRUST IS ME.

YOU'RE GOING OFF THE DEEP END, STONE. LISTEN TO YOUR FRIENDS.

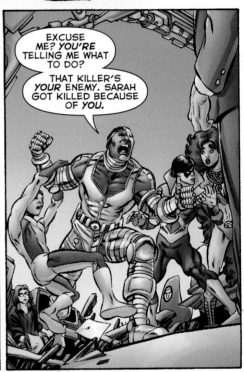

EXCUSE ME? YOU'RE TELLING ME WHAT TO DO?

THAT KILLER'S YOUR ENEMY. SARAH GOT KILLED BECAUSE OF YOU.

WHAT--?

THIS IS YOUR FAULT!!

WHAT ARE--

NO, JOE. DON'T--

YOU HAVEN'T GIVEN US A CHOICE.

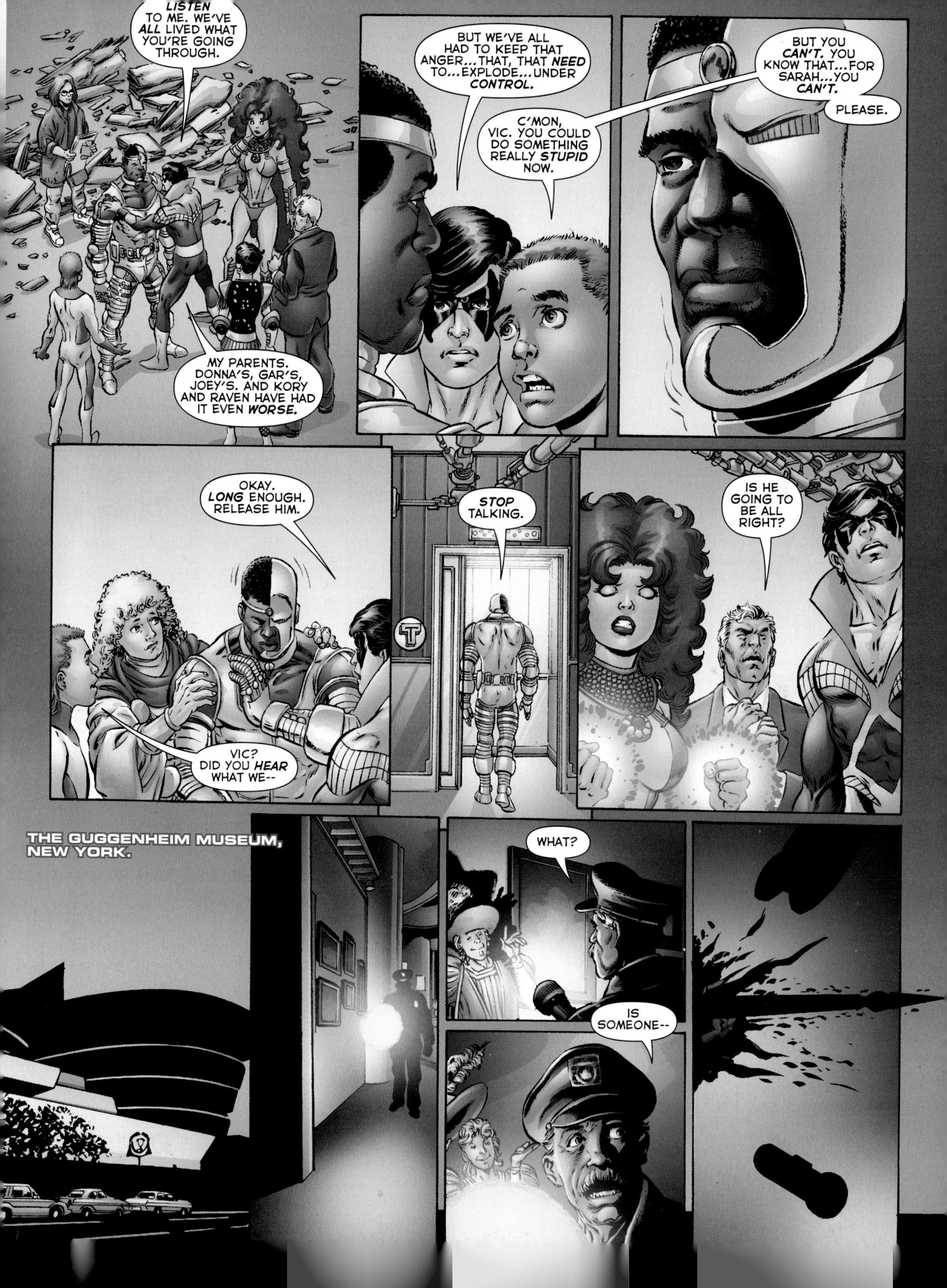
LISTEN TO ME. WE'VE ALL LIVED WHAT YOU'RE GOING THROUGH.
MY PARENTS. DONNA'S, GAR'S, JOEY'S. AND KORY AND RAVEN HAVE HAD IT EVEN WORSE.
BUT WE'VE ALL HAD TO KEEP THAT ANGER...THAT, THAT NEED TO...EXPLODE...UNDER CONTROL.
C'MON, VIC. YOU COULD DO SOMETHING REALLY STUPID NOW.
BUT YOU CAN'T. YOU KNOW THAT...FOR SARAH...YOU CAN'T.
PLEASE.
OKAY. LONG ENOUGH. RELEASE HIM.
VIC? DID YOU HEAR WHAT WE--
STOP TALKING.
IS HE GOING TO BE ALL RIGHT?
THE GUGGENHEIM MUSEUM, NEW YORK.
WHAT?
IS SOMEONE--

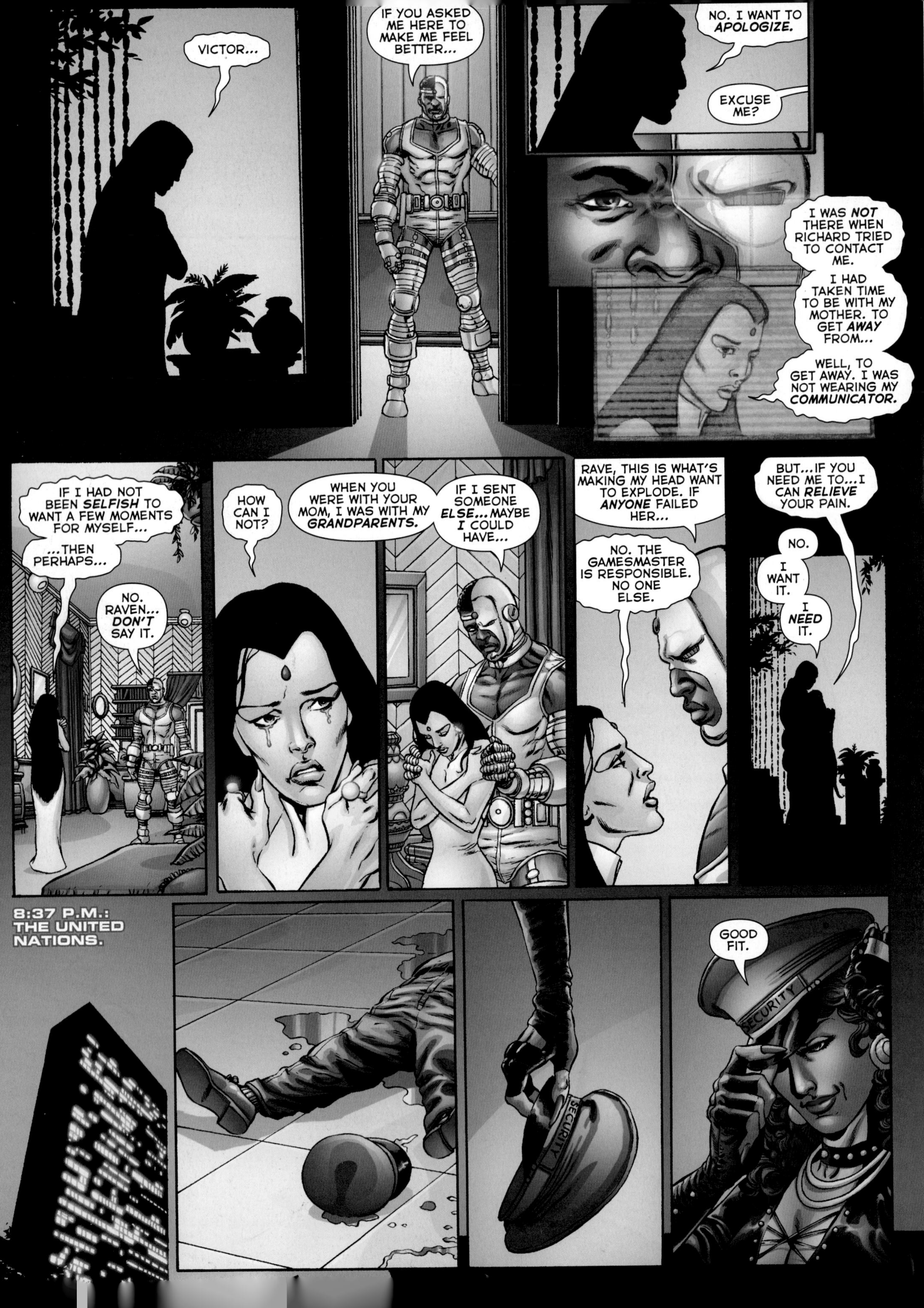
VICTOR...
IF YOU ASKED ME HERE TO MAKE ME FEEL BETTER...
NO. I WANT TO APOLOGIZE.
EXCUSE ME?
I WAS NOT THERE WHEN RICHARD TRIED TO CONTACT ME.
I HAD TAKEN TIME TO BE WITH MY MOTHER. TO GET AWAY FROM...
WELL, TO GET AWAY. I WAS NOT WEARING MY COMMUNICATOR.
IF I HAD NOT BEEN SELFISH TO WANT A FEW MOMENTS FOR MYSELF...
...THEN PERHAPS...
NO. RAVEN... DON'T SAY IT.
HOW CAN I NOT?
WHEN YOU WERE WITH YOUR MOM, I WAS WITH MY GRANDPARENTS.
IF I SENT SOMEONE ELSE... MAYBE I COULD HAVE...
RAVE, THIS IS WHAT'S MAKING MY HEAD WANT TO EXPLODE. IF ANYONE FAILED HER...
NO. THE GAMESMASTER IS RESPONSIBLE. NO ONE ELSE.
BUT... IF YOU NEED ME TO... I CAN RELIEVE YOUR PAIN.
NO.
I WANT IT.
I NEED IT.
8:37 P.M.: THE UNITED NATIONS.
SECURITY
SECURITY
GOOD FIT.

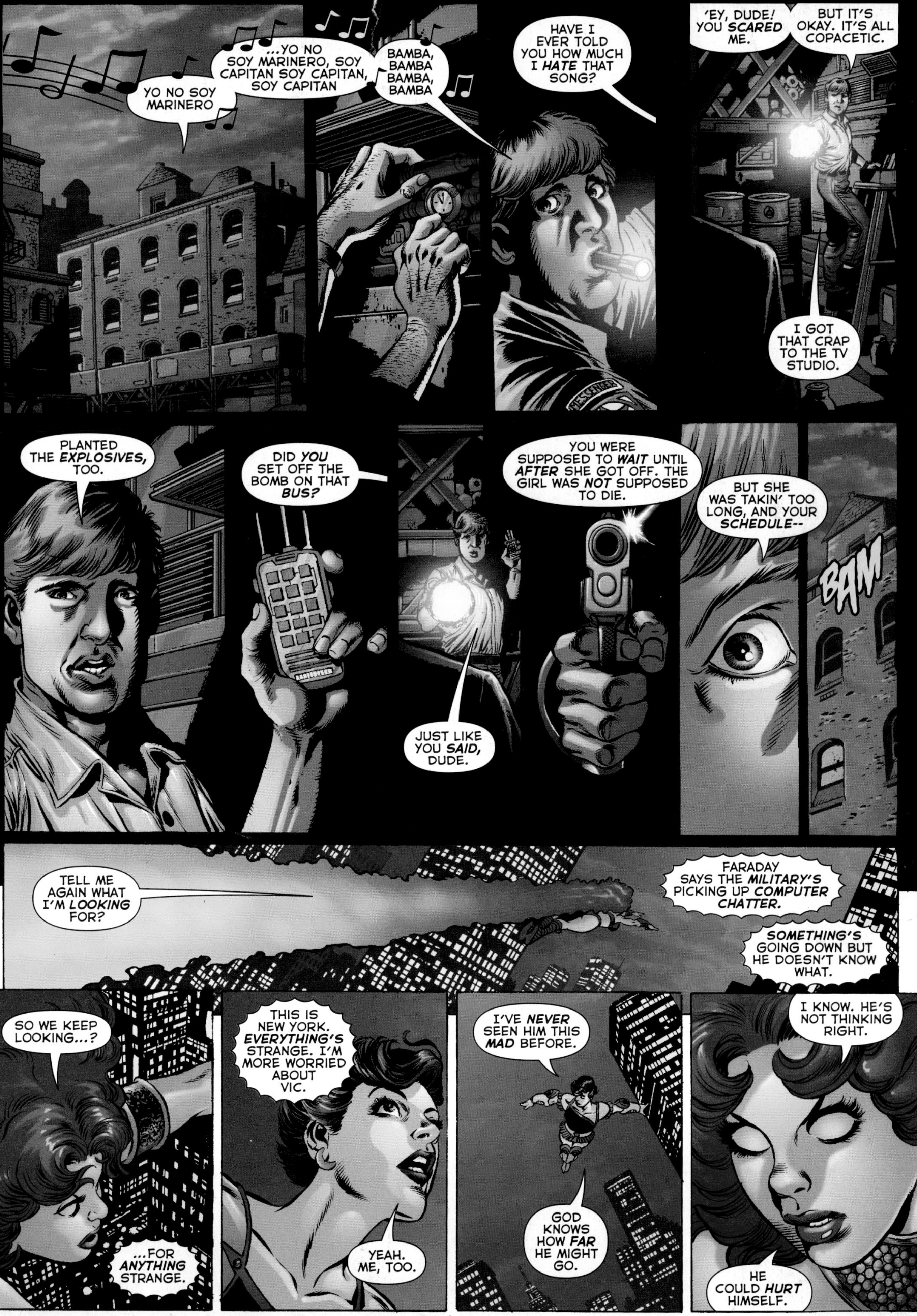
YO NO SOY MARINERO
...YO NO SOY MARINERO, SOY CAPITAN SOY CAPITAN, SOY CAPITAN
BAMBA, BAMBA BAMBA, BAMBA
HAVE I EVER TOLD YOU HOW MUCH I HATE THAT SONG?
'EY, DUDE! YOU SCARED ME.
BUT IT'S OKAY. IT'S ALL COPACETIC.
I GOT THAT CRAP TO THE TV STUDIO.
PLANTED THE EXPLOSIVES, TOO.
DID YOU SET OFF THE BOMB ON THAT BUS?
JUST LIKE YOU SAID, DUDE.
YOU WERE SUPPOSED TO WAIT UNTIL AFTER SHE GOT OFF. THE GIRL WAS NOT SUPPOSED TO DIE.
BUT SHE WAS TAKIN' TOO LONG, AND YOUR SCHEDULE--
BAM
TELL ME AGAIN WHAT I'M LOOKING FOR?
FARADAY SAYS THE MILITARY'S PICKING UP COMPUTER CHATTER.
SOMETHING'S GOING DOWN BUT HE DOESN'T KNOW WHAT.
SO WE KEEP LOOKING...?
...FOR ANYTHING STRANGE.
THIS IS NEW YORK. EVERYTHING'S STRANGE. I'M MORE WORRIED ABOUT VIC.
YEAH. ME, TOO.
I'VE NEVER SEEN HIM THIS MAD BEFORE.
GOD KNOWS HOW FAR HE MIGHT GO.
I KNOW. HE'S NOT THINKING RIGHT.
HE COULD HURT HIMSELF.

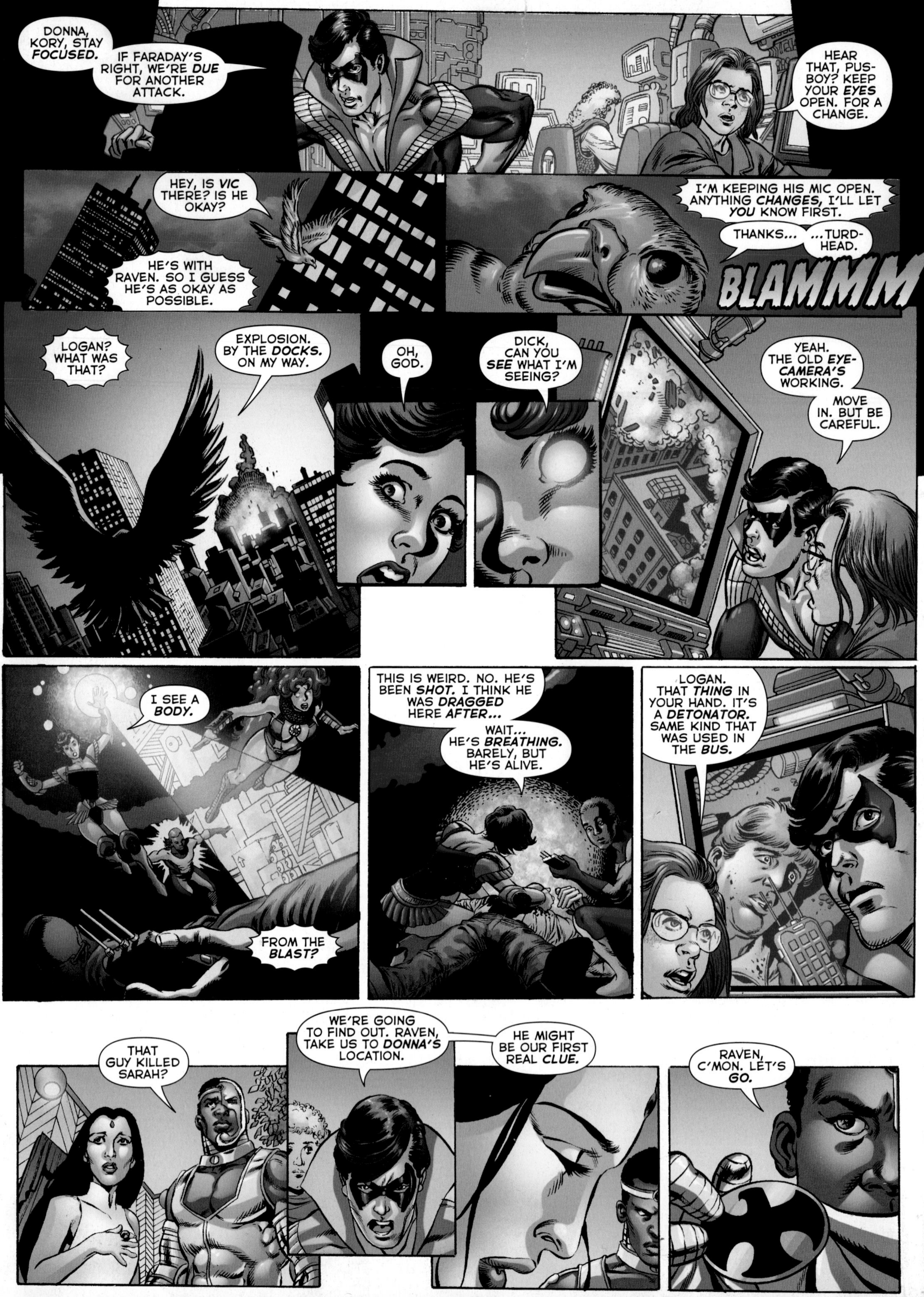
DONNA, KORY, STAY FOCUSED.
IF FARADAY'S RIGHT, WE'RE DUE FOR ANOTHER ATTACK.
HEAR THAT, PUS-BOY? KEEP YOUR EYES OPEN. FOR A CHANGE.
HEY, IS VIC THERE? IS HE OKAY?
HE'S WITH RAVEN. SO I GUESS HE'S AS OKAY AS POSSIBLE.
I'M KEEPING HIS MIC OPEN. ANYTHING CHANGES, I'LL LET YOU KNOW FIRST.
THANKS...
...TURD-HEAD.
BLAMMM
LOGAN? WHAT WAS THAT?
EXPLOSION. BY THE DOCKS. ON MY WAY.
OH, GOD.
DICK, CAN YOU SEE WHAT I'M SEEING?
YEAH. THE OLD EYE-CAMERA'S WORKING.
MOVE IN. BUT BE CAREFUL.
I SEE A BODY.
FROM THE BLAST?
THIS IS WEIRD. NO. HE'S BEEN SHOT. I THINK HE WAS DRAGGED HERE AFTER...
WAIT... HE'S BREATHING. BARELY, BUT HE'S ALIVE.
LOGAN. THAT THING IN YOUR HAND. IT'S A DETONATOR. SAME KIND THAT WAS USED IN THE BUS.
THAT GUY KILLED SARAH?
WE'RE GOING TO FIND OUT. RAVEN, TAKE US TO DONNA'S LOCATION.
HE MIGHT BE OUR FIRST REAL CLUE.
RAVEN, C'MON. LET'S GO.

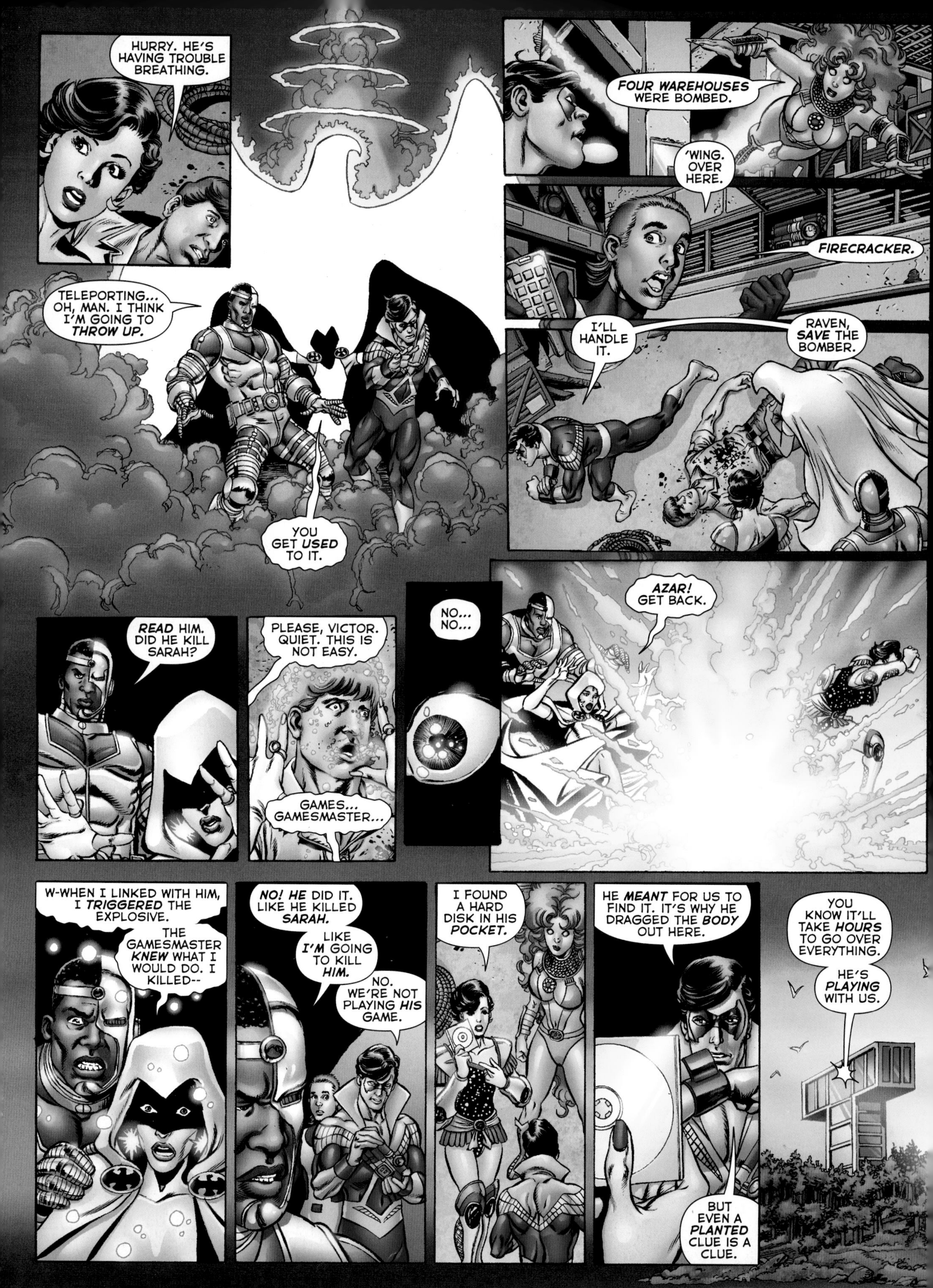
HURRY. HE'S HAVING TROUBLE BREATHING.
TELEPORTING... OH, MAN. I THINK I'M GOING TO THROW UP.
YOU GET USED TO IT.
FOUR WAREHOUSES WERE BOMBED.
'WING. OVER HERE.
FIRECRACKER.
I'LL HANDLE IT.
RAVEN, SAVE THE BOMBER.
READ HIM. DID HE KILL SARAH?
PLEASE, VICTOR. QUIET. THIS IS NOT EASY.
GAMES... GAMESMASTER...
NO... NO...
AZAR! GET BACK.
W-WHEN I LINKED WITH HIM, I TRIGGERED THE EXPLOSIVE.
THE GAMESMASTER KNEW WHAT I WOULD DO. I KILLED--
NO! HE DID IT. LIKE HE KILLED SARAH.
LIKE I'M GOING TO KILL HIM.
NO. WE'RE NOT PLAYING HIS GAME.
I FOUND A HARD DISK IN HIS POCKET.
HE MEANT FOR US TO FIND IT. IT'S WHY HE DRAGGED THE BODY OUT HERE.
BUT EVEN A PLANTED CLUE IS A CLUE.
YOU KNOW IT'LL TAKE HOURS TO GO OVER EVERYTHING.
HE'S PLAYING WITH US.

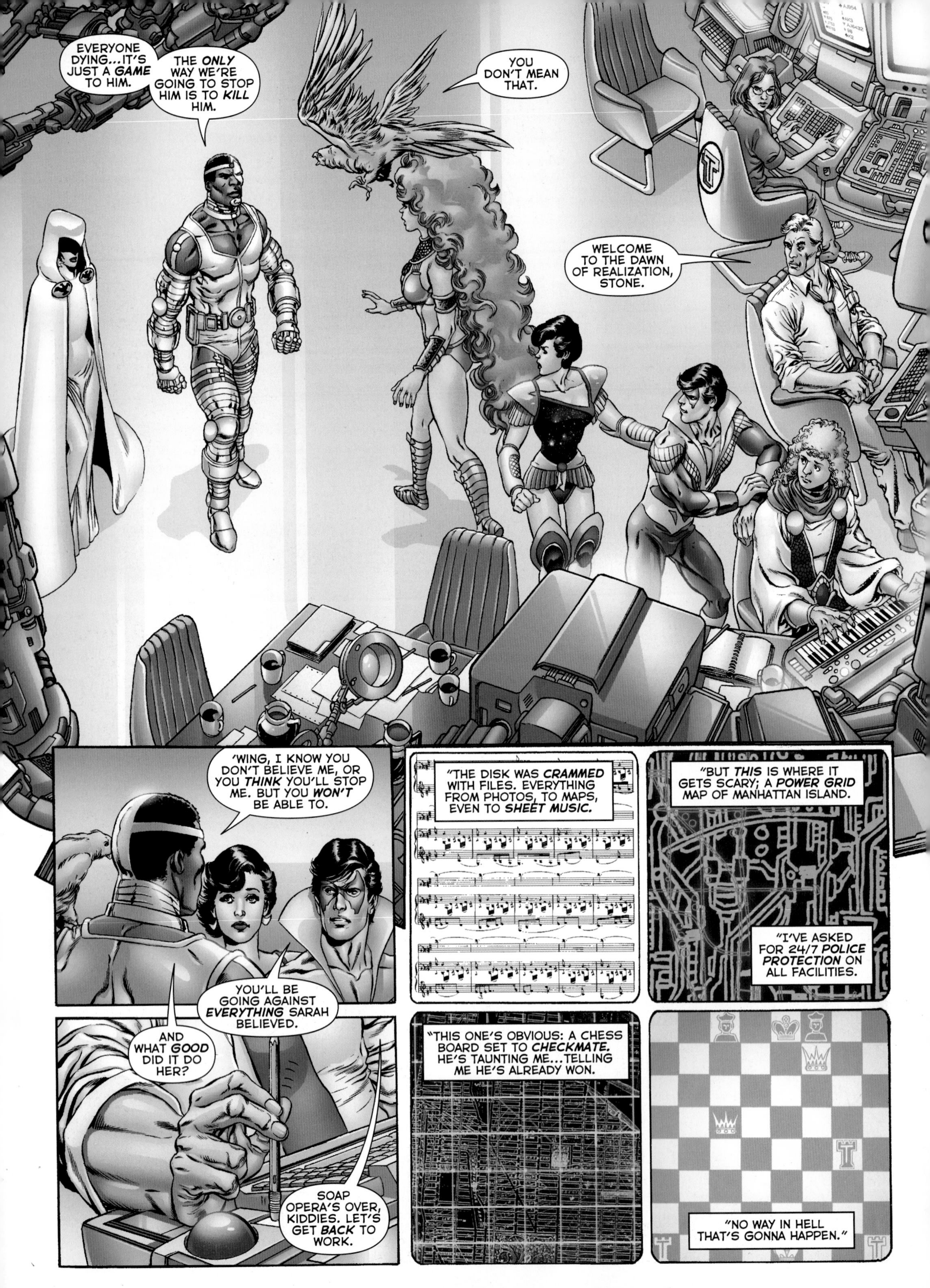
EVERYONE DYING...IT'S JUST A GAME TO HIM.
THE ONLY WAY WE'RE GOING TO STOP HIM IS TO KILL HIM.
YOU DON'T MEAN THAT.
WELCOME TO THE DAWN OF REALIZATION, STONE.
'WING, I KNOW YOU DON'T BELIEVE ME, OR YOU THINK YOU'LL STOP ME. BUT YOU WON'T BE ABLE TO.
YOU'LL BE GOING AGAINST EVERYTHING SARAH BELIEVED.
AND WHAT GOOD DID IT DO HER?
SOAP OPERA'S OVER, KIDDIES. LET'S GET BACK TO WORK.
"THE DISK WAS CRAMMED WITH FILES. EVERYTHING FROM PHOTOS, TO MAPS, EVEN TO SHEET MUSIC.
"BUT THIS IS WHERE IT GETS SCARY; A POWER GRID MAP OF MANHATTAN ISLAND.
"I'VE ASKED FOR 24/7 POLICE PROTECTION ON ALL FACILITIES.
"THIS ONE'S OBVIOUS: A CHESS BOARD SET TO CHECKMATE. HE'S TAUNTING ME...TELLING ME HE'S ALREADY WON.
"NO WAY IN HELL THAT'S GONNA HAPPEN."

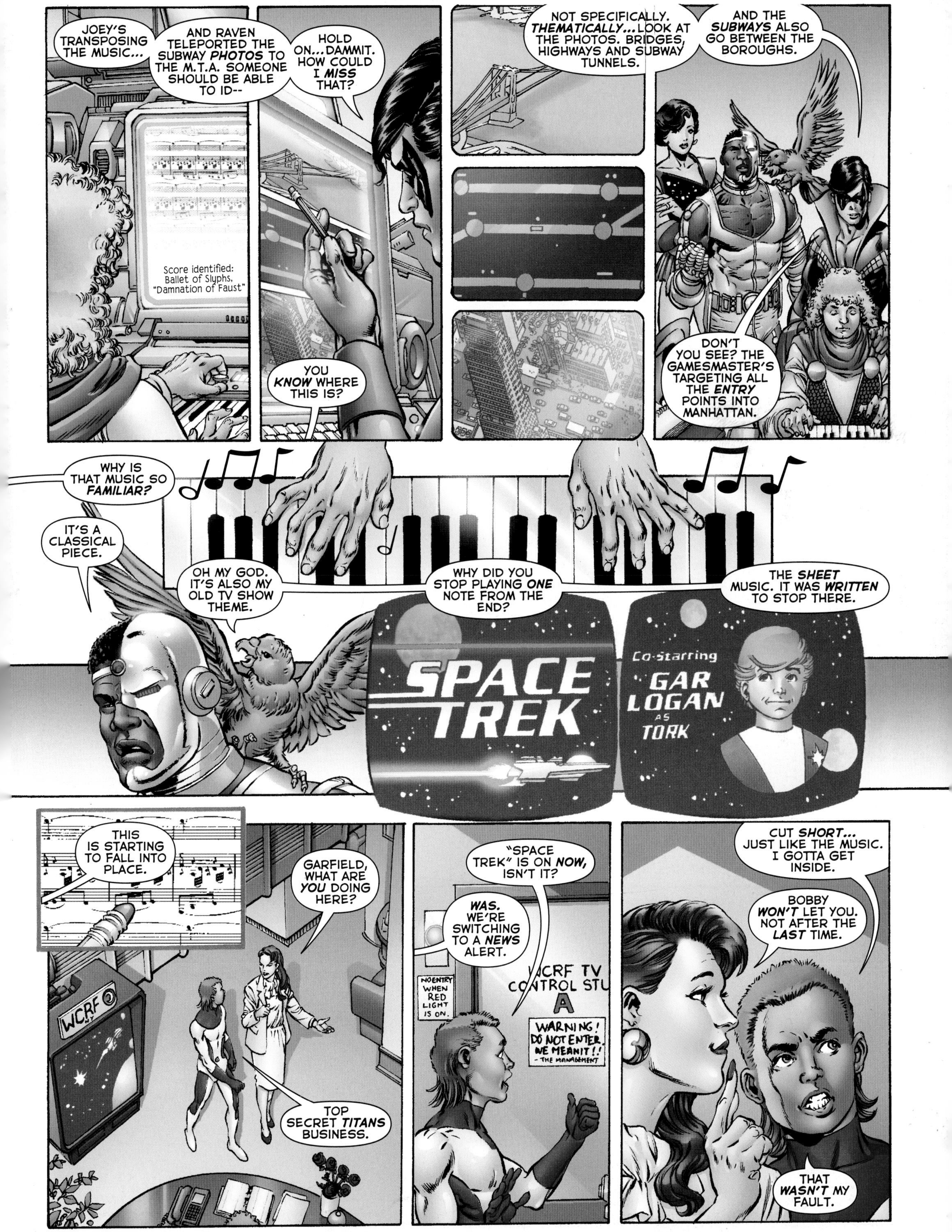
JOEY'S TRANSPOSING THE MUSIC...
AND RAVEN TELEPORTED THE SUBWAY PHOTOS TO THE M.T.A. SOMEONE SHOULD BE ABLE TO ID--
Score identified: Ballet of Slyphs, "Damnation of Faust"
HOLD ON...DAMMIT. HOW COULD I MISS THAT?
YOU KNOW WHERE THIS IS?
NOT SPECIFICALLY. THEMATICALLY...LOOK AT THE PHOTOS. BRIDGES, HIGHWAYS AND SUBWAY TUNNELS.
AND THE SUBWAYS ALSO GO BETWEEN THE BOROUGHS.
DON'T YOU SEE? THE GAMESMASTER'S TARGETING ALL THE ENTRY POINTS INTO MANHATTAN.
WHY IS THAT MUSIC SO FAMILIAR?
IT'S A CLASSICAL PIECE.
OH MY GOD. IT'S ALSO MY OLD TV SHOW THEME.
WHY DID YOU STOP PLAYING ONE NOTE FROM THE END?
THE SHEET MUSIC. IT WAS WRITTEN TO STOP THERE.
SPACE TREK
Co-starring GAR LOGAN AS TORK
THIS IS STARTING TO FALL INTO PLACE.
GARFIELD, WHAT ARE YOU DOING HERE?
WCRF
TOP SECRET TITANS BUSINESS.
"SPACE TREK" IS ON NOW, ISN'T IT?
WAS. WE'RE SWITCHING TO A NEWS ALERT.
NO ENTRY WHEN RED LIGHT IS ON.
WCRF TV CONTROL STU
A
WARNING! DO NOT ENTER. WE MEAN IT!! - THE MANAGEMENT
CUT SHORT... JUST LIKE THE MUSIC. I GOTTA GET INSIDE.
BOBBY WON'T LET YOU. NOT AFTER THE LAST TIME.
THAT WASN'T MY FAULT.

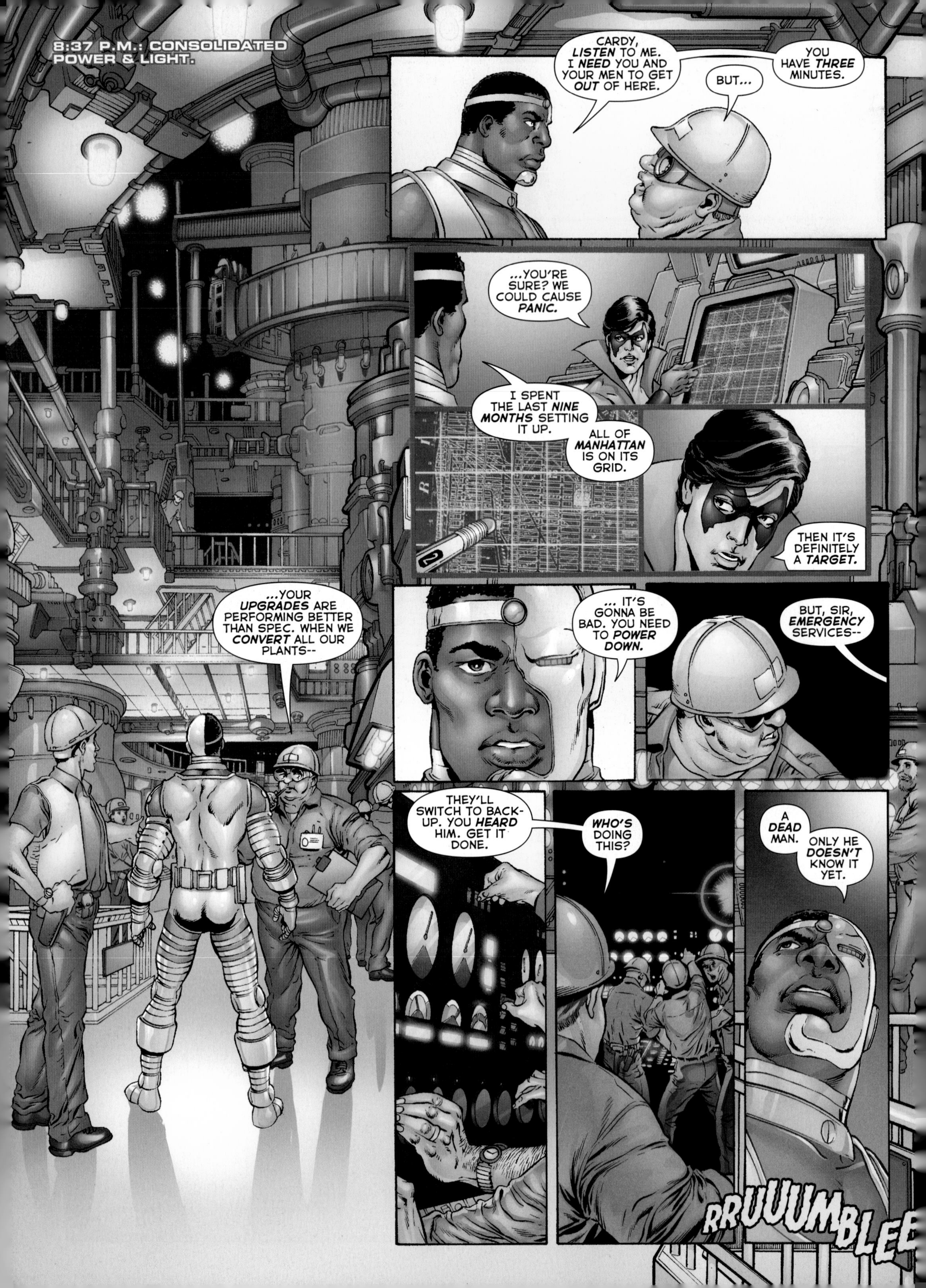

8:37 P.M.: CONSOLIDATED POWER & LIGHT.
CARDY, LISTEN TO ME. I NEED YOU AND YOUR MEN TO GET OUT OF HERE.
BUT...
YOU HAVE THREE MINUTES.
...YOU'RE SURE? WE COULD CAUSE PANIC.
I SPENT THE LAST NINE MONTHS SETTING IT UP.
ALL OF MANHATTAN IS ON ITS GRID.
THEN IT'S DEFINITELY A TARGET.
...YOUR UPGRADES ARE PERFORMING BETTER THAN SPEC. WHEN WE CONVERT ALL OUR PLANTS--
... IT'S GONNA BE BAD. YOU NEED TO POWER DOWN.
BUT, SIR, EMERGENCY SERVICES--
THEY'LL SWITCH TO BACK-UP. YOU HEARD HIM. GET IT DONE.
WHO'S DOING THIS?
A DEAD MAN.
ONLY HE DOESN'T KNOW IT YET.
RRUUUMBLEE

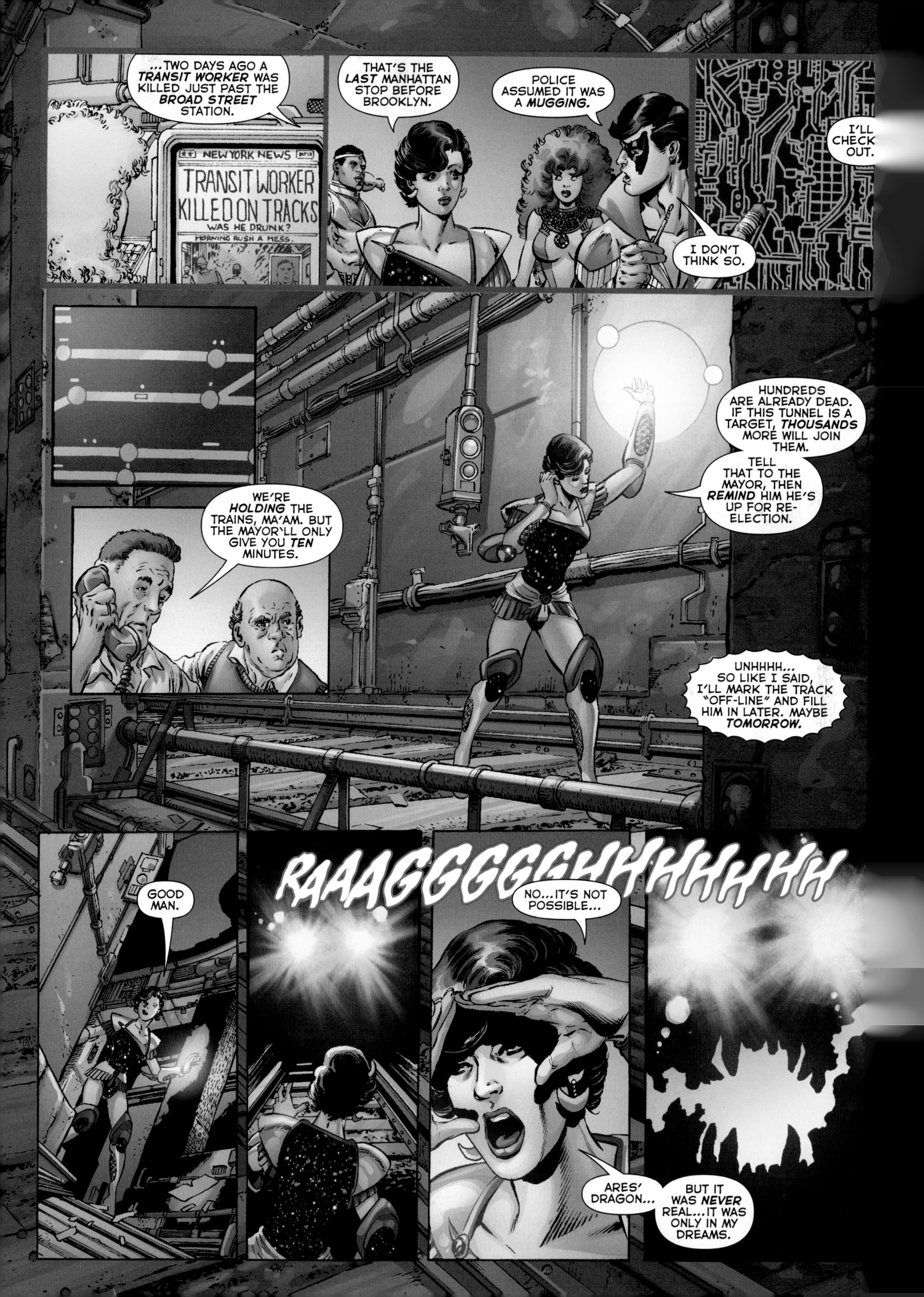
...TWO DAYS AGO A TRANSIT WORKER WAS KILLED JUST PAST THE BROAD STREET STATION.
NEW YORK NEWS
TRANSIT WORKER KILLED ON TRACKS
WAS HE DRUNK?
MORNING RUSH A MESS.
THAT'S THE LAST MANHATTAN STOP BEFORE BROOKLYN.
POLICE ASSUMED IT WAS A MUGGING.
I DON'T THINK SO.
I'LL CHECK OUT.
WE'RE HOLDING THE TRAINS, MA'AM. BUT THE MAYOR'LL ONLY GIVE YOU TEN MINUTES.
HUNDREDS ARE ALREADY DEAD. IF THIS TUNNEL IS A TARGET, THOUSANDS MORE WILL JOIN THEM.
TELL THAT TO THE MAYOR, THEN REMIND HIM HE'S UP FOR RE-ELECTION.
UNHHHH... SO LIKE I SAID, I'LL MARK THE TRACK "OFF-LINE" AND FILL HIM IN LATER. MAYBE TOMORROW.
GOOD MAN.
RAAAGGGGGHHHHHHHH
NO...IT'S NOT POSSIBLE...
ARES' DRAGON...
BUT IT WAS NEVER REAL...IT WAS ONLY IN MY DREAMS.

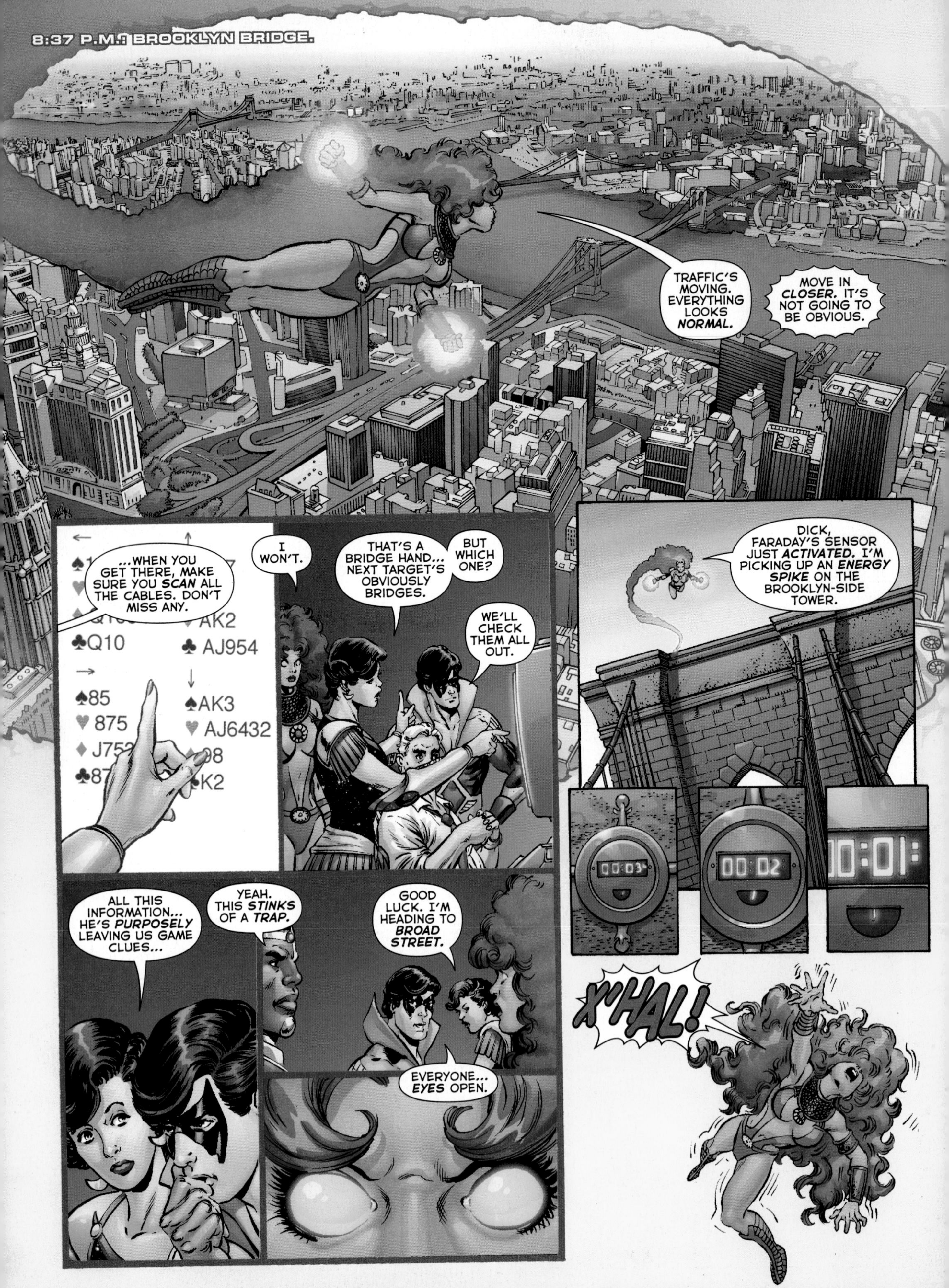
8:37 P.M.: BROOKLYN BRIDGE.
TRAFFIC'S MOVING. EVERYTHING LOOKS NORMAL.
MOVE IN CLOSER. IT'S NOT GOING TO BE OBVIOUS.
...WHEN YOU GET THERE, MAKE SURE YOU SCAN ALL THE CABLES. DON'T MISS ANY.
♥AK2
♣Q10
♣AJ954
♠85
♥875
♠AK3
♥AJ6432
I WON'T.
THAT'S A BRIDGE HAND... NEXT TARGET'S OBVIOUSLY BRIDGES.
BUT WHICH ONE?
WE'LL CHECK THEM ALL OUT.
DICK, FARADAY'S SENSOR JUST ACTIVATED. I'M PICKING UP AN ENERGY SPIKE ON THE BROOKLYN-SIDE TOWER.
00:03
00:02
00:01
ALL THIS INFORMATION... HE'S PURPOSELY LEAVING US GAME CLUES...
YEAH. THIS STINKS OF A TRAP.
GOOD LUCK. I'M HEADING TO BROAD STREET.
EVERYONE... EYES OPEN.
X'HAL!

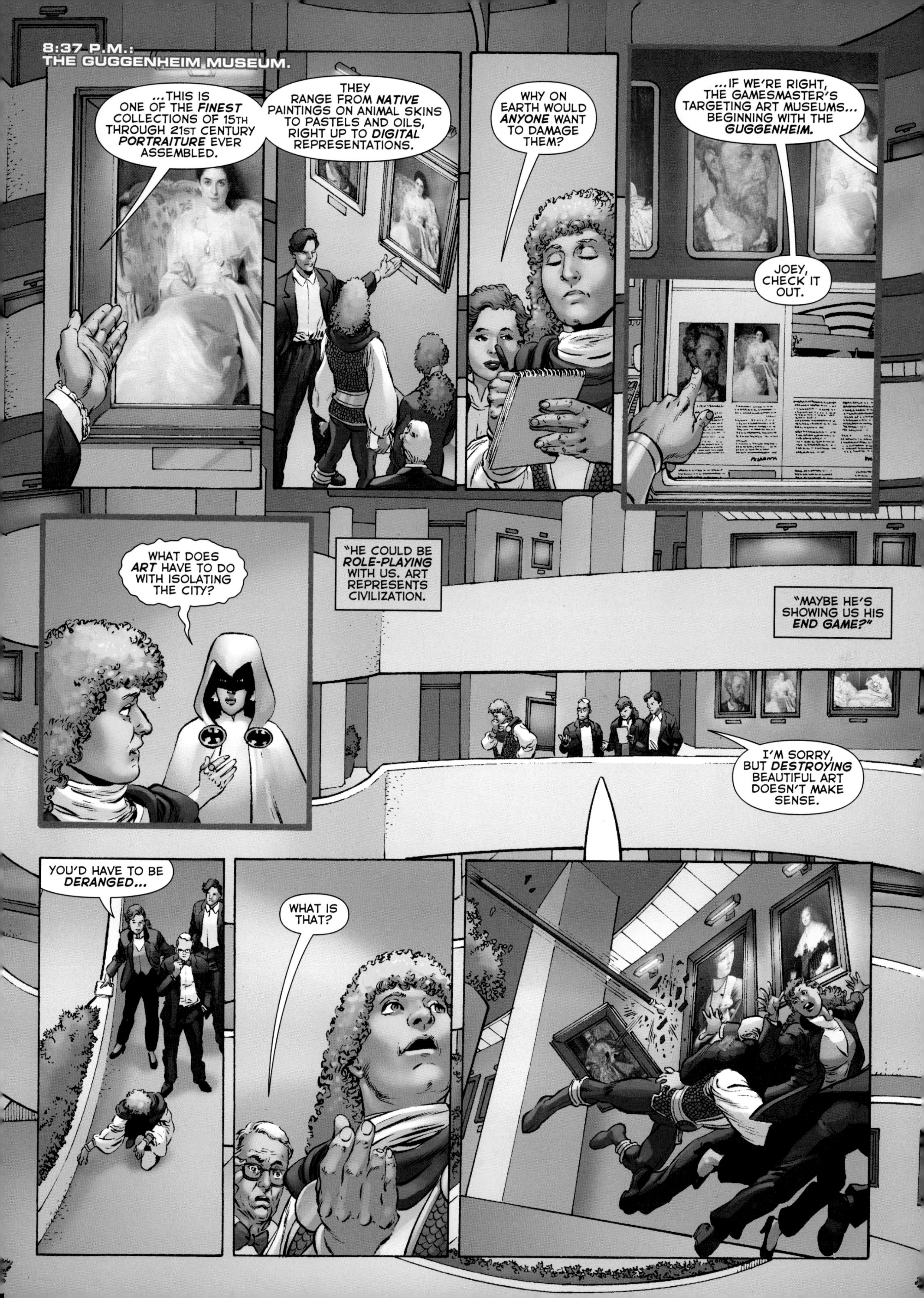
8:37 P.M.: THE GUGGENHEIM MUSEUM.
...THIS IS ONE OF THE FINEST COLLECTIONS OF 15TH THROUGH 21ST CENTURY PORTRAITURE EVER ASSEMBLED.
THEY RANGE FROM NATIVE PAINTINGS ON ANIMAL SKINS TO PASTELS AND OILS, RIGHT UP TO DIGITAL REPRESENTATIONS.
WHY ON EARTH WOULD ANYONE WANT TO DAMAGE THEM?
...IF WE'RE RIGHT, THE GAMESMASTER'S TARGETING ART MUSEUMS... BEGINNING WITH THE GUGGENHEIM.
JOEY, CHECK IT OUT.
WHAT DOES ART HAVE TO DO WITH ISOLATING THE CITY?
"HE COULD BE ROLE-PLAYING WITH US. ART REPRESENTS CIVILIZATION.
"MAYBE HE'S SHOWING US HIS END GAME?"
I'M SORRY, BUT DESTROYING BEAUTIFUL ART DOESN'T MAKE SENSE.
YOU'D HAVE TO BE DERANGED...
WHAT IS THAT?

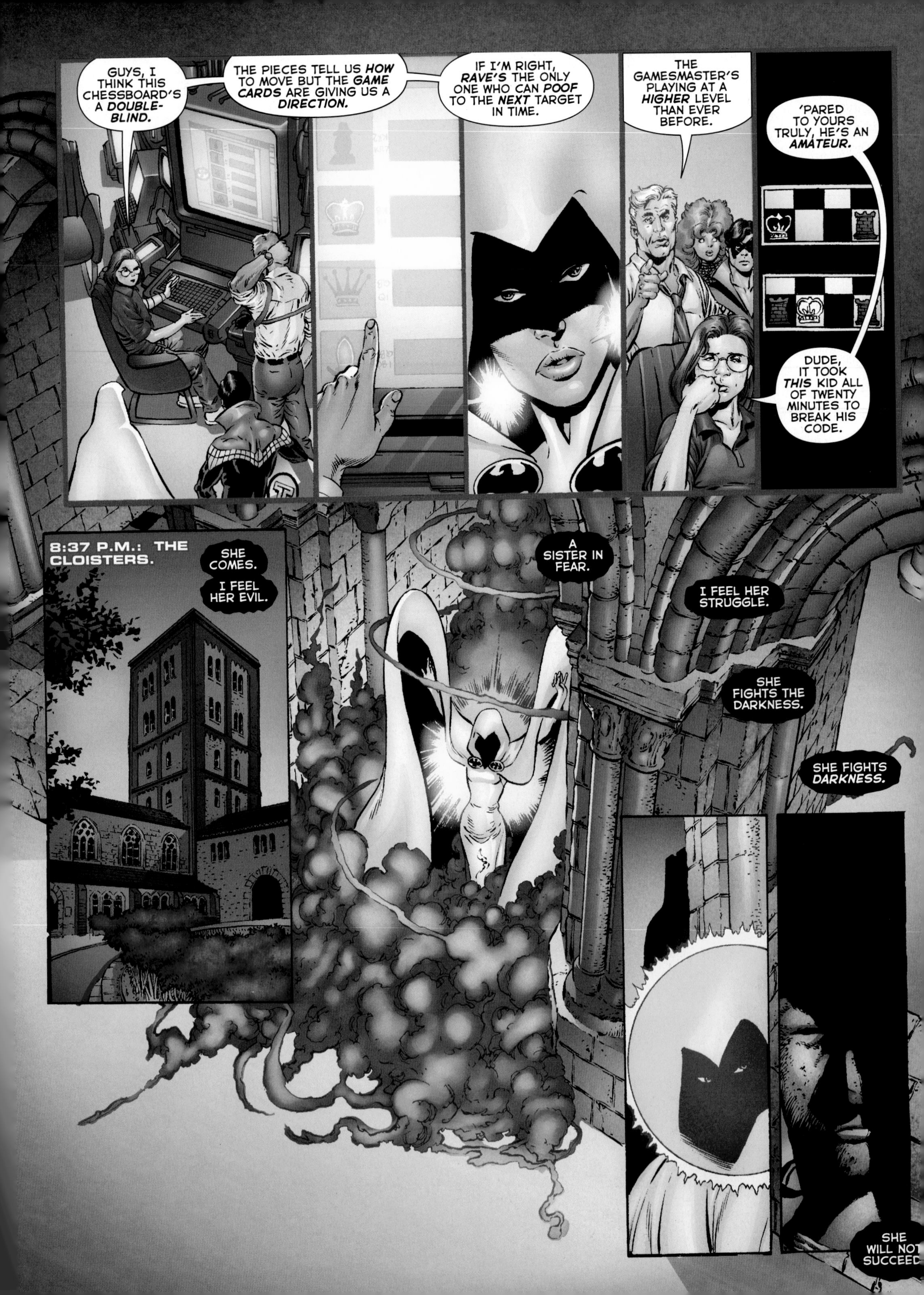

GUYS, I THINK THIS CHESSBOARD'S A DOUBLE-BLIND.
THE PIECES TELL US HOW TO MOVE BUT THE GAME CARDS ARE GIVING US A DIRECTION.
IF I'M RIGHT, RAVE'S THE ONLY ONE WHO CAN POOF TO THE NEXT TARGET IN TIME.
THE GAMESMASTER'S PLAYING AT A HIGHER LEVEL THAN EVER BEFORE.
'PARED TO YOURS TRULY, HE'S AN AMATEUR.
DUDE, IT TOOK THIS KID ALL OF TWENTY MINUTES TO BREAK HIS CODE.
8:37 P.M.: THE CLOISTERS.
SHE COMES.
I FEEL HER EVIL.
A SISTER IN FEAR.
I FEEL HER STRUGGLE.
SHE FIGHTS THE DARKNESS.
SHE FIGHTS DARKNESS.
SHE WILL NOT SUCCEED.

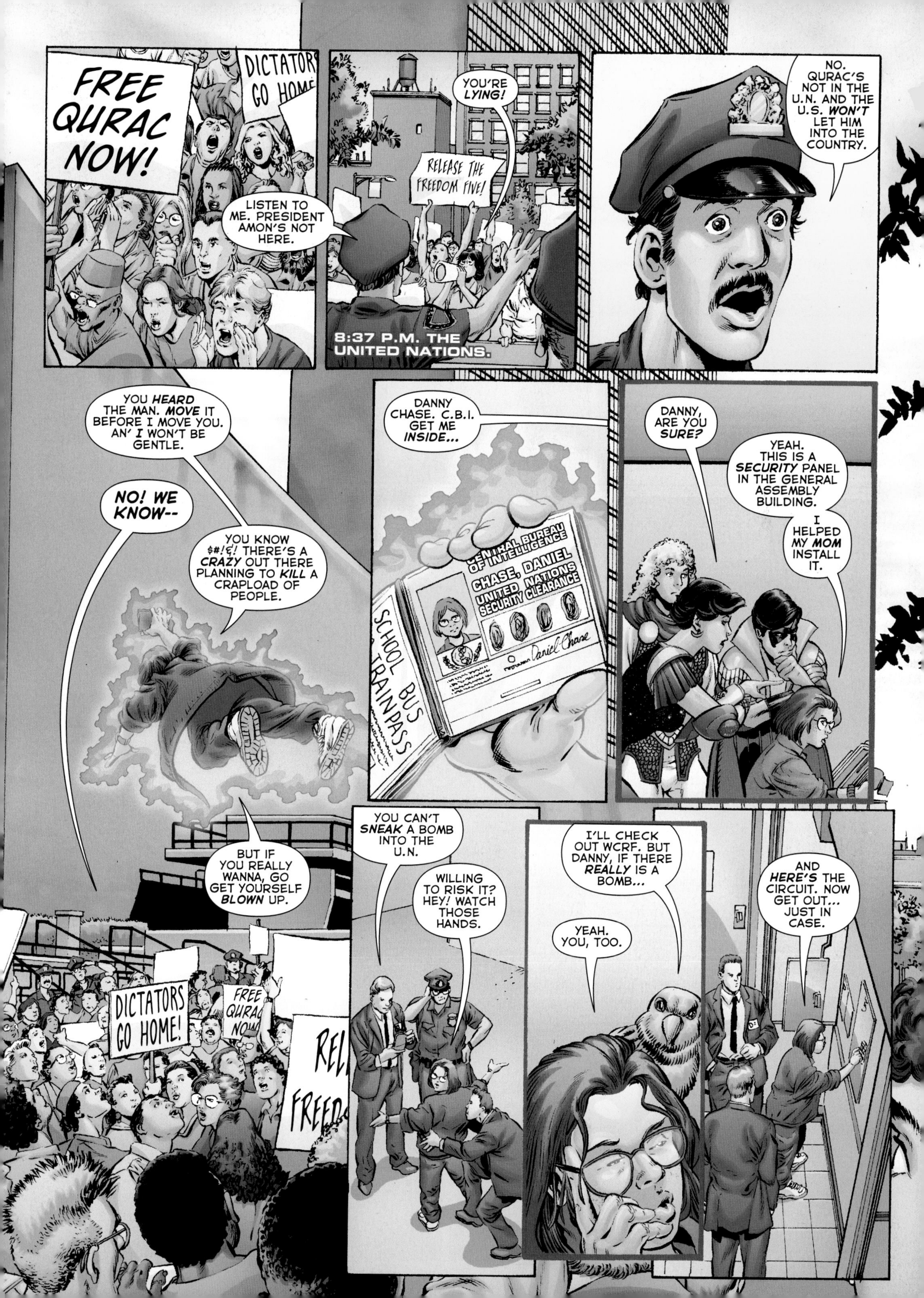
FREE QURAC NOW!
DICTATORS GO HOME
LISTEN TO ME. PRESIDENT AMON'S NOT HERE.
YOU'RE LYING!
RELEASE THE FREEDOM FIVE!
8:37 P.M. THE UNITED NATIONS.
NO. QURAC'S NOT IN THE U.N. AND THE U.S. WON'T LET HIM INTO THE COUNTRY.
YOU HEARD THE MAN. MOVE IT BEFORE I MOVE YOU. AN' I WON'T BE GENTLE.
NO! WE KNOW--
YOU KNOW $#!&! THERE'S A CRAZY OUT THERE PLANNING TO KILL A CRAPLOAD OF PEOPLE.
BUT IF YOU REALLY WANNA, GO GET YOURSELF BLOWN UP.
DICTATORS GO HOME!
FREE QURAC NOW
DANNY CHASE. C.B.I. GET ME INSIDE...
CENTRAL BUREAU OF INTELLIGENCE
CHASE, DANIEL
UNITED NATIONS SECURITY CLEARANCE
Daniel Chase
SCHOOL BUS TRAINPASS
DANNY, ARE YOU SURE?
YEAH. THIS IS A SECURITY PANEL IN THE GENERAL ASSEMBLY BUILDING.
I HELPED MY MOM INSTALL IT.
YOU CAN'T SNEAK A BOMB INTO THE U.N.
WILLING TO RISK IT? HEY! WATCH THOSE HANDS.
I'LL CHECK OUT WCRF. BUT DANNY, IF THERE REALLY IS A BOMB...
YEAH. YOU, TOO.
AND HERE'S THE CIRCUIT. NOW GET OUT... JUST IN CASE.

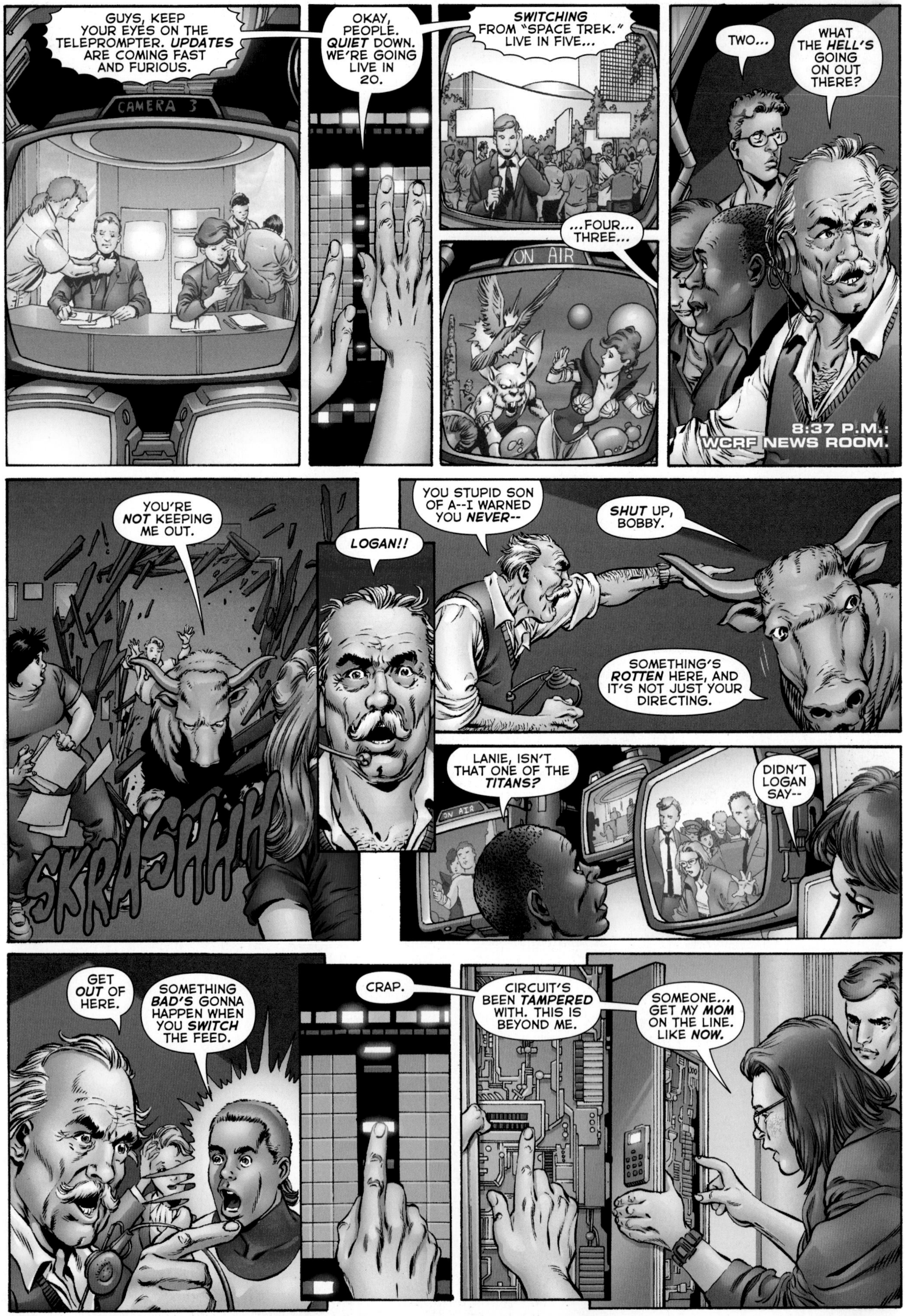
GUYS, KEEP YOUR EYES ON THE TELEPROMPTER. UPDATES ARE COMING FAST AND FURIOUS.
CAMERA 3
OKAY, PEOPLE. QUIET DOWN. WE'RE GOING LIVE IN 20.
SWITCHING FROM "SPACE TREK." LIVE IN FIVE...
...FOUR... THREE...
ON AIR
TWO...
WHAT THE HELL'S GOING ON OUT THERE?
8:37 P.M.: WCRF NEWS ROOM.
YOU'RE NOT KEEPING ME OUT.
SKRASHHH
LOGAN!!
YOU STUPID SON OF A--I WARNED YOU NEVER--
SHUT UP, BOBBY.
SOMETHING'S ROTTEN HERE, AND IT'S NOT JUST YOUR DIRECTING.
LANIE, ISN'T THAT ONE OF THE TITANS?
ON AIR
DIDN'T LOGAN SAY--
GET OUT OF HERE.
SOMETHING BAD'S GONNA HAPPEN WHEN YOU SWITCH THE FEED.
CRAP.
CIRCUIT'S BEEN TAMPERED WITH. THIS IS BEYOND ME.
SOMEONE... GET MY MOM ON THE LINE. LIKE NOW.

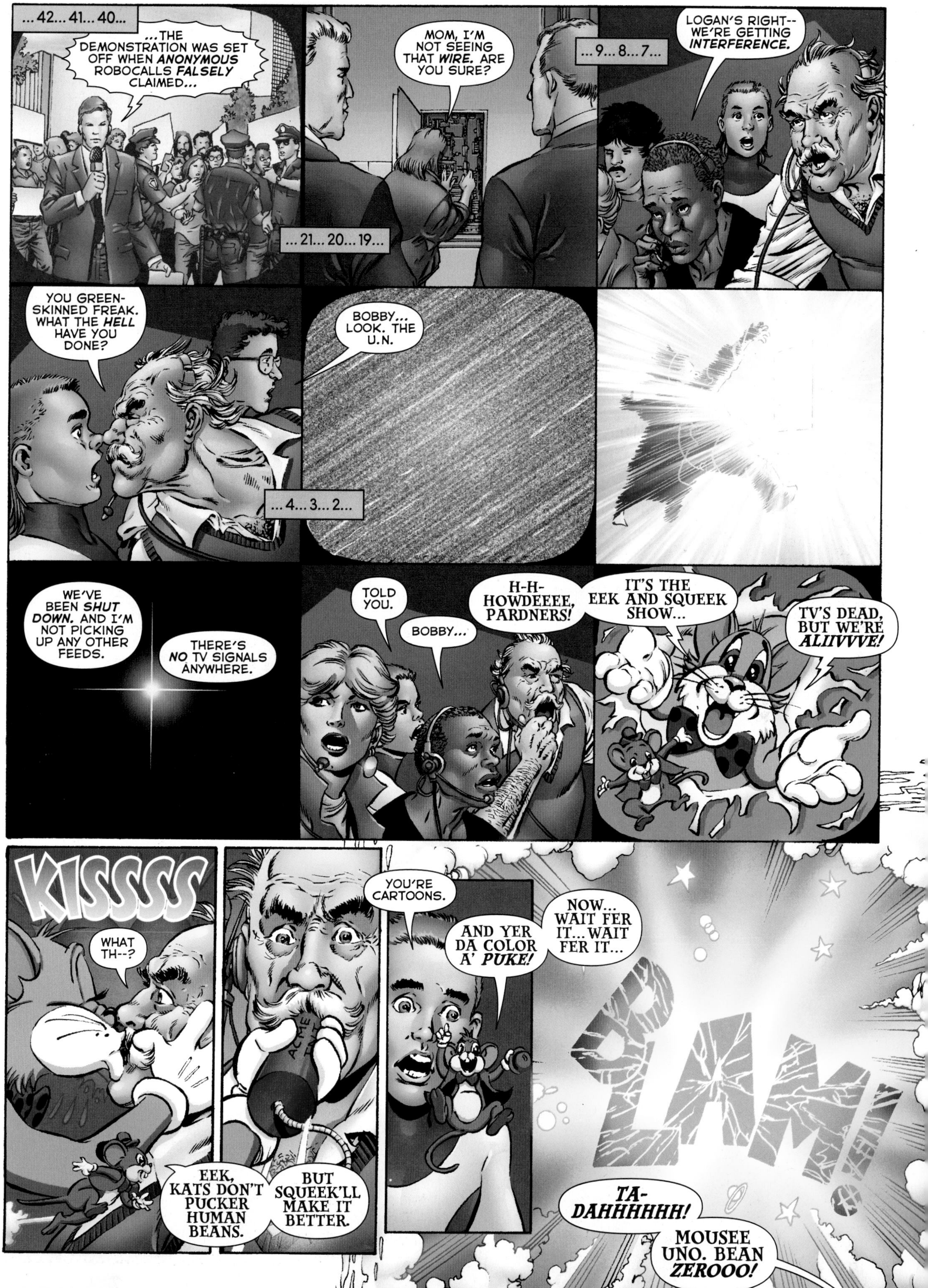
...42... 41... 40...
...THE DEMONSTRATION WAS SET OFF WHEN ANONYMOUS ROBOCALLS FALSELY CLAIMED...
...21... 20... 19...
MOM, I'M NOT SEEING THAT WIRE. ARE YOU SURE?
...9... 8... 7...
LOGAN'S RIGHT-- WE'RE GETTING INTERFERENCE.
YOU GREEN-SKINNED FREAK. WHAT THE HELL HAVE YOU DONE?
...4... 3... 2...
BOBBY... LOOK. THE U.N.
WE'VE BEEN SHUT DOWN. AND I'M NOT PICKING UP ANY OTHER FEEDS.
THERE'S NO TV SIGNALS ANYWHERE.
TOLD YOU.
BOBBY...
H-H-HOWDEEEE, PARDNERS!
IT'S THE EEK AND SQUEEK SHOW...
TV'S DEAD, BUT WE'RE ALIIVVVE!
KISSSS
WHAT TH--?
EEK, KATS DON'T PUCKER HUMAN BEANS.
BUT SQUEEK'LL MAKE IT BETTER.
ACME TNT
YOU'RE CARTOONS.
AND YER DA COLOR A' PUKE!
NOW... WAIT FER IT... WAIT FER IT...
BLAM!
TA-DAHHHHHH!
MOUSEE UNO. BEAN ZEROOO!

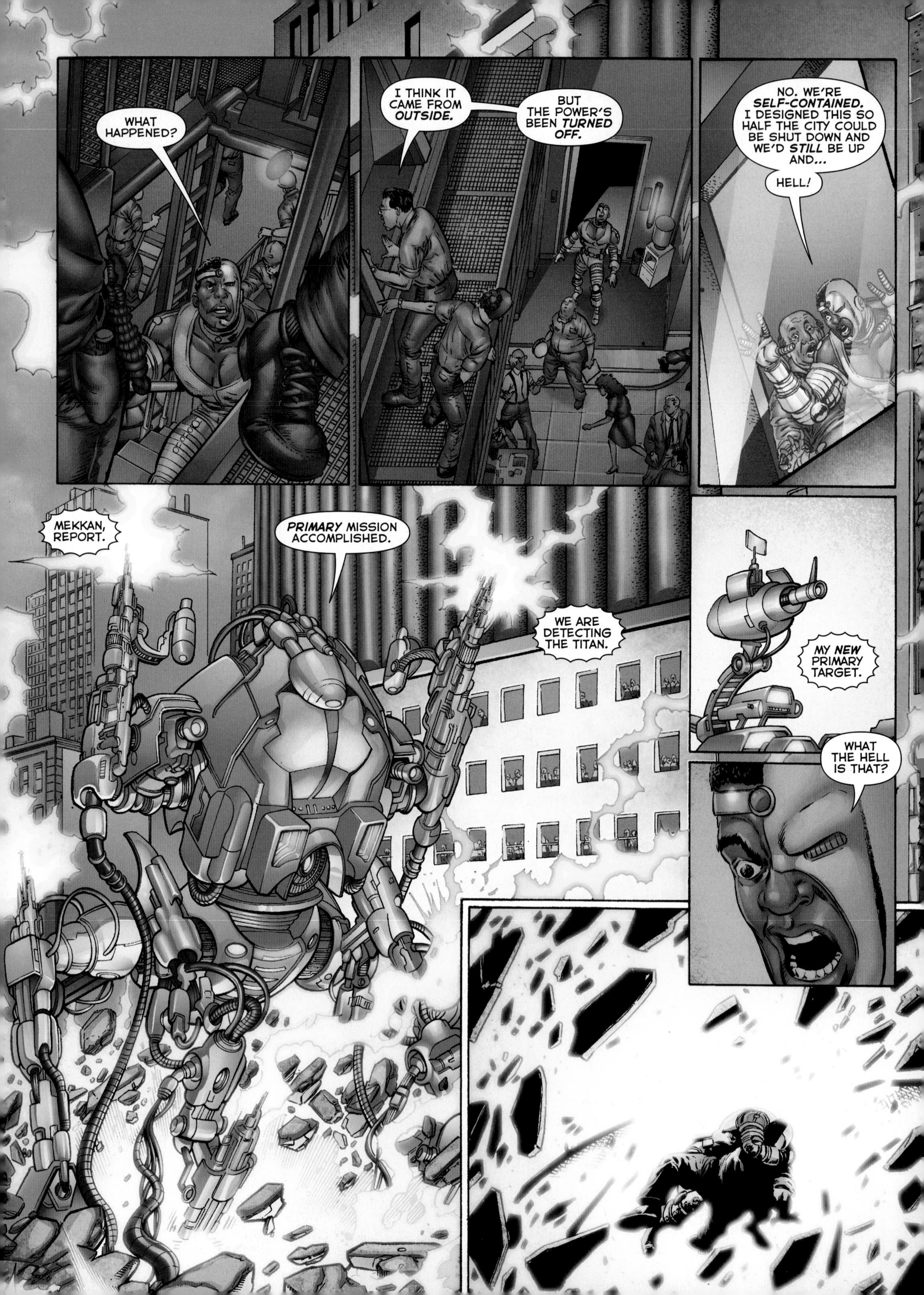
WHAT HAPPENED?
I THINK IT CAME FROM OUTSIDE.
BUT THE POWER'S BEEN TURNED OFF.
NO. WE'RE SELF-CONTAINED. I DESIGNED THIS SO HALF THE CITY COULD BE SHUT DOWN AND WE'D STILL BE UP AND...
HELL!
MEKKAN, REPORT.
PRIMARY MISSION ACCOMPLISHED.
WE ARE DETECTING THE TITAN.
MY NEW PRIMARY TARGET.
WHAT THE HELL IS THAT?

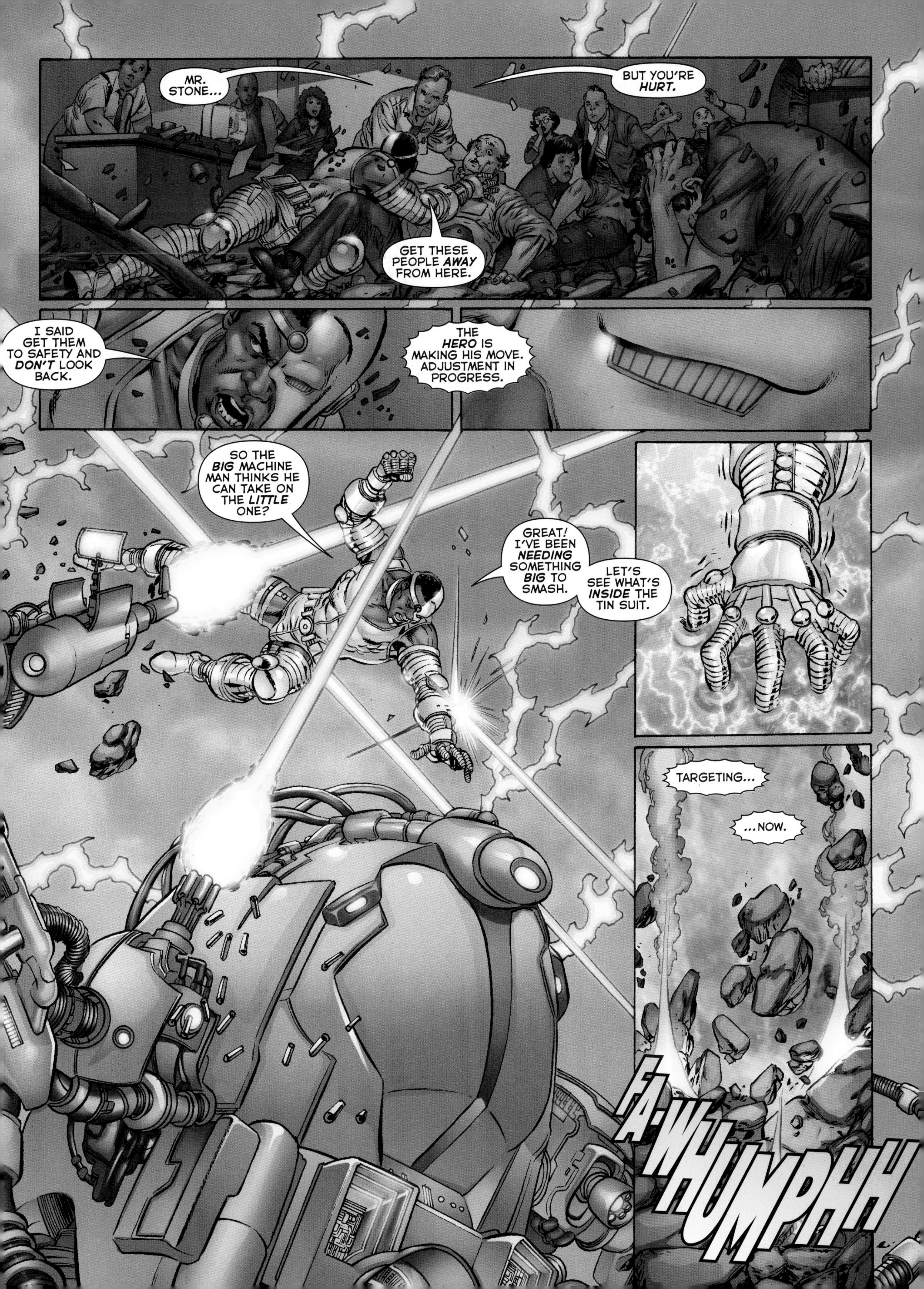

MR. STONE...
BUT YOU'RE *HURT.*
GET THESE PEOPLE *AWAY* FROM HERE.
I SAID GET THEM TO SAFETY AND *DON'T* LOOK BACK.
THE *HERO* IS MAKING HIS MOVE. ADJUSTMENT IN PROGRESS.
SO THE *BIG* MACHINE MAN THINKS HE CAN TAKE ON THE *LITTLE* ONE?
GREAT! I'VE BEEN *NEEDING* SOMETHING *BIG* TO SMASH.
LET'S SEE WHAT'S *INSIDE* THE TIN SUIT.
TARGETING...
...NOW.
FA-WHUMPHH

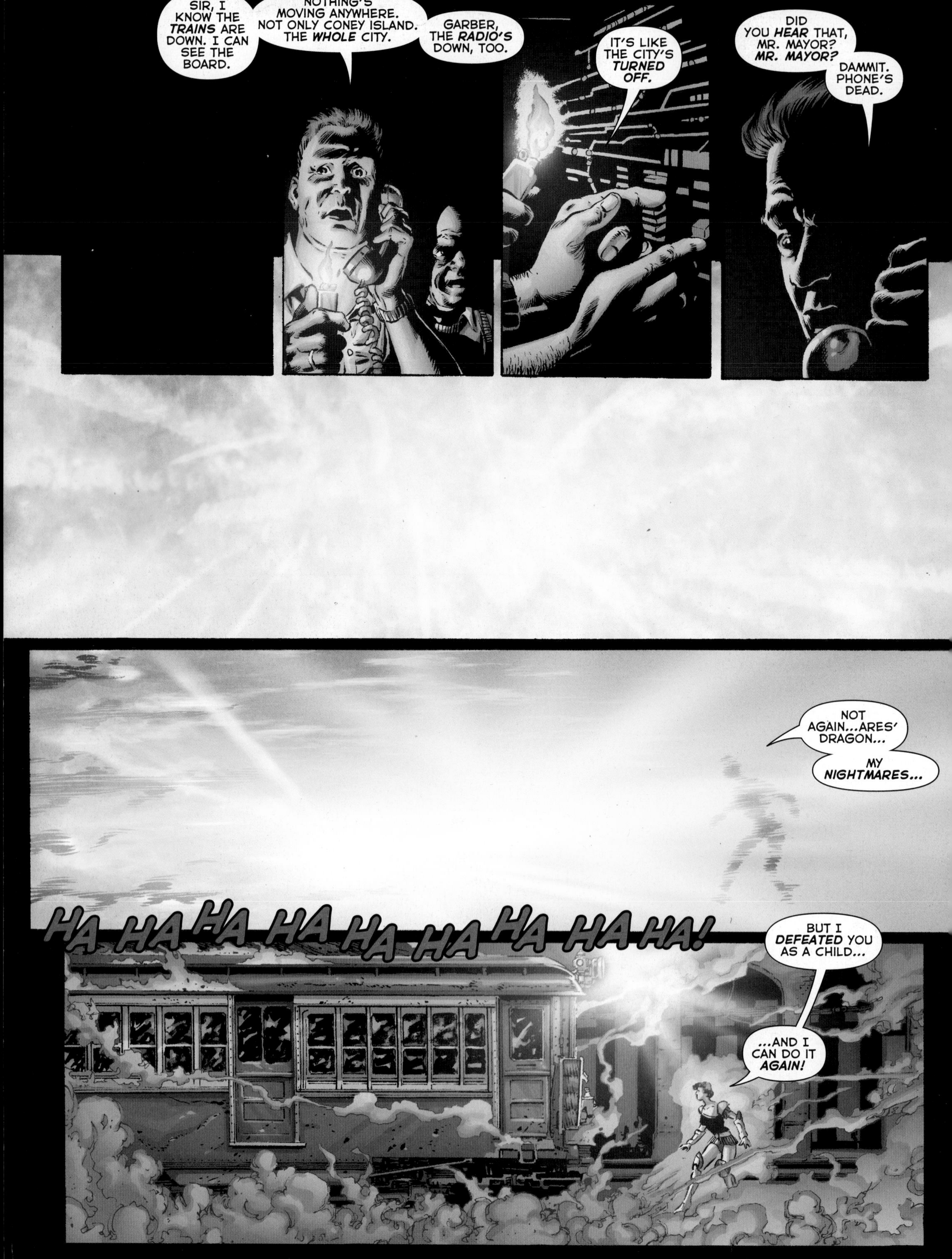
SIR, I KNOW THE TRAINS ARE DOWN. I CAN SEE THE BOARD.
NOTHING'S MOVING ANYWHERE. NOT ONLY CONEY ISLAND. THE WHOLE CITY.
GARBER, THE RADIO'S DOWN, TOO.
IT'S LIKE THE CITY'S TURNED OFF.
DID YOU HEAR THAT, MR. MAYOR? MR. MAYOR?
DAMMIT. PHONE'S DEAD.
NOT AGAIN...ARES' DRAGON...
MY NIGHTMARES...
HA HA HA HA HA HA HA HA HA!
BUT I DEFEATED YOU AS A CHILD...
...AND I CAN DO IT AGAIN!

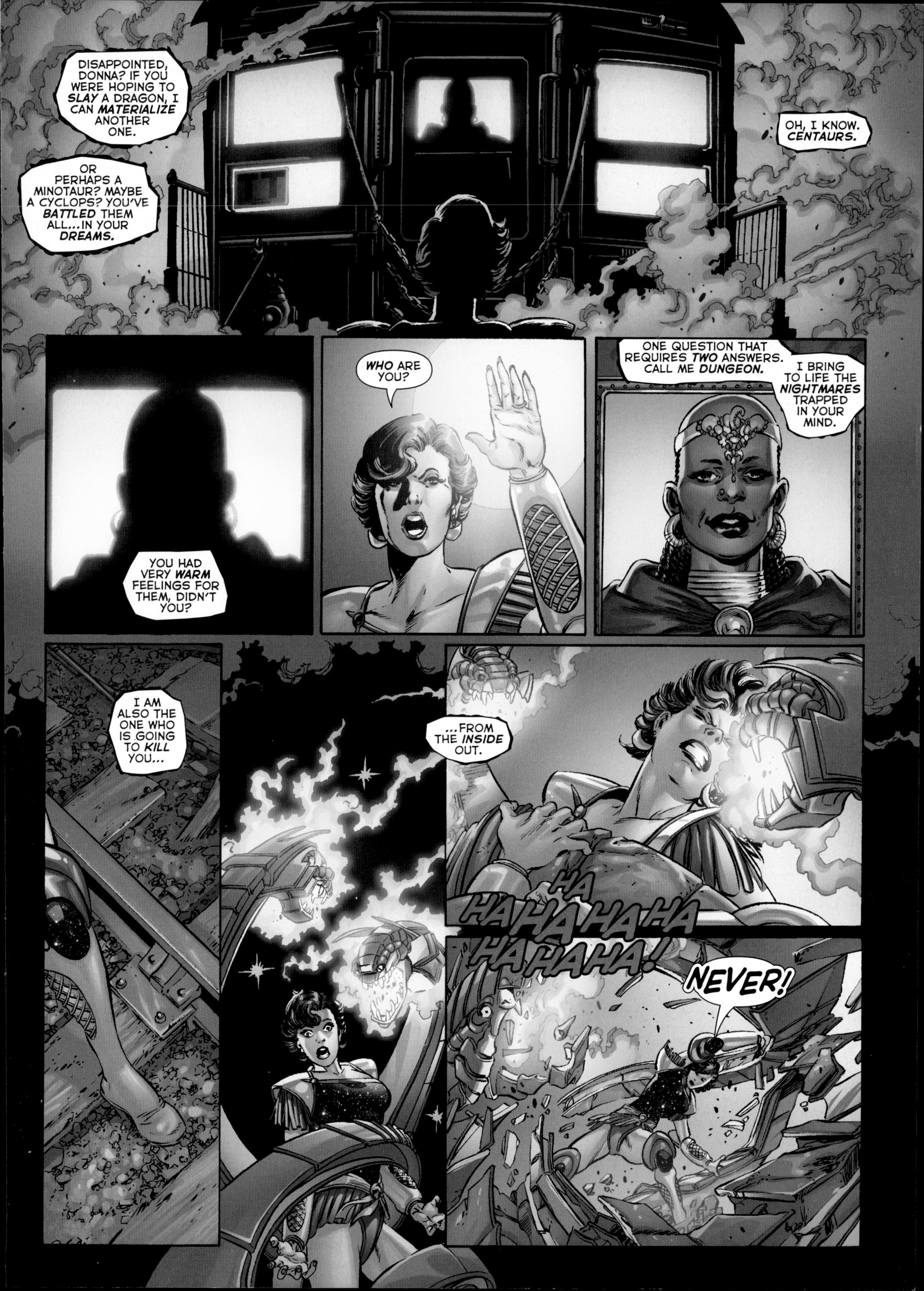
DISAPPOINTED, DONNA? IF YOU WERE HOPING TO SLAY A DRAGON, I CAN MATERIALIZE ANOTHER ONE.
OR PERHAPS A MINOTAUR? MAYBE A CYCLOPS? YOU'VE BATTLED THEM ALL...IN YOUR DREAMS.
OH, I KNOW. CENTAURS.
YOU HAD VERY WARM FEELINGS FOR THEM, DIDN'T YOU?
WHO ARE YOU?
ONE QUESTION THAT REQUIRES TWO ANSWERS. CALL ME DUNGEON.
I BRING TO LIFE THE NIGHTMARES TRAPPED IN YOUR MIND.
I AM ALSO THE ONE WHO IS GOING TO KILL YOU...
...FROM THE INSIDE OUT.
HA HAHAHAHAHA HAHAHA!
NEVER!

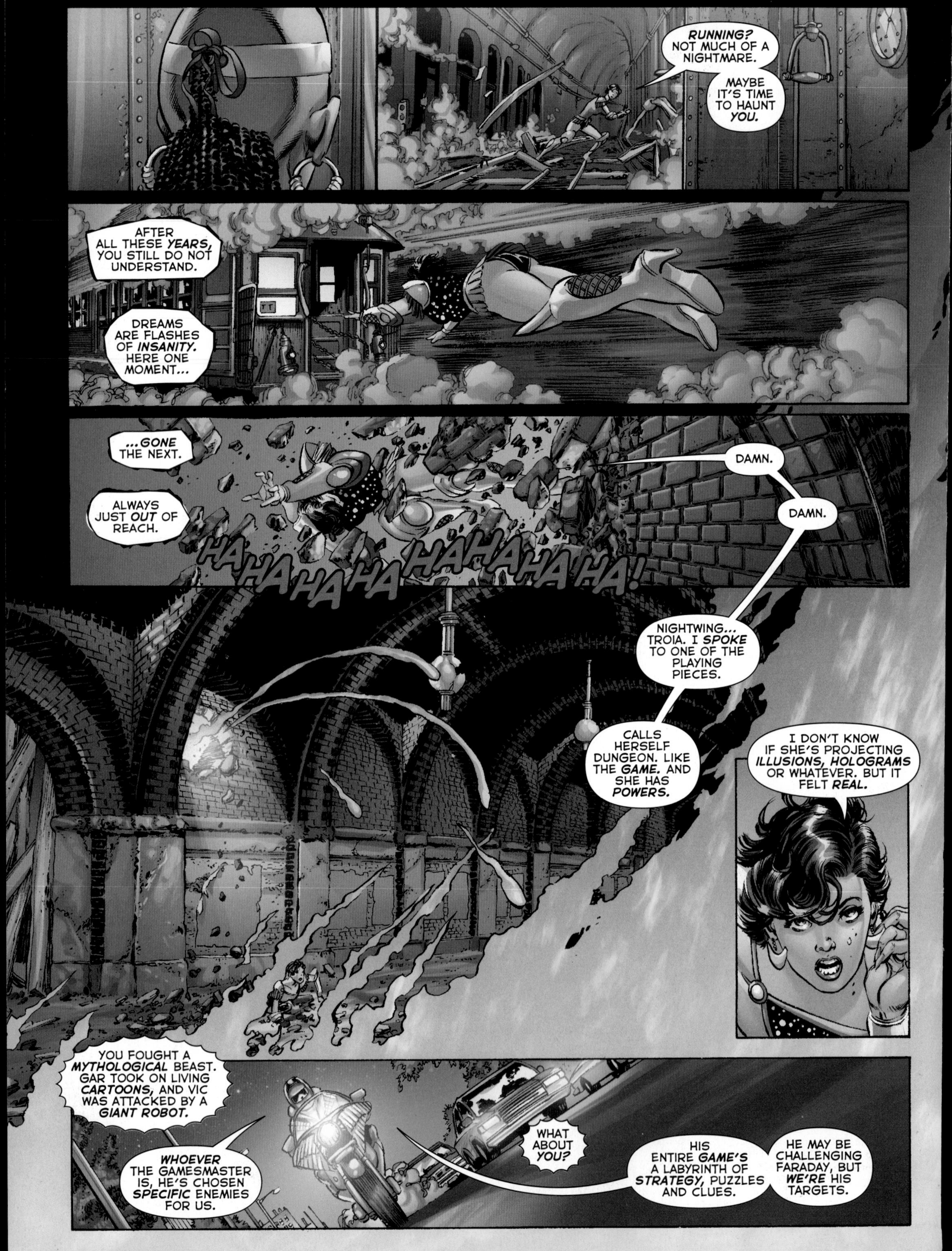
RUNNING? NOT MUCH OF A NIGHTMARE.
MAYBE IT'S TIME TO HAUNT YOU.
AFTER ALL THESE YEARS, YOU STILL DO NOT UNDERSTAND.
DREAMS ARE FLASHES OF INSANITY. HERE ONE MOMENT...
...GONE THE NEXT.
ALWAYS JUST OUT OF REACH.
DAMN.
DAMN.
HAHAHAHA HAHAHAHAHA!
NIGHTWING... TROIA. I SPOKE TO ONE OF THE PLAYING PIECES.
CALLS HERSELF DUNGEON. LIKE THE GAME. AND SHE HAS POWERS.
I DON'T KNOW IF SHE'S PROJECTING ILLUSIONS, HOLOGRAMS OR WHATEVER. BUT IT FELT REAL.
YOU FOUGHT A MYTHOLOGICAL BEAST. GAR TOOK ON LIVING CARTOONS, AND VIC WAS ATTACKED BY A GIANT ROBOT.
WHOEVER THE GAMESMASTER IS, HE'S CHOSEN SPECIFIC ENEMIES FOR US.
WHAT ABOUT YOU?
HIS ENTIRE GAME'S A LABYRINTH OF STRATEGY, PUZZLES AND CLUES.
HE MAY BE CHALLENGING FARADAY, BUT WE'RE HIS TARGETS.

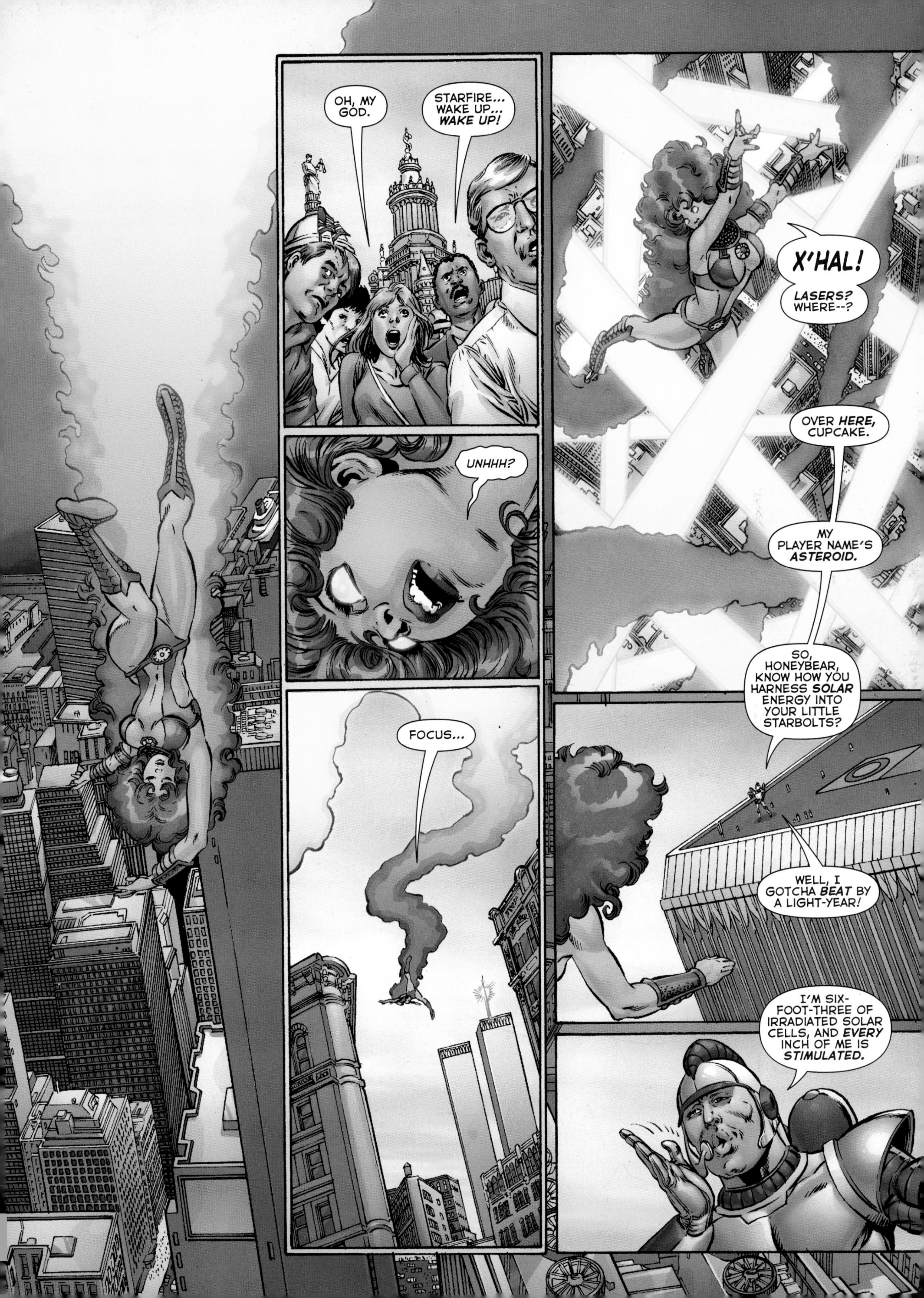
OH, MY GOD.
STARFIRE... WAKE UP... WAKE UP!
UNHHH?
FOCUS...
X'HAL!
LASERS? WHERE--?
OVER HERE, CUPCAKE.
MY PLAYER NAME'S ASTEROID.
SO, HONEYBEAR, KNOW HOW YOU HARNESS SOLAR ENERGY INTO YOUR LITTLE STARBOLTS?
WELL, I GOTCHA BEAT BY A LIGHT-YEAR!
I'M SIX-FOOT-THREE OF IRRADIATED SOLAR CELLS, AND EVERY INCH OF ME IS STIMULATED.

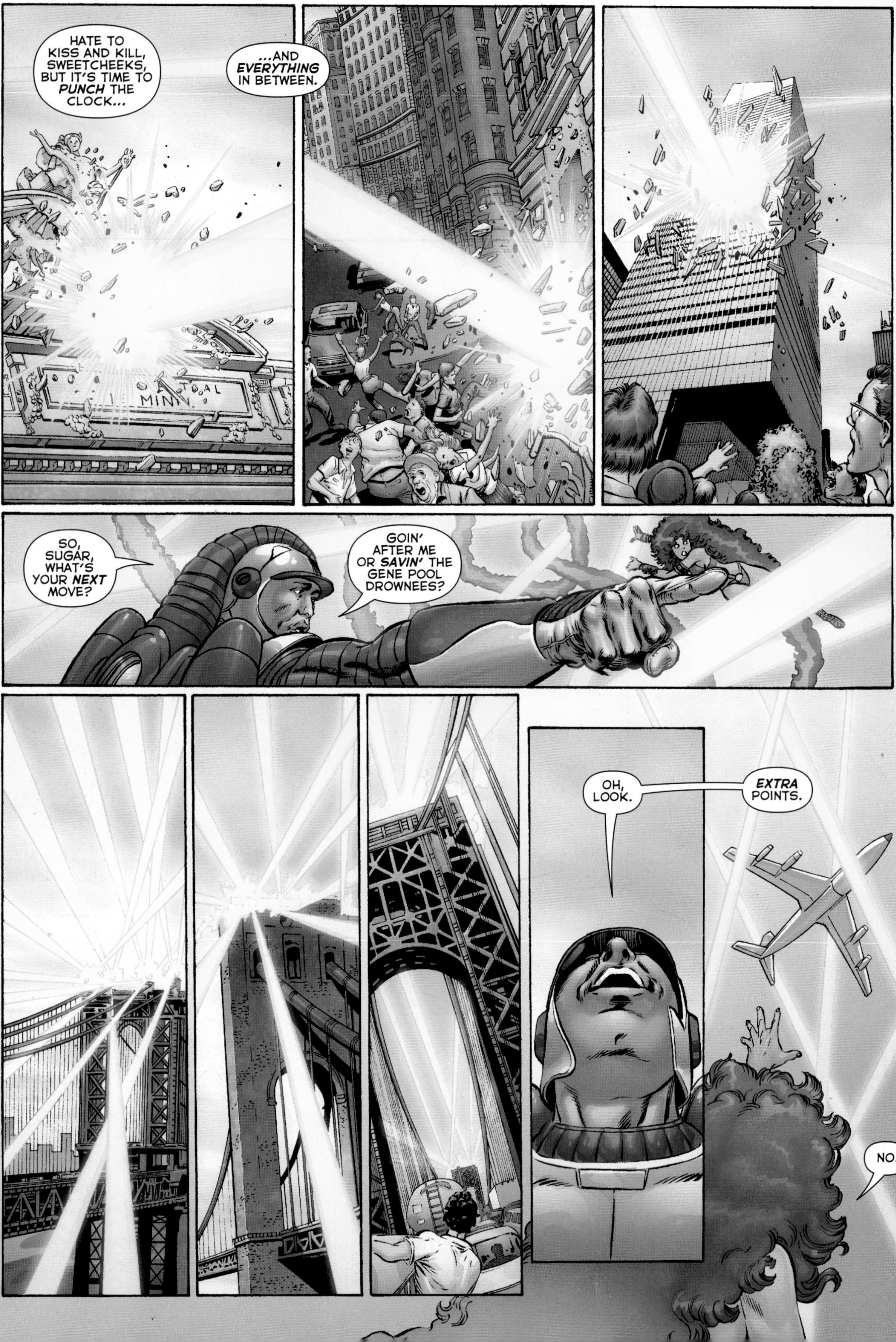
HATE TO KISS AND KILL, SWEETCHEEKS, BUT IT'S TIME TO PUNCH THE CLOCK...
...AND EVERYTHING IN BETWEEN.
SO, SUGAR, WHAT'S YOUR NEXT MOVE?
GOIN' AFTER ME OR SAVIN' THE GENE POOL DROWNEES?
OH, LOOK.
EXTRA POINTS.
NO.

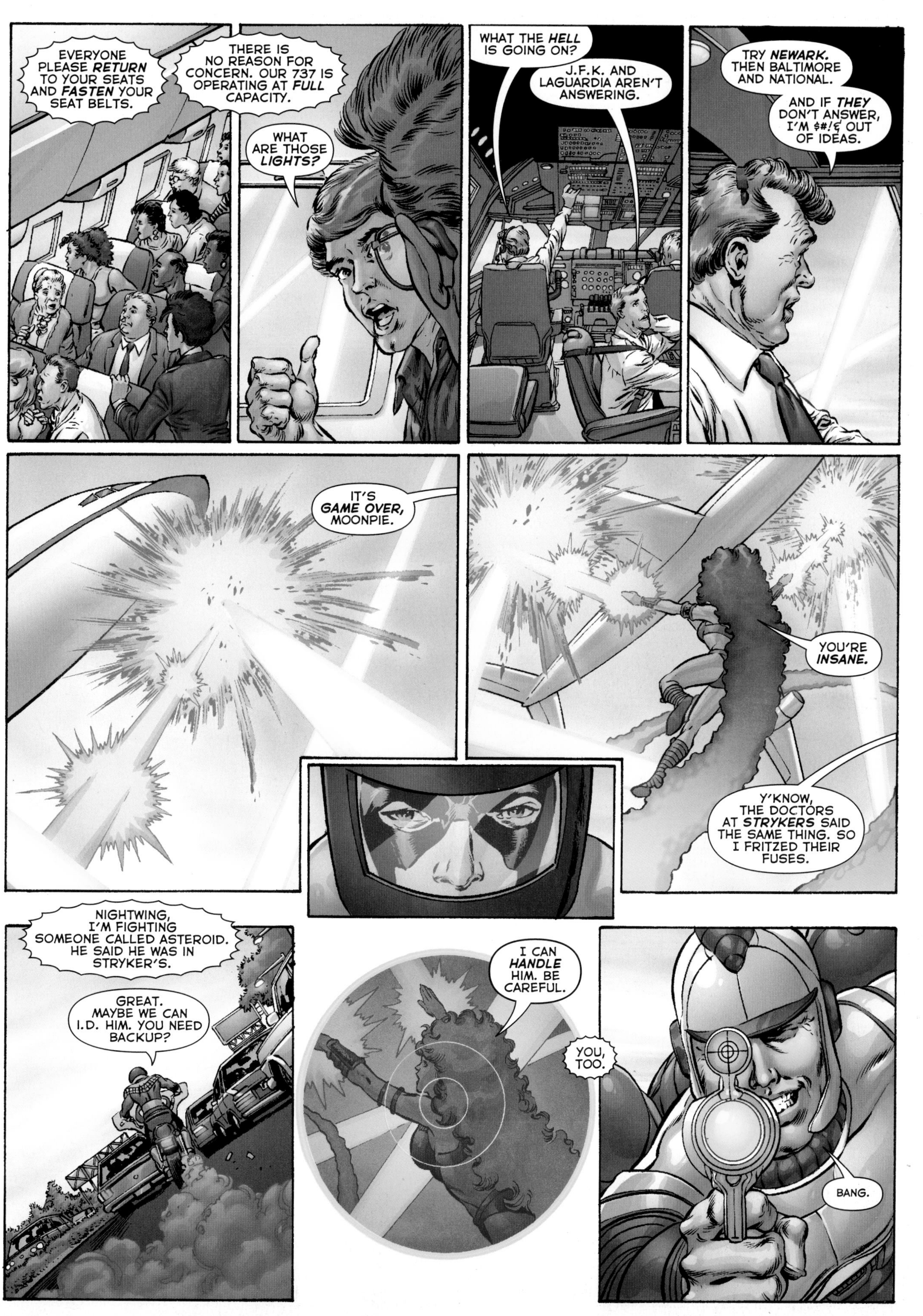
EVERYONE PLEASE RETURN TO YOUR SEATS AND FASTEN YOUR SEAT BELTS.
THERE IS NO REASON FOR CONCERN. OUR 737 IS OPERATING AT FULL CAPACITY.
WHAT ARE THOSE LIGHTS?
WHAT THE HELL IS GOING ON?
J.F.K. AND LAGUARDIA AREN'T ANSWERING.
TRY NEWARK. THEN BALTIMORE AND NATIONAL.
AND IF THEY DON'T ANSWER, I'M $#!¢ OUT OF IDEAS.
IT'S GAME OVER, MOONPIE.
YOU'RE INSANE.
Y'KNOW, THE DOCTORS AT STRYKERS SAID THE SAME THING. SO I FRITZED THEIR FUSES.
NIGHTWING, I'M FIGHTING SOMEONE CALLED ASTEROID. HE SAID HE WAS IN STRYKER'S.
GREAT. MAYBE WE CAN I.D. HIM. YOU NEED BACKUP?
I CAN HANDLE HIM. BE CAREFUL.
YOU, TOO.
BANG.

THUKK

OH, NONONONONO. THAT *PAINTING'S* WORTH MILLIONS...

I-IT'S *IRREPLACEABLE.*

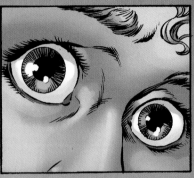

"*SQUIRE* REPORTING. IT'S LIKE YOU SAID. THE TITANS SENT THE *SILENT* ONE.

"*APROPOS,* SINCE *KNIGHT* CAN'T TALK, EITHER.

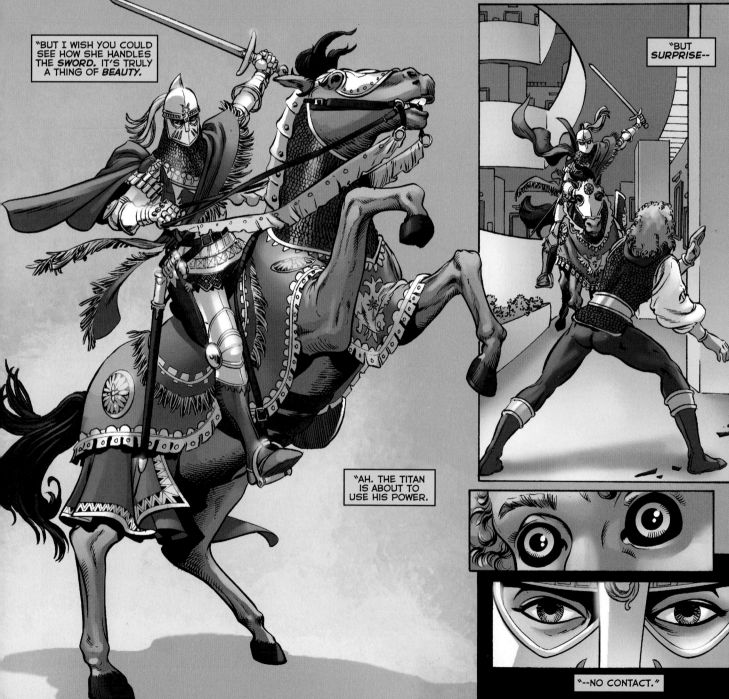

"BUT I WISH YOU COULD SEE HOW SHE HANDLES THE *SWORD.* IT'S TRULY A THING OF *BEAUTY.*

"AH. THE TITAN IS ABOUT TO USE HIS POWER.

"BUT *SURPRISE--*

"--NO CONTACT."

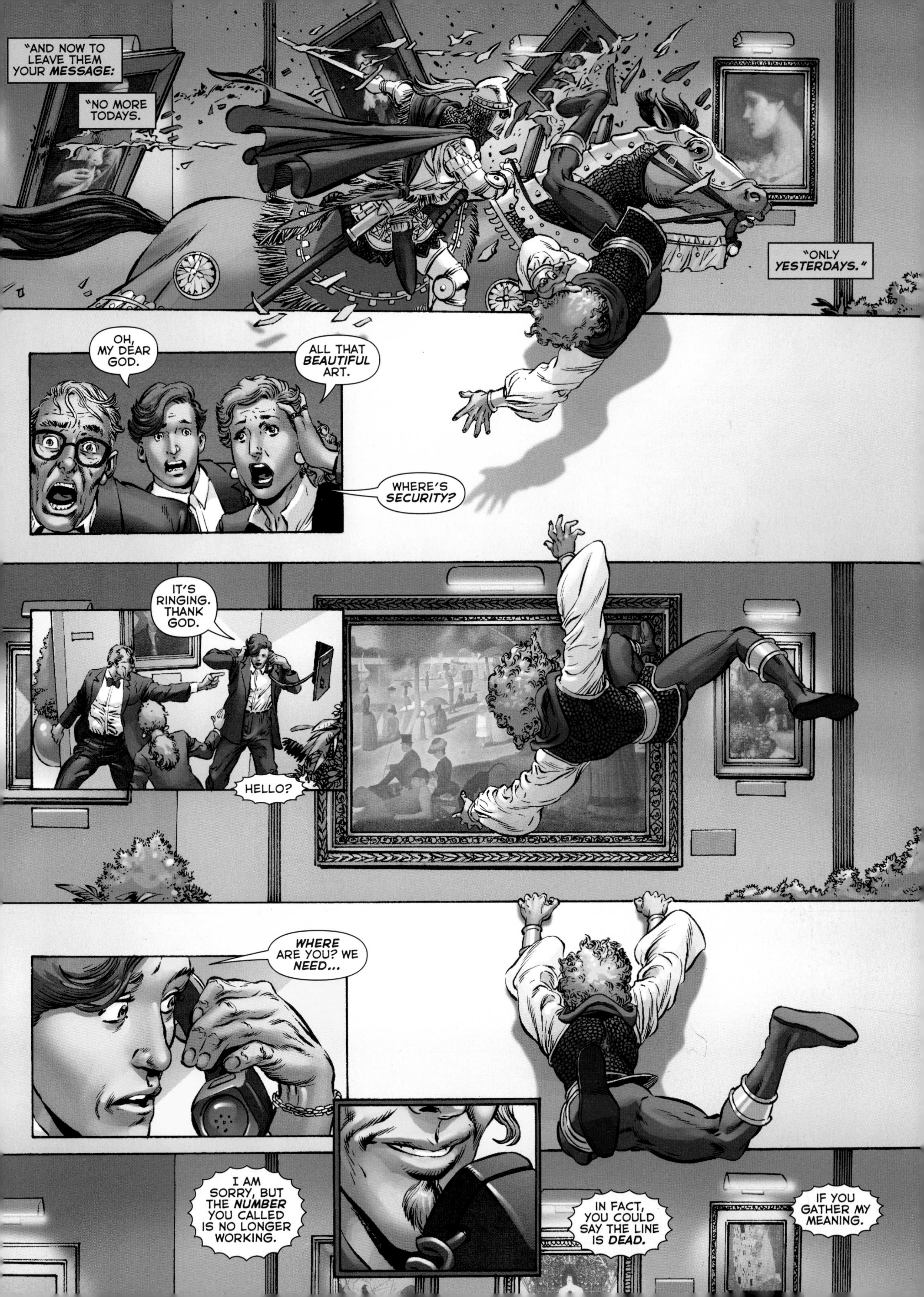
"AND NOW TO LEAVE THEM YOUR MESSAGE:
"NO MORE TODAYS.
"ONLY YESTERDAYS."
OH, MY DEAR GOD.
ALL THAT BEAUTIFUL ART.
WHERE'S SECURITY?
IT'S RINGING. THANK GOD.
HELLO?
WHERE ARE YOU? WE NEED...
I AM SORRY, BUT THE NUMBER YOU CALLED IS NO LONGER WORKING.
IN FACT, YOU COULD SAY THE LINE IS DEAD.
IF YOU GATHER MY MEANING.

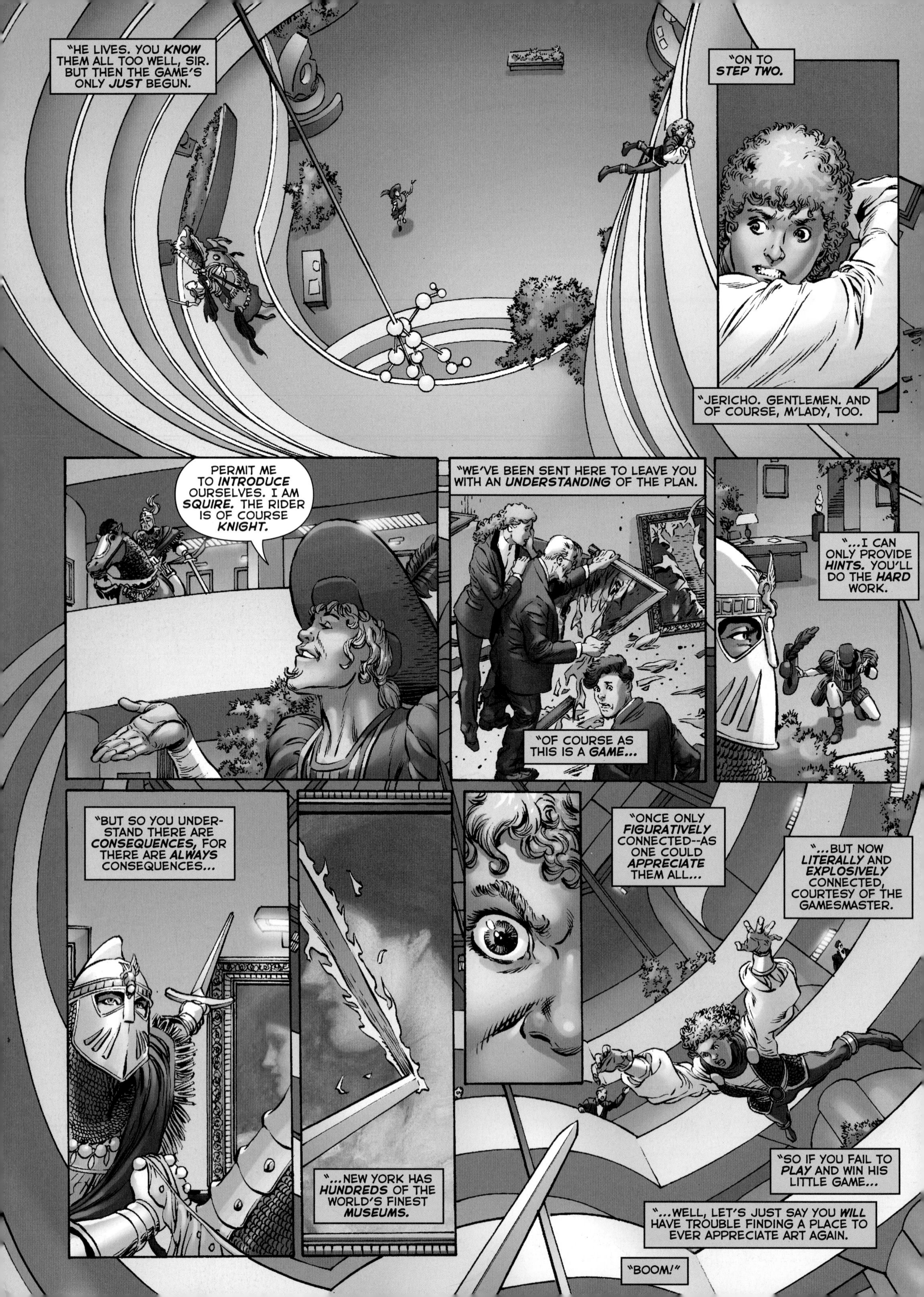

"HE LIVES. YOU KNOW THEM ALL TOO WELL, SIR. BUT THEN THE GAME'S ONLY JUST BEGUN.
"ON TO STEP TWO.
"JERICHO. GENTLEMEN. AND OF COURSE, M'LADY, TOO.
PERMIT ME TO INTRODUCE OURSELVES. I AM SQUIRE. THE RIDER IS OF COURSE KNIGHT.
"WE'VE BEEN SENT HERE TO LEAVE YOU WITH AN UNDERSTANDING OF THE PLAN.
"OF COURSE AS THIS IS A GAME...
"...I CAN ONLY PROVIDE HINTS. YOU'LL DO THE HARD WORK.
"BUT SO YOU UNDERSTAND THERE ARE CONSEQUENCES, FOR THERE ARE ALWAYS CONSEQUENCES...
"...NEW YORK HAS HUNDREDS OF THE WORLD'S FINEST MUSEUMS.
"ONCE ONLY FIGURATIVELY CONNECTED--AS ONE COULD APPRECIATE THEM ALL...
"...BUT NOW LITERALLY AND EXPLOSIVELY CONNECTED, COURTESY OF THE GAMESMASTER.
"SO IF YOU FAIL TO PLAY AND WIN HIS LITTLE GAME...
"...WELL, LET'S JUST SAY YOU WILL HAVE TROUBLE FINDING A PLACE TO EVER APPRECIATE ART AGAIN.
"BOOM!"

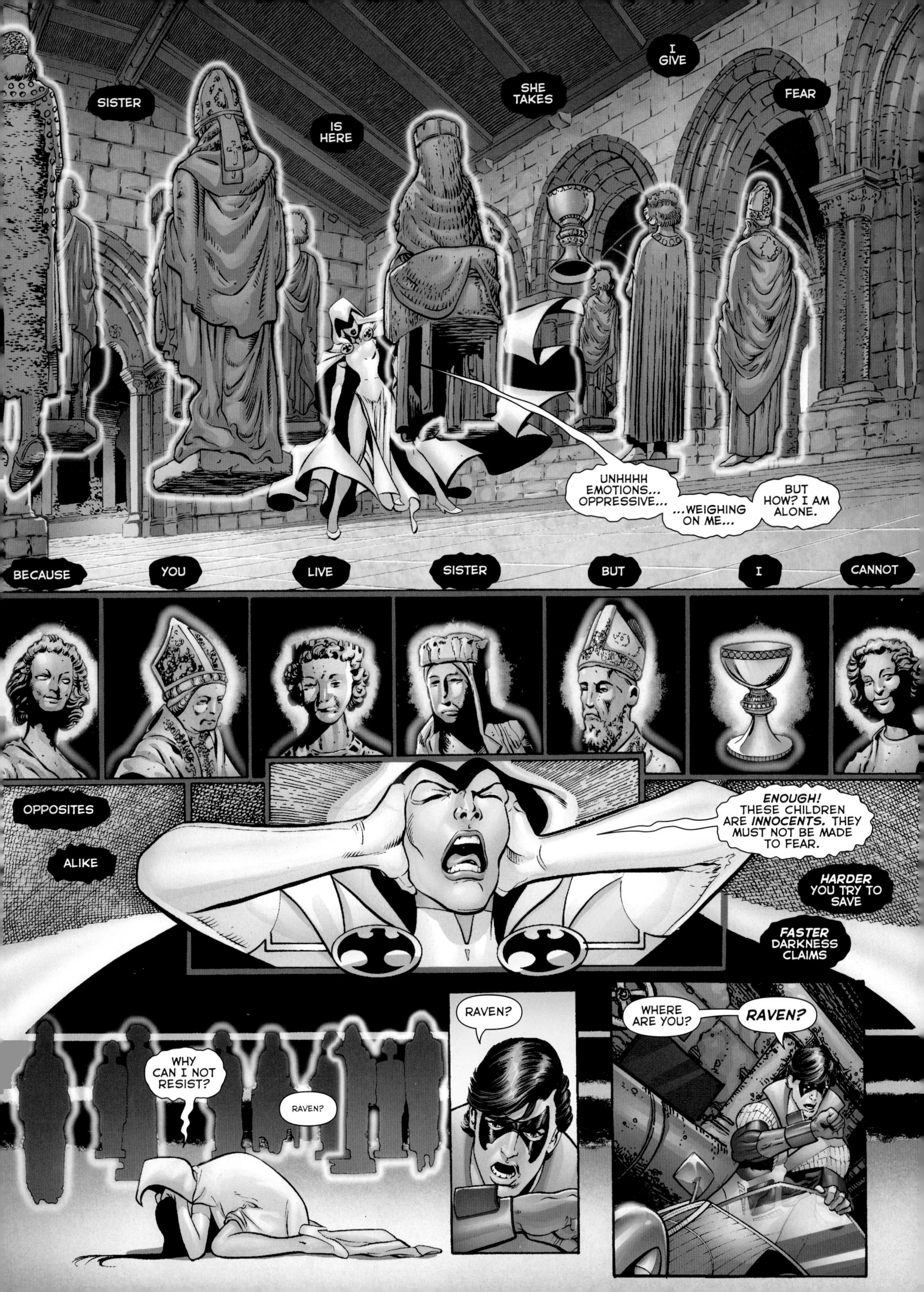
SISTER
IS HERE
SHE TAKES
I GIVE
FEAR
UNHHHH EMOTIONS... OPPRESSIVE...
...WEIGHING ON ME...
BUT HOW? I AM ALONE.
BECAUSE
YOU
LIVE
SISTER
BUT
I
CANNOT
OPPOSITES
ALIKE
ENOUGH! THESE CHILDREN ARE INNOCENTS. THEY MUST NOT BE MADE TO FEAR.
HARDER YOU TRY TO SAVE
FASTER DARKNESS CLAIMS
WHY CAN I NOT RESIST?
RAVEN?
RAVEN?
WHERE ARE YOU?
RAVEN?

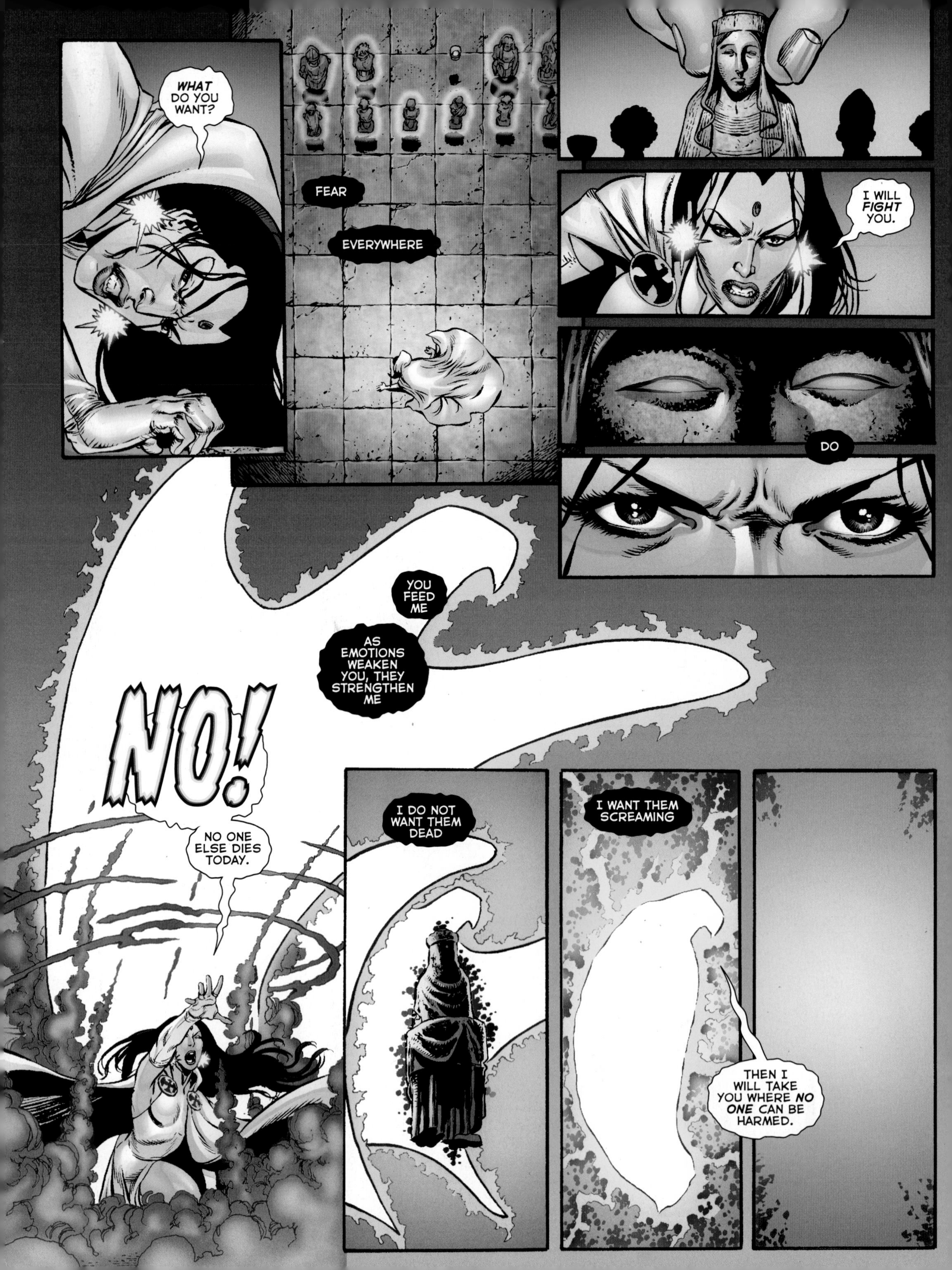
WHAT DO YOU WANT?
FEAR
EVERYWHERE
I WILL FIGHT YOU.
DO
YOU FEED ME
AS EMOTIONS WEAKEN YOU, THEY STRENGTHEN ME
NO!
NO ONE ELSE DIES TODAY.
I DO NOT WANT THEM DEAD
I WANT THEM SCREAMING
THEN I WILL TAKE YOU WHERE NO ONE CAN BE HARMED.

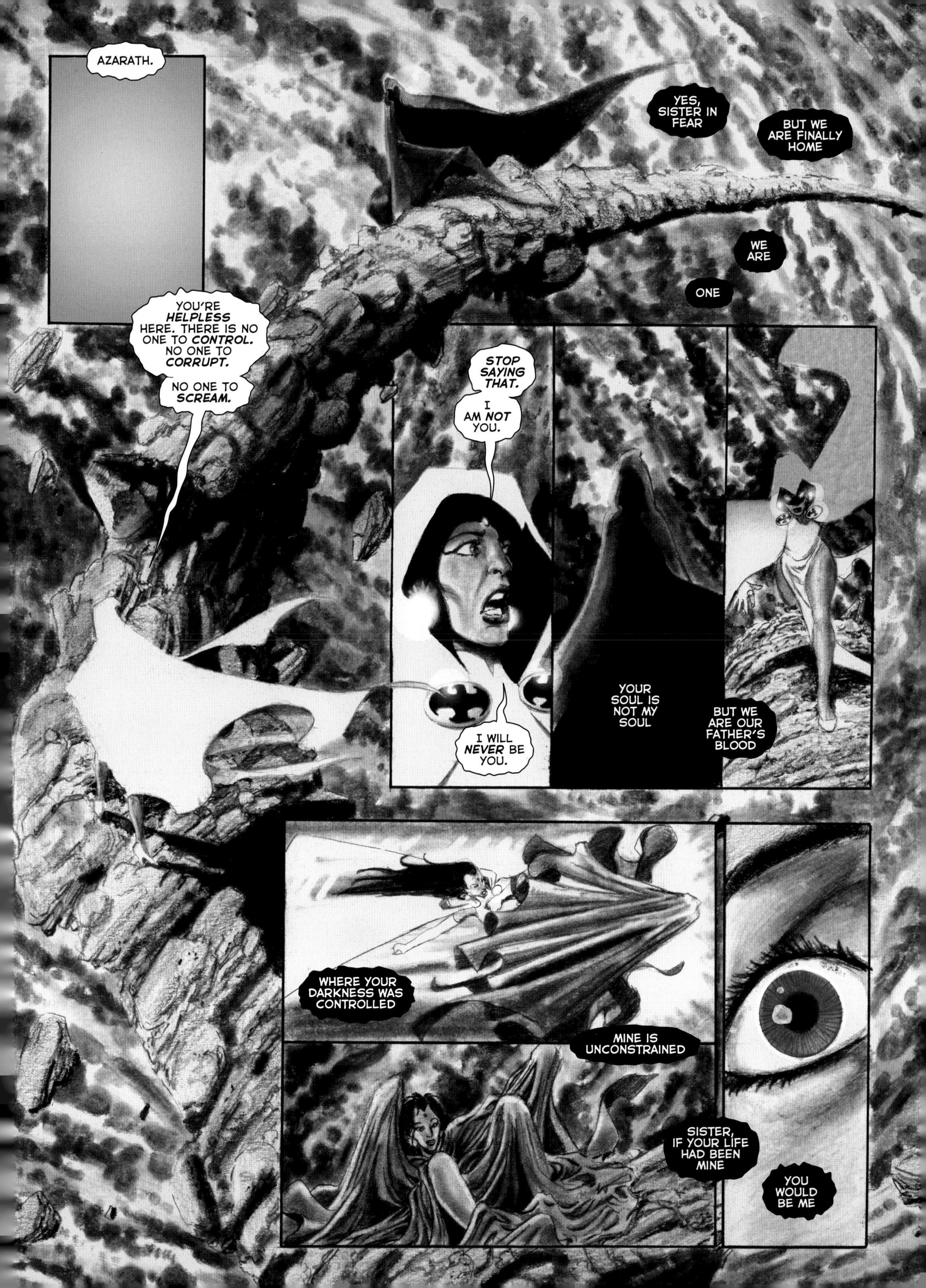
AZARATH.
YES, SISTER IN FEAR
BUT WE ARE FINALLY HOME
WE ARE
ONE
YOU'RE *HELPLESS* HERE. THERE IS NO ONE TO *CONTROL.* NO ONE TO *CORRUPT.*
NO ONE TO *SCREAM.*
STOP SAYING THAT.
I AM *NOT* YOU.
I WILL *NEVER* BE YOU.
YOUR SOUL IS NOT MY SOUL
BUT WE ARE OUR FATHER'S BLOOD
WHERE YOUR DARKNESS WAS CONTROLLED
MINE IS UNCONSTRAINED
SISTER, IF YOUR LIFE HAD BEEN MINE
YOU WOULD BE ME

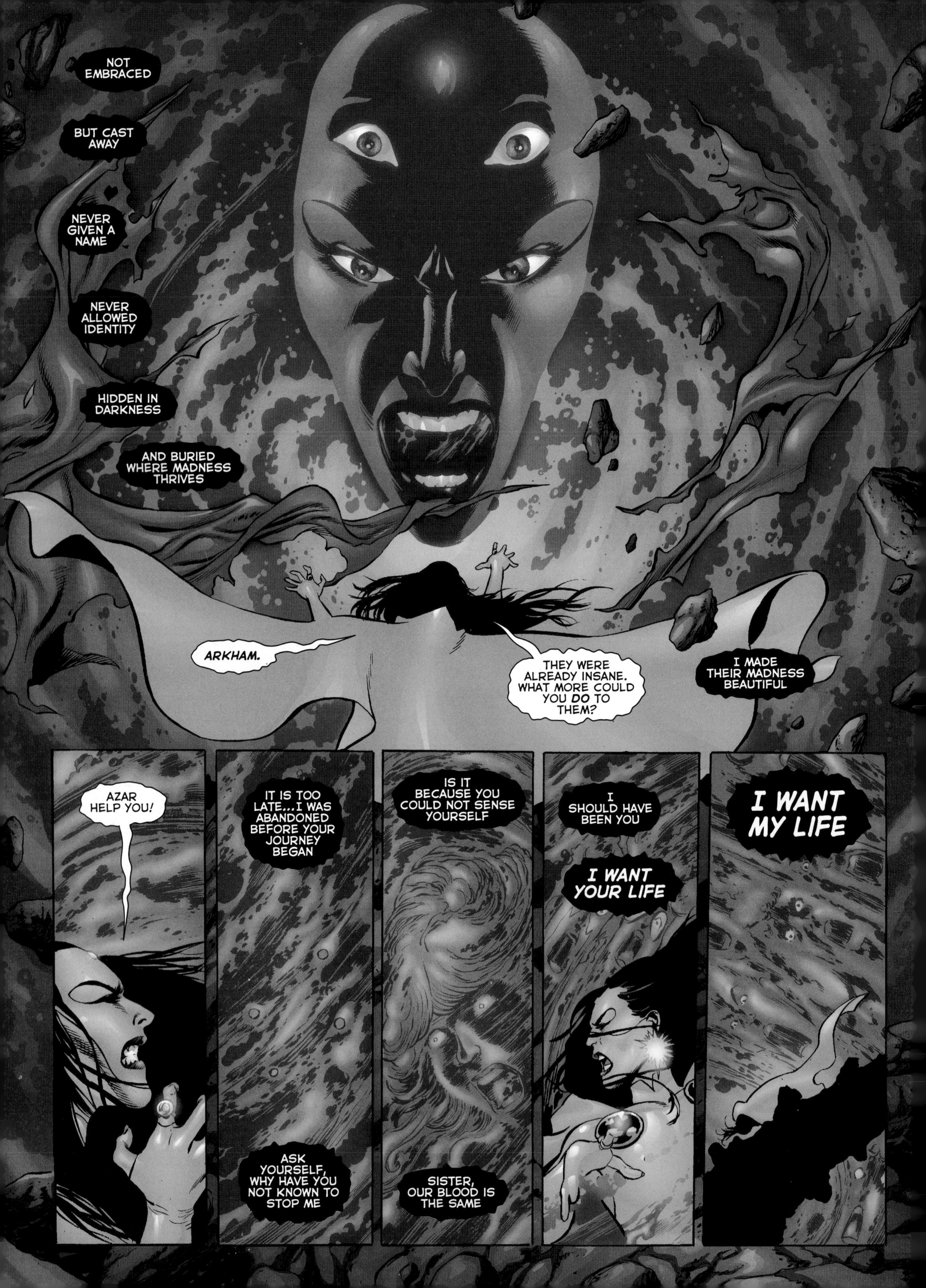

NOT EMBRACED
BUT CAST AWAY
NEVER GIVEN A NAME
NEVER ALLOWED IDENTITY
HIDDEN IN DARKNESS
AND BURIED WHERE MADNESS THRIVES
ARKHAM.
THEY WERE ALREADY INSANE. WHAT MORE COULD YOU DO TO THEM?
I MADE THEIR MADNESS BEAUTIFUL
AZAR HELP YOU!
IT IS TOO LATE...I WAS ABANDONED BEFORE YOUR JOURNEY BEGAN
ASK YOURSELF, WHY HAVE YOU NOT KNOWN TO STOP ME
IS IT BECAUSE YOU COULD NOT SENSE YOURSELF
SISTER, OUR BLOOD IS THE SAME
I SHOULD HAVE BEEN YOU
I WANT YOUR LIFE
I WANT MY LIFE

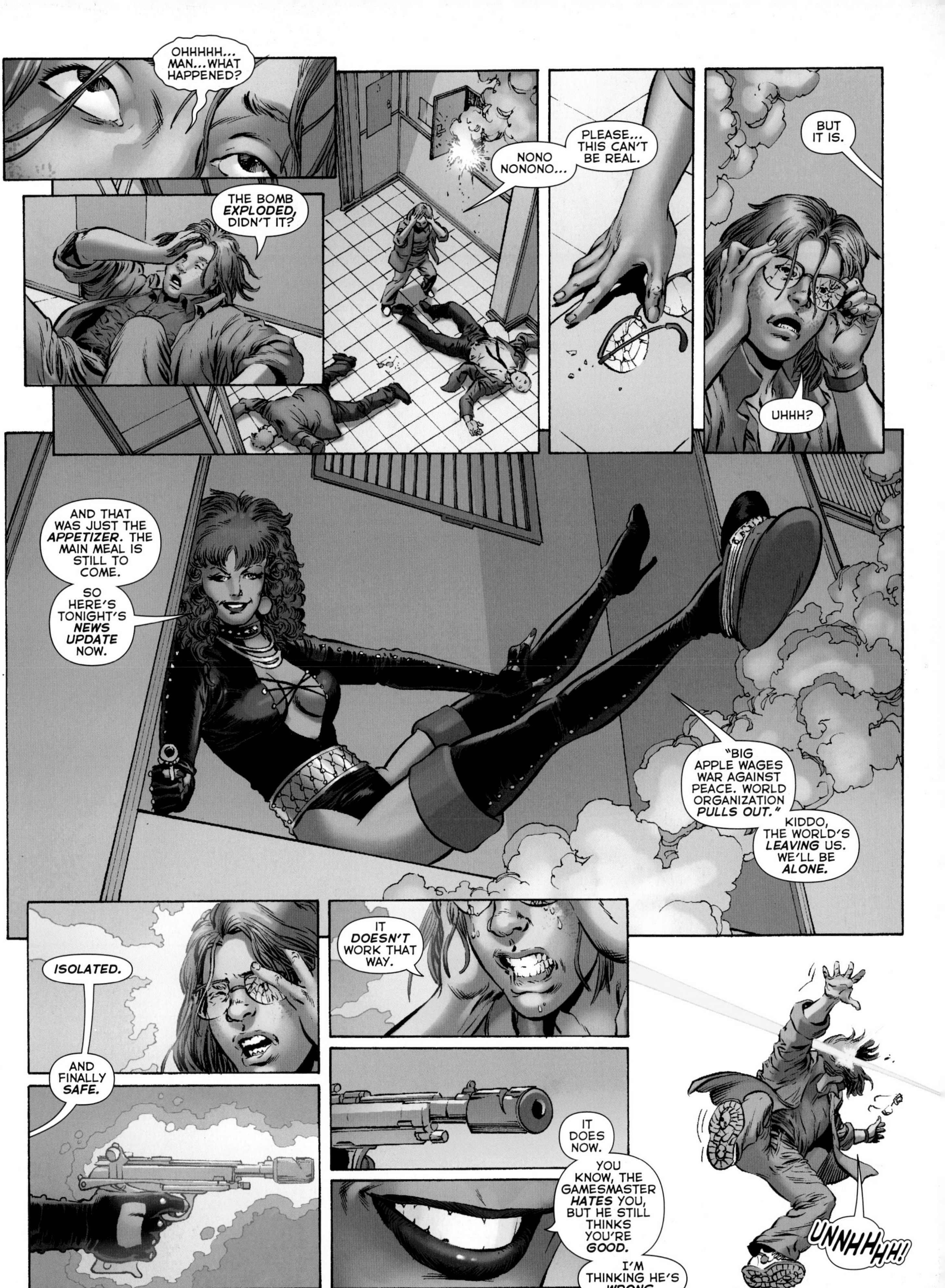

OHHHHH... MAN...WHAT HAPPENED?
THE BOMB *EXPLODED,* DIDN'T IT?
NONO NONONO...
PLEASE... THIS CAN'T BE REAL.
BUT IT IS.
UHHH?
AND THAT WAS JUST THE *APPETIZER.* THE MAIN MEAL IS STILL TO COME.
SO HERE'S TONIGHT'S *NEWS UPDATE* NOW.
"BIG APPLE WAGES WAR AGAINST PEACE. WORLD ORGANIZATION *PULLS OUT."*
KIDDO, THE WORLD'S *LEAVING* US. WE'LL BE *ALONE.*
ISOLATED.
AND FINALLY *SAFE.*
IT *DOESN'T* WORK THAT WAY.
IT DOES NOW.
YOU KNOW, THE GAMESMASTER *HATES* YOU, BUT HE STILL THINKS YOU'RE *GOOD.*
I'M THINKING HE'S *WRONG.*
UNNHHH!

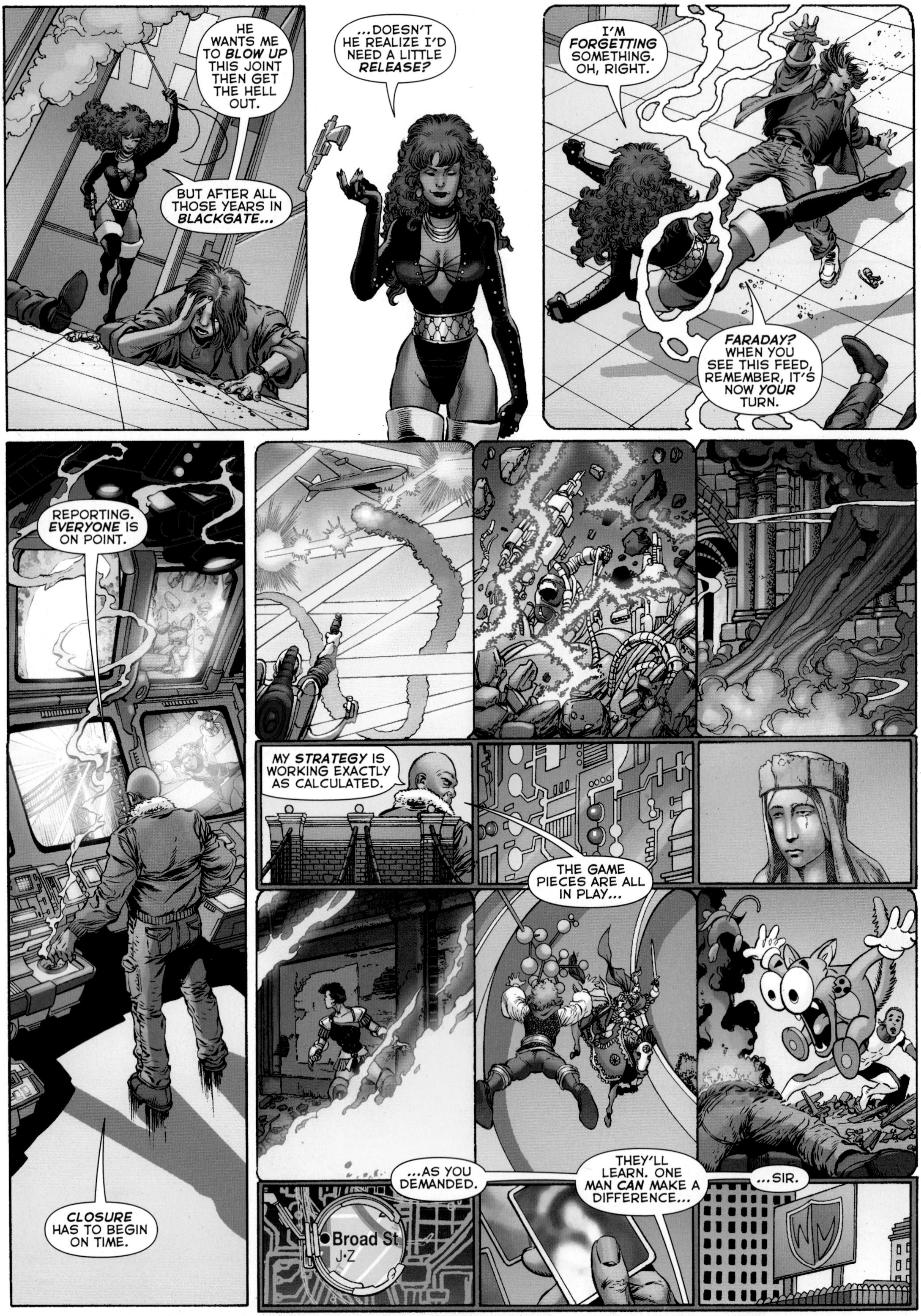
HE WANTS ME TO BLOW UP THIS JOINT THEN GET THE HELL OUT.
BUT AFTER ALL THOSE YEARS IN BLACKGATE...
...DOESN'T HE REALIZE I'D NEED A LITTLE RELEASE?
I'M FORGETTING SOMETHING. OH, RIGHT.
FARADAY? WHEN YOU SEE THIS FEED, REMEMBER, IT'S NOW YOUR TURN.
REPORTING. EVERYONE IS ON POINT.
MY STRATEGY IS WORKING EXACTLY AS CALCULATED.
THE GAME PIECES ARE ALL IN PLAY...
CLOSURE HAS TO BEGIN ON TIME.
...AS YOU DEMANDED.
THEY'LL LEARN. ONE MAN CAN MAKE A DIFFERENCE...
...SIR.
Broad St
J·Z

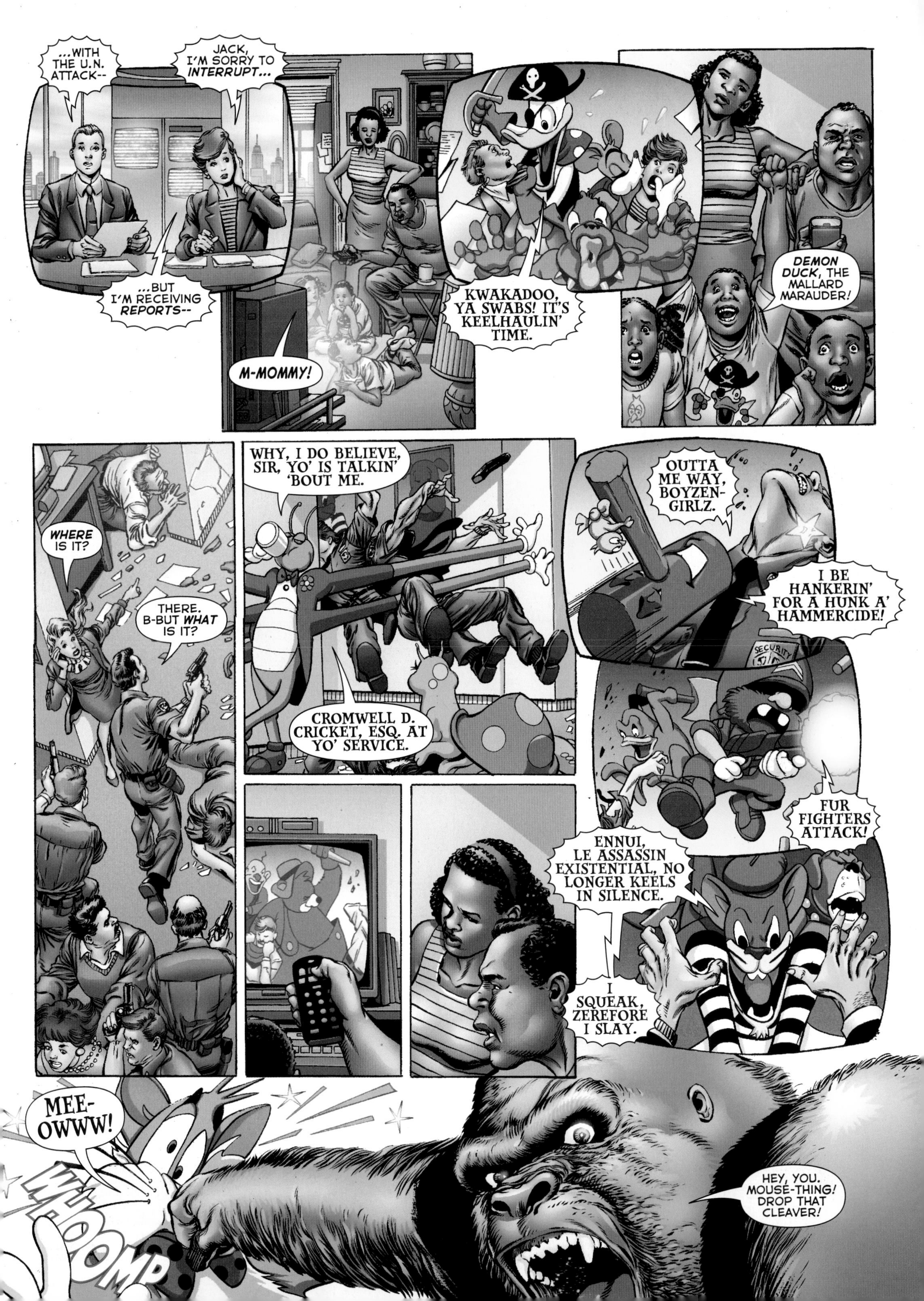
...WITH THE U.N. ATTACK--
JACK, I'M SORRY TO INTERRUPT...
...BUT I'M RECEIVING REPORTS--
M-MOMMY!
KWAKADOO, YA SWABS! IT'S KEELHAULIN' TIME.
DEMON DUCK, THE MALLARD MARAUDER!
WHERE IS IT?
THERE. B-BUT WHAT IS IT?
WHY, I DO BELIEVE, SIR, YO' IS TALKIN' 'BOUT ME.
CROMWELL D. CRICKET, ESQ. AT YO' SERVICE.
OUTTA ME WAY, BOYZEN-GIRLZ.
I BE HANKERIN' FOR A HUNK A' HAMMERCIDE!
SECURITY
FUR FIGHTERS ATTACK!
ENNUI, LE ASSASSIN EXISTENTIAL, NO LONGER KEELS IN SILENCE.
I SQUEAK, ZEREFORE I SLAY.
MEE-OWWW!
WHOOMP
HEY, YOU. MOUSE-THING! DROP THAT CLEAVER!

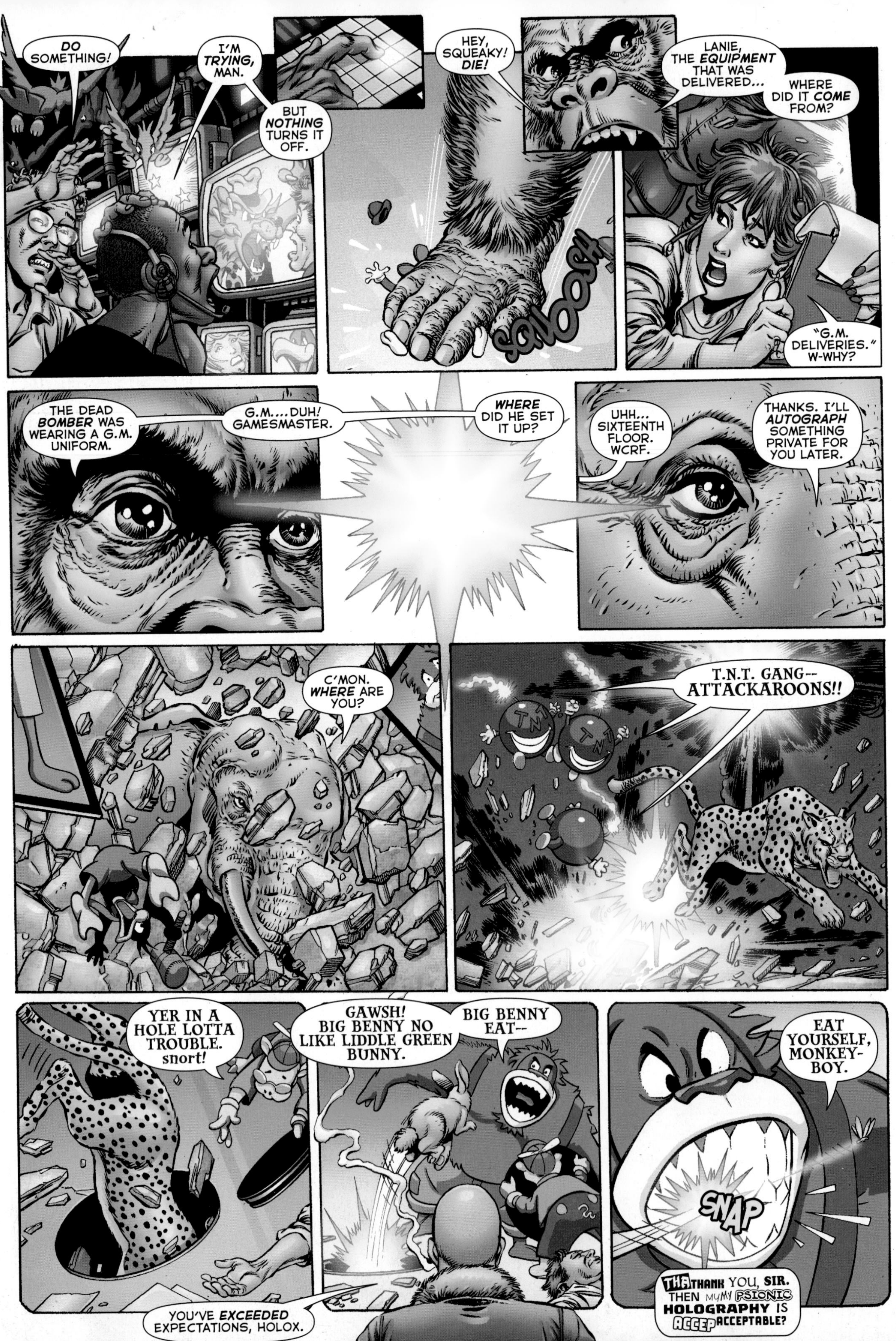
DO SOMETHING!
I'M TRYING, MAN.
BUT NOTHING TURNS IT OFF.
HEY, SQUEAKY! DIE!
SQLOOSH
LANIE, THE EQUIPMENT THAT WAS DELIVERED...
WHERE DID IT COME FROM?
"G.M. DELIVERIES." W-WHY?
THE DEAD BOMBER WAS WEARING A G.M. UNIFORM.
G.M.... DUH! GAMESMASTER.
WHERE DID HE SET IT UP?
UHH... SIXTEENTH FLOOR. WCRF.
THANKS. I'LL AUTOGRAPH SOMETHING PRIVATE FOR YOU LATER.
C'MON. WHERE ARE YOU?
T.N.T. GANG-- ATTACKAROONS!!
YER IN A HOLE LOTTA TROUBLE. snort!
GAWSH! BIG BENNY NO LIKE LIDDLE GREEN BUNNY.
BIG BENNY EAT--
EAT YOURSELF, MONKEY-BOY.
SNAP
YOU'VE EXCEEDED EXPECTATIONS, HOLOX.
THA THANK YOU, SIR. THEN MY MY PSIONIC HOLOGRAPHY IS ACCEP ACCEPTABLE?

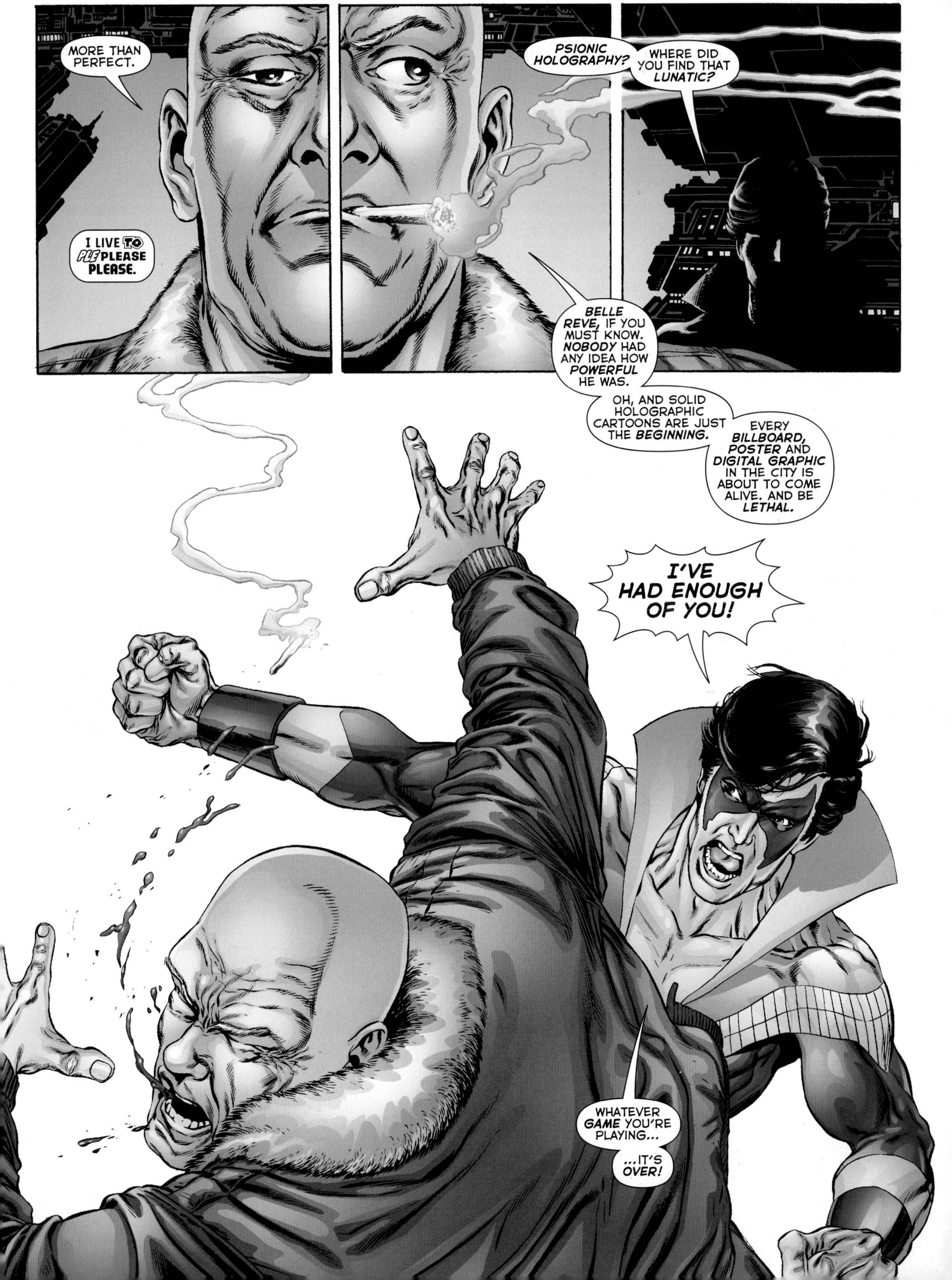
MORE THAN PERFECT.
I LIVE TO PLE PLEASE PLEASE.
PSIONIC HOLOGRAPHY?
WHERE DID YOU FIND THAT LUNATIC?
BELLE REVE, IF YOU MUST KNOW. NOBODY HAD ANY IDEA HOW POWERFUL HE WAS.
OH, AND SOLID HOLOGRAPHIC CARTOONS ARE JUST THE BEGINNING.
EVERY BILLBOARD, POSTER AND DIGITAL GRAPHIC IN THE CITY IS ABOUT TO COME ALIVE. AND BE LETHAL.
I'VE HAD ENOUGH OF YOU!
WHATEVER GAME YOU'RE PLAYING...
...IT'S OVER!

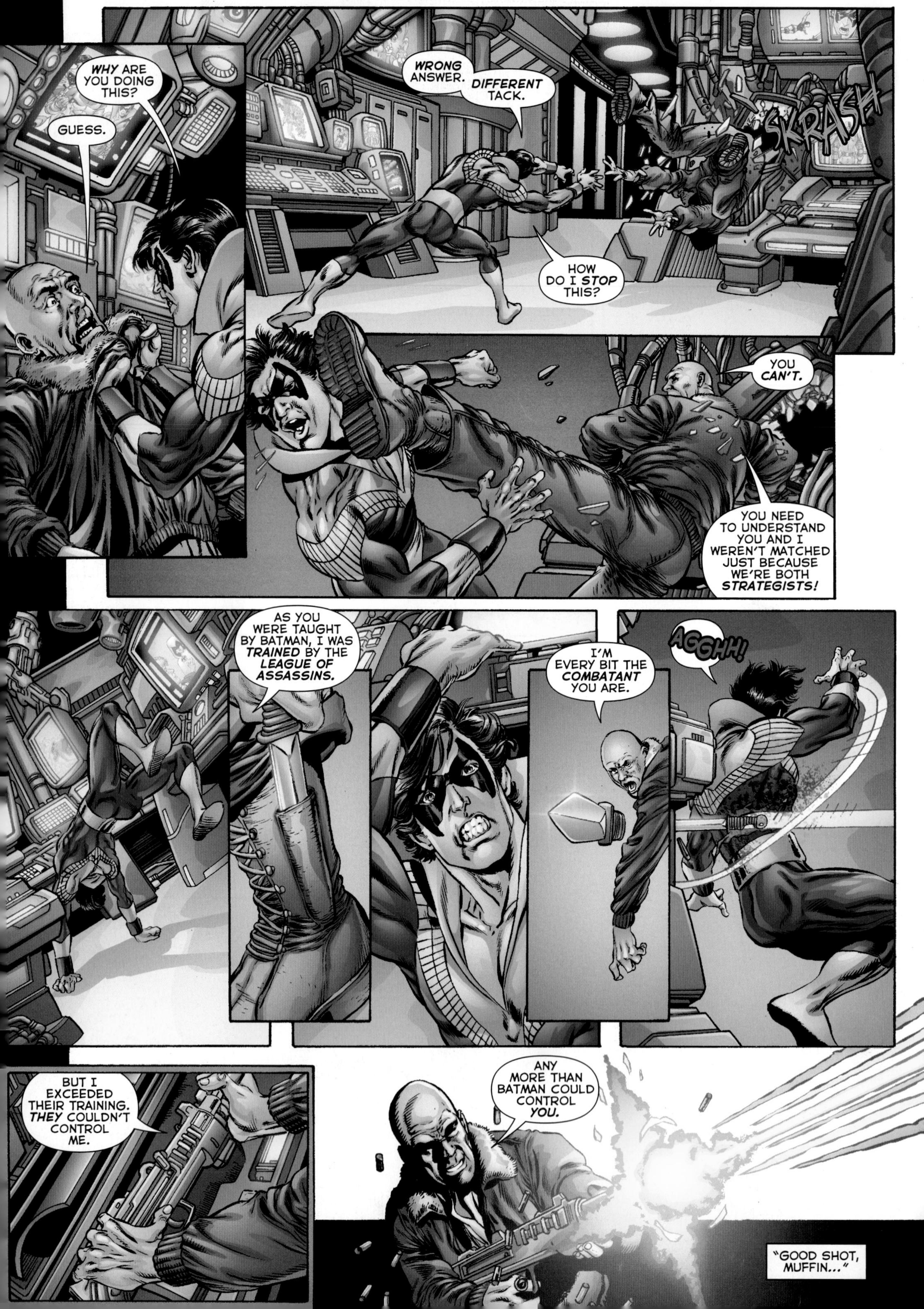

WHY ARE YOU DOING THIS?
GUESS.
WRONG ANSWER. DIFFERENT TACK.
SKRASH
HOW DO I STOP THIS?
YOU CAN'T.
YOU NEED TO UNDERSTAND YOU AND I WEREN'T MATCHED JUST BECAUSE WE'RE BOTH STRATEGISTS!
AS YOU WERE TAUGHT BY BATMAN, I WAS TRAINED BY THE LEAGUE OF ASSASSINS.
I'M EVERY BIT THE COMBATANT YOU ARE.
AGGHH!
BUT I EXCEEDED THEIR TRAINING. THEY COULDN'T CONTROL ME.
ANY MORE THAN BATMAN COULD CONTROL YOU.
"GOOD SHOT, MUFFIN..."

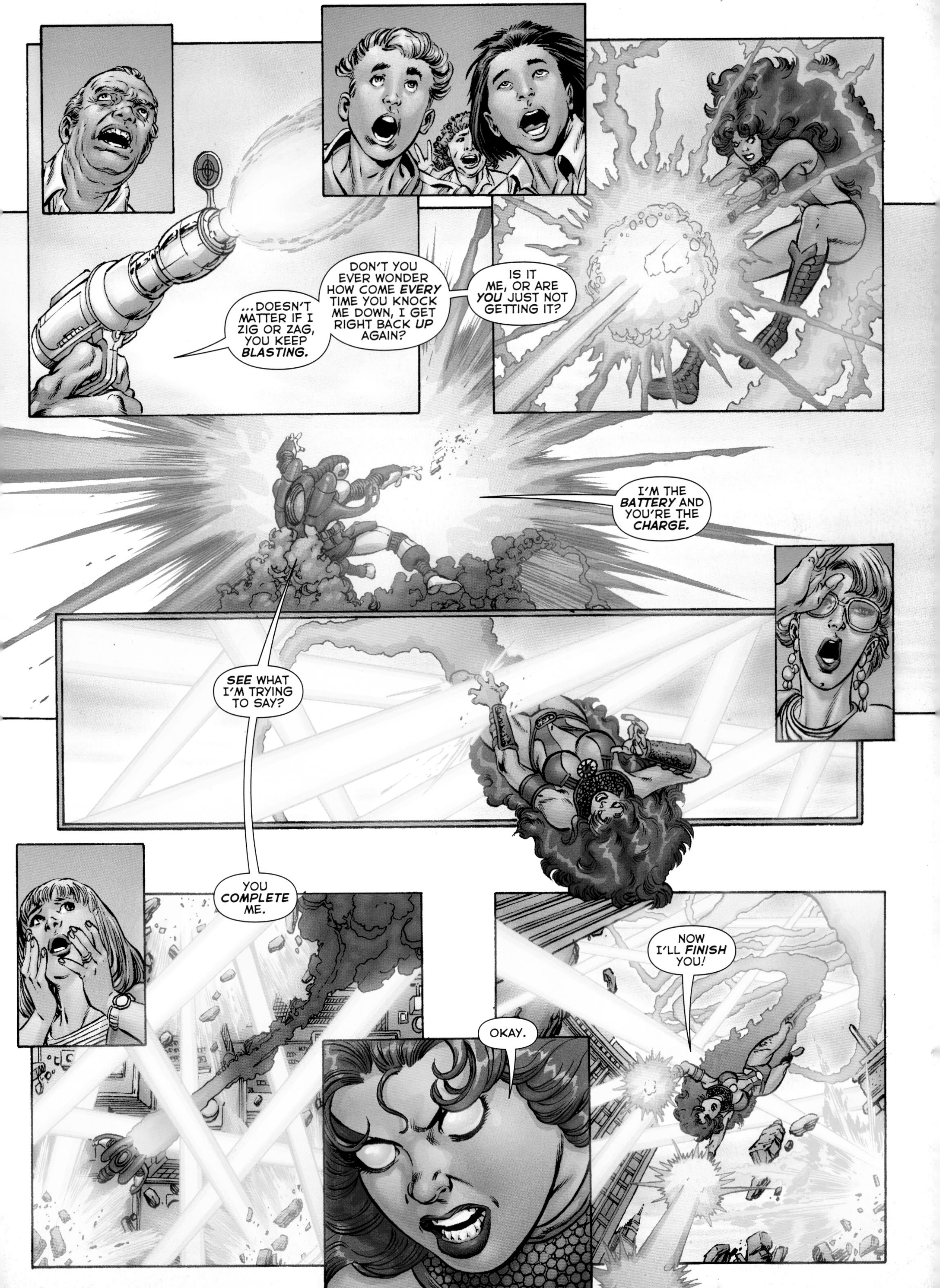

...DOESN'T MATTER IF I ZIG OR ZAG, YOU KEEP BLASTING.
DON'T YOU EVER WONDER HOW COME EVERY TIME YOU KNOCK ME DOWN, I GET RIGHT BACK UP AGAIN?
IS IT ME, OR ARE YOU JUST NOT GETTING IT?
I'M THE BATTERY AND YOU'RE THE CHARGE.
SEE WHAT I'M TRYING TO SAY?
YOU COMPLETE ME.
NOW I'LL FINISH YOU!
OKAY.

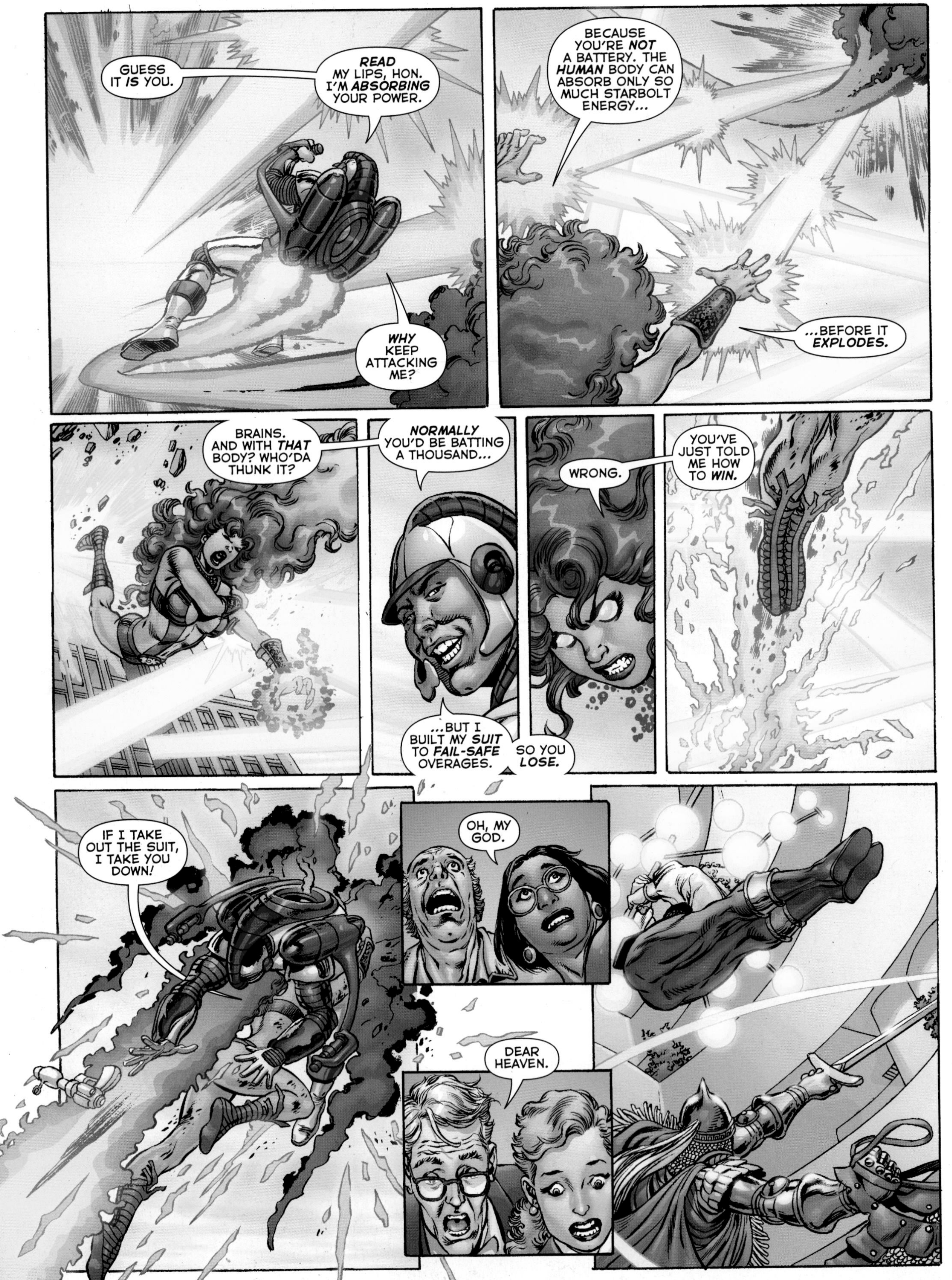
GUESS IT IS YOU.
READ MY LIPS, HON. I'M ABSORBING YOUR POWER.
WHY KEEP ATTACKING ME?
BECAUSE YOU'RE NOT A BATTERY. THE HUMAN BODY CAN ABSORB ONLY SO MUCH STARBOLT ENERGY...
...BEFORE IT EXPLODES.
BRAINS. AND WITH THAT BODY? WHO'DA THUNK IT?
NORMALLY YOU'D BE BATTING A THOUSAND...
...BUT I BUILT MY SUIT TO FAIL-SAFE OVERAGES.
SO YOU LOSE.
WRONG.
YOU'VE JUST TOLD ME HOW TO WIN.
IF I TAKE OUT THE SUIT, I TAKE YOU DOWN!
OH, MY GOD.
DEAR HEAVEN.

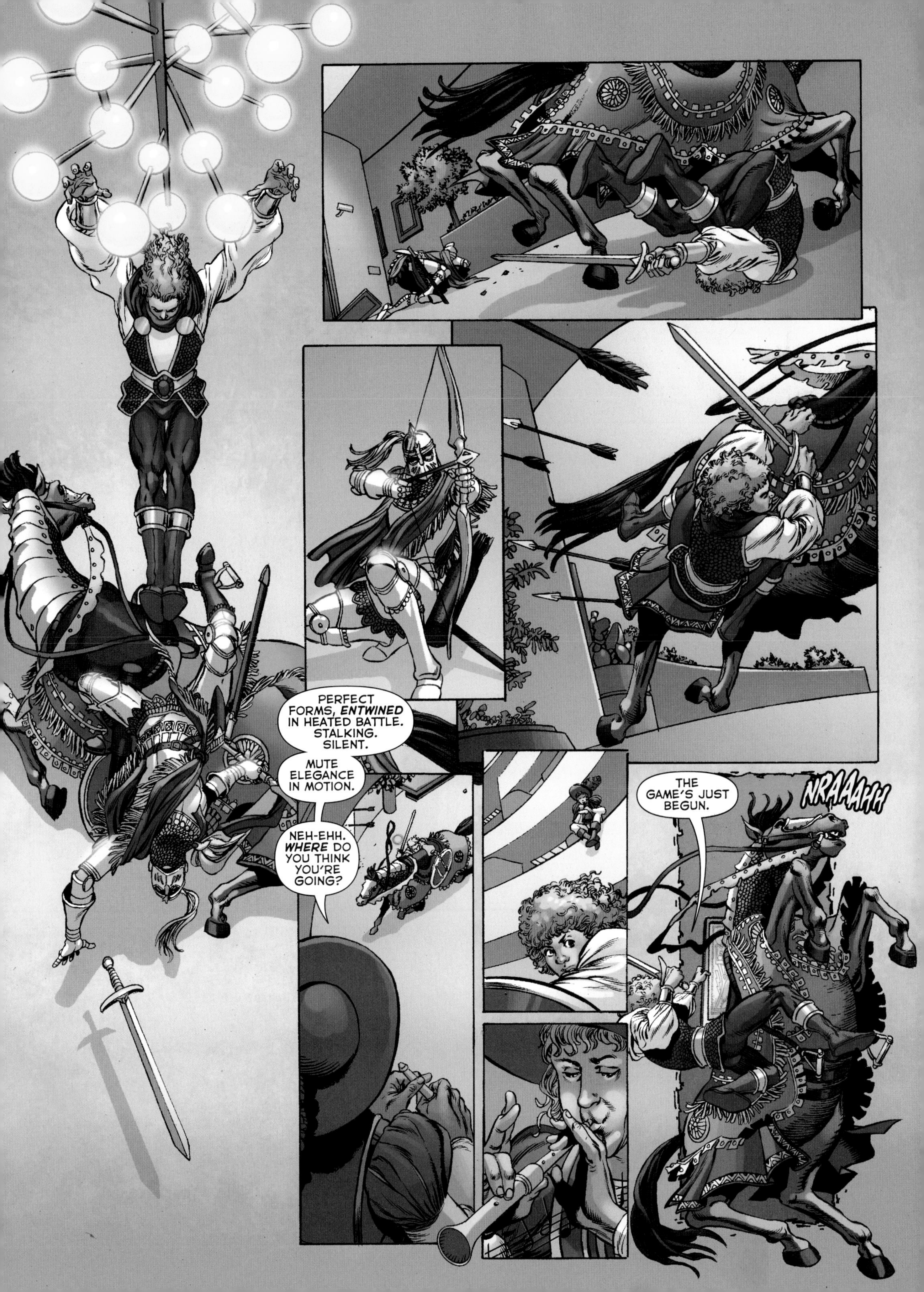
PERFECT FORMS, ***ENTWINED*** IN HEATED BATTLE. STALKING. SILENT.
MUTE ELEGANCE IN MOTION.
NEH-EHH. ***WHERE*** DO YOU THINK YOU'RE GOING?
THE GAME'S JUST BEGUN.
NRAAAHH

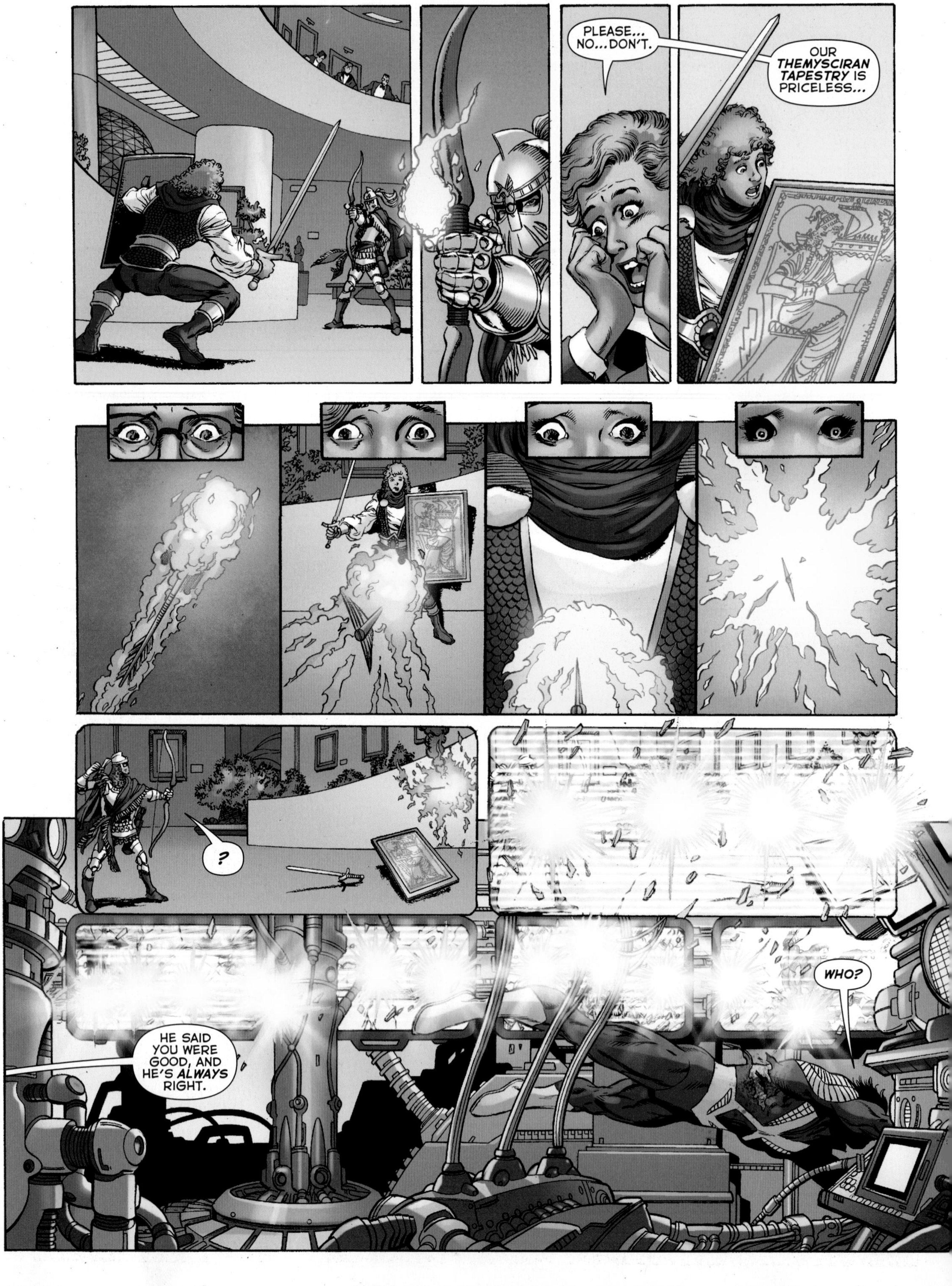

PLEASE... NO...DON'T.
OUR *THEMYSCIRAN TAPESTRY* IS PRICELESS...
?
HE SAID YOU WERE GOOD, AND HE'S *ALWAYS* RIGHT.
WHO?

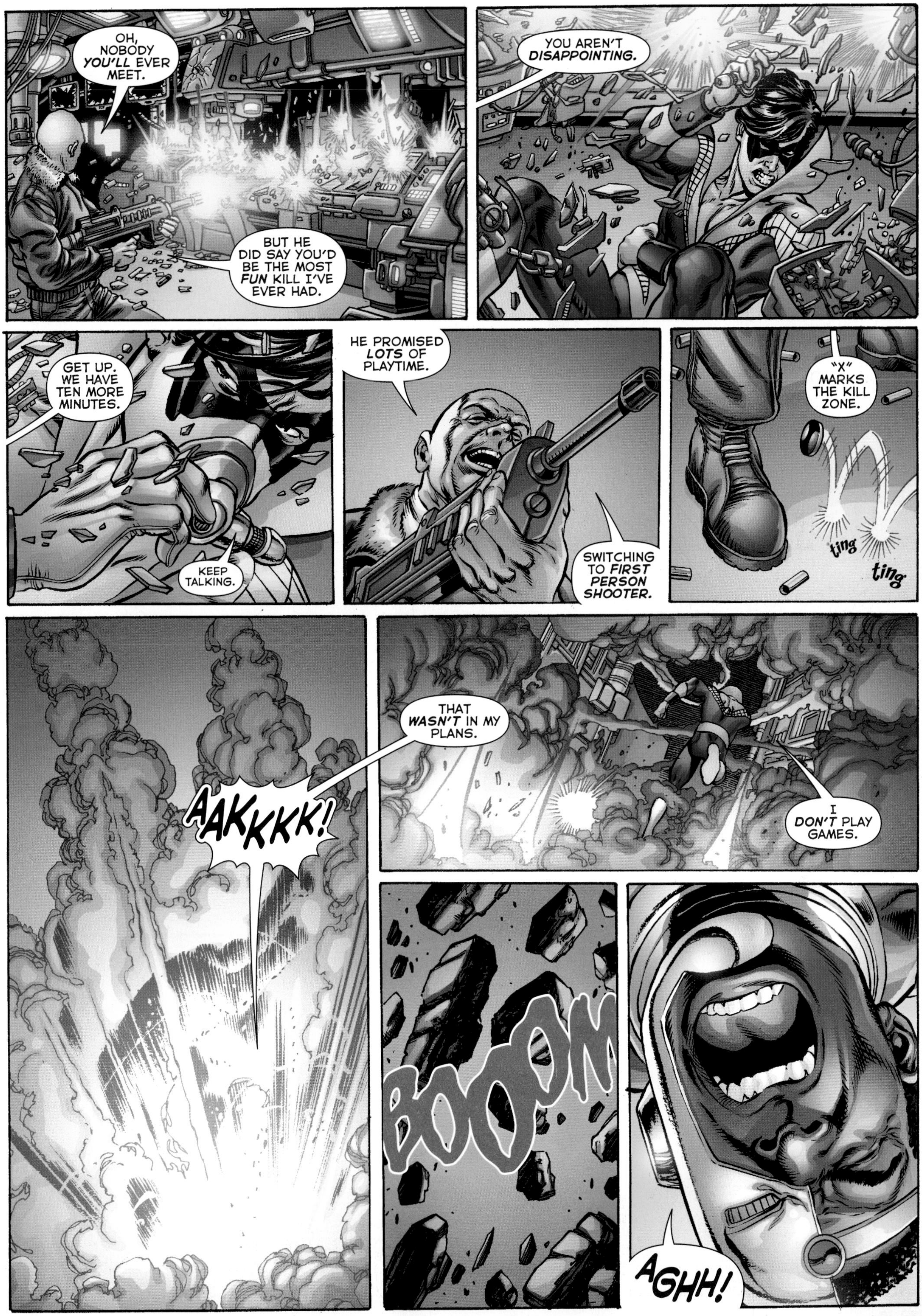

OH, NOBODY YOU'LL EVER MEET.
BUT HE DID SAY YOU'D BE THE MOST FUN KILL I'VE EVER HAD.
YOU AREN'T DISAPPOINTING.
GET UP. WE HAVE TEN MORE MINUTES.
KEEP TALKING.
HE PROMISED LOTS OF PLAYTIME.
SWITCHING TO FIRST PERSON SHOOTER.
"X" MARKS THE KILL ZONE.
ting
ting
AAKKKK!
THAT WASN'T IN MY PLANS.
I DON'T PLAY GAMES.
BOOOM
AGHH!

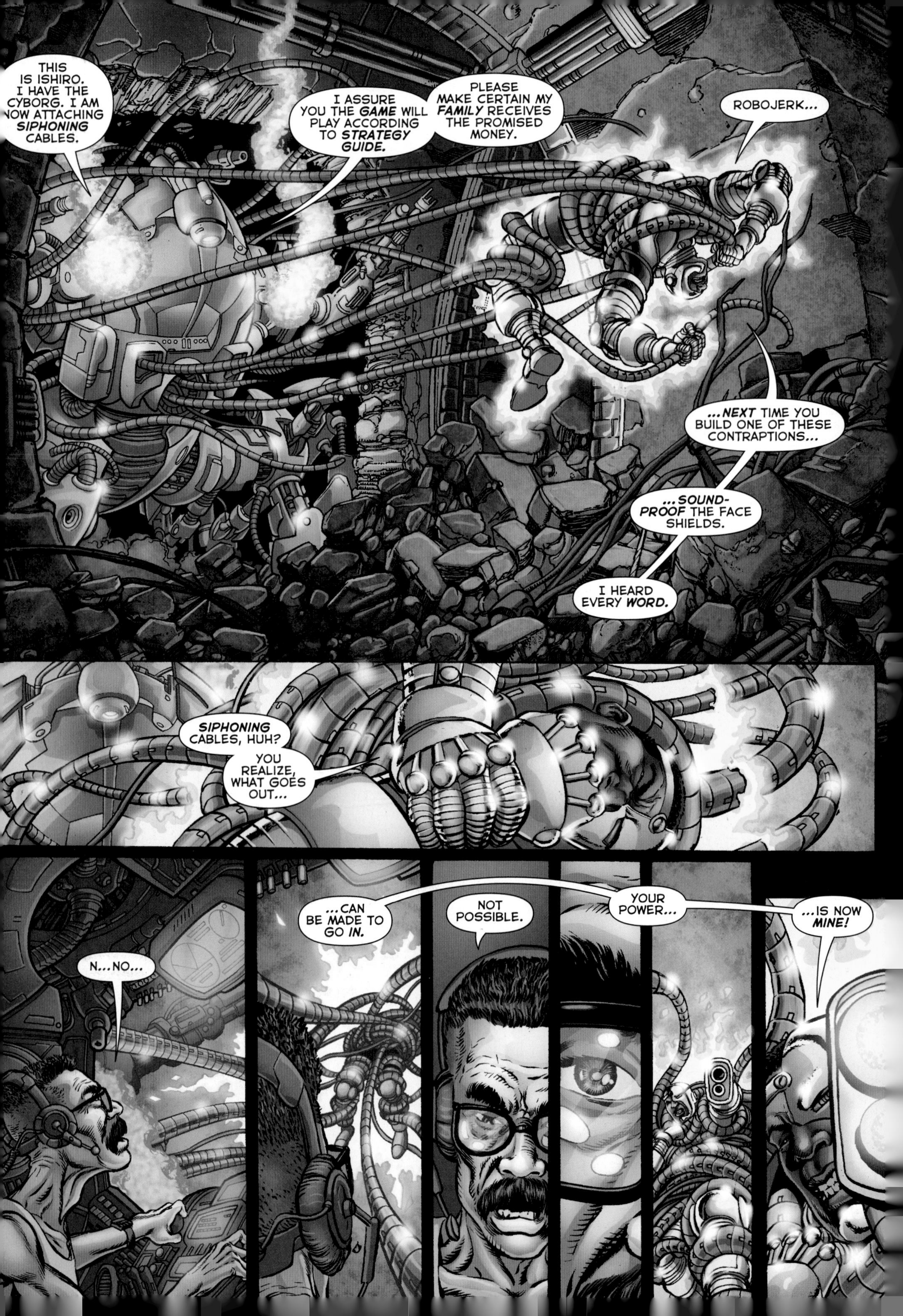
THIS IS ISHIRO. I HAVE THE CYBORG. I AM NOW ATTACHING SIPHONING CABLES.
I ASSURE YOU THE GAME WILL PLAY ACCORDING TO STRATEGY GUIDE.
PLEASE MAKE CERTAIN MY FAMILY RECEIVES THE PROMISED MONEY.
ROBOJERK...
...NEXT TIME YOU BUILD ONE OF THESE CONTRAPTIONS...
...SOUND-PROOF THE FACE SHIELDS.
I HEARD EVERY WORD.
SIPHONING CABLES, HUH?
YOU REALIZE, WHAT GOES OUT...
N...NO...
...CAN BE MADE TO GO IN.
NOT POSSIBLE.
YOUR POWER...
...IS NOW MINE!

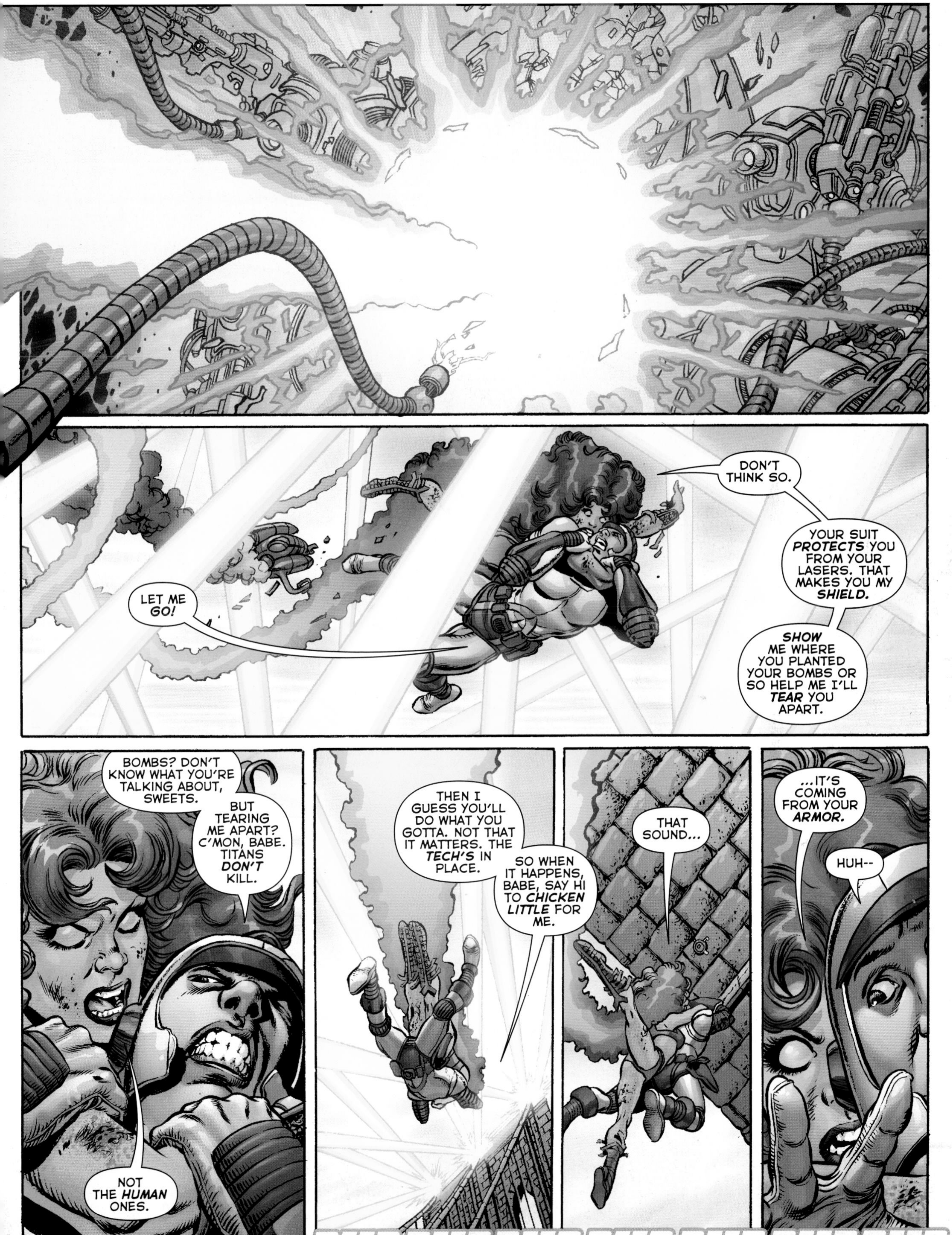
DON'T THINK SO.
YOUR SUIT PROTECTS YOU FROM YOUR LASERS. THAT MAKES YOU MY SHIELD.
LET ME GO!
SHOW ME WHERE YOU PLANTED YOUR BOMBS OR SO HELP ME I'LL TEAR YOU APART.
BOMBS? DON'T KNOW WHAT YOU'RE TALKING ABOUT, SWEETS.
BUT TEARING ME APART? C'MON, BABE. TITANS DON'T KILL.
NOT THE HUMAN ONES.
THEN I GUESS YOU'LL DO WHAT YOU GOTTA. NOT THAT IT MATTERS. THE TECH'S IN PLACE.
SO WHEN IT HAPPENS, BABE, SAY HI TO CHICKEN LITTLE FOR ME.
THAT SOUND...
...IT'S COMING FROM YOUR ARMOR.
HUH--
BEEP BEEP BEEP BEEP BEEP BEEP BEEP

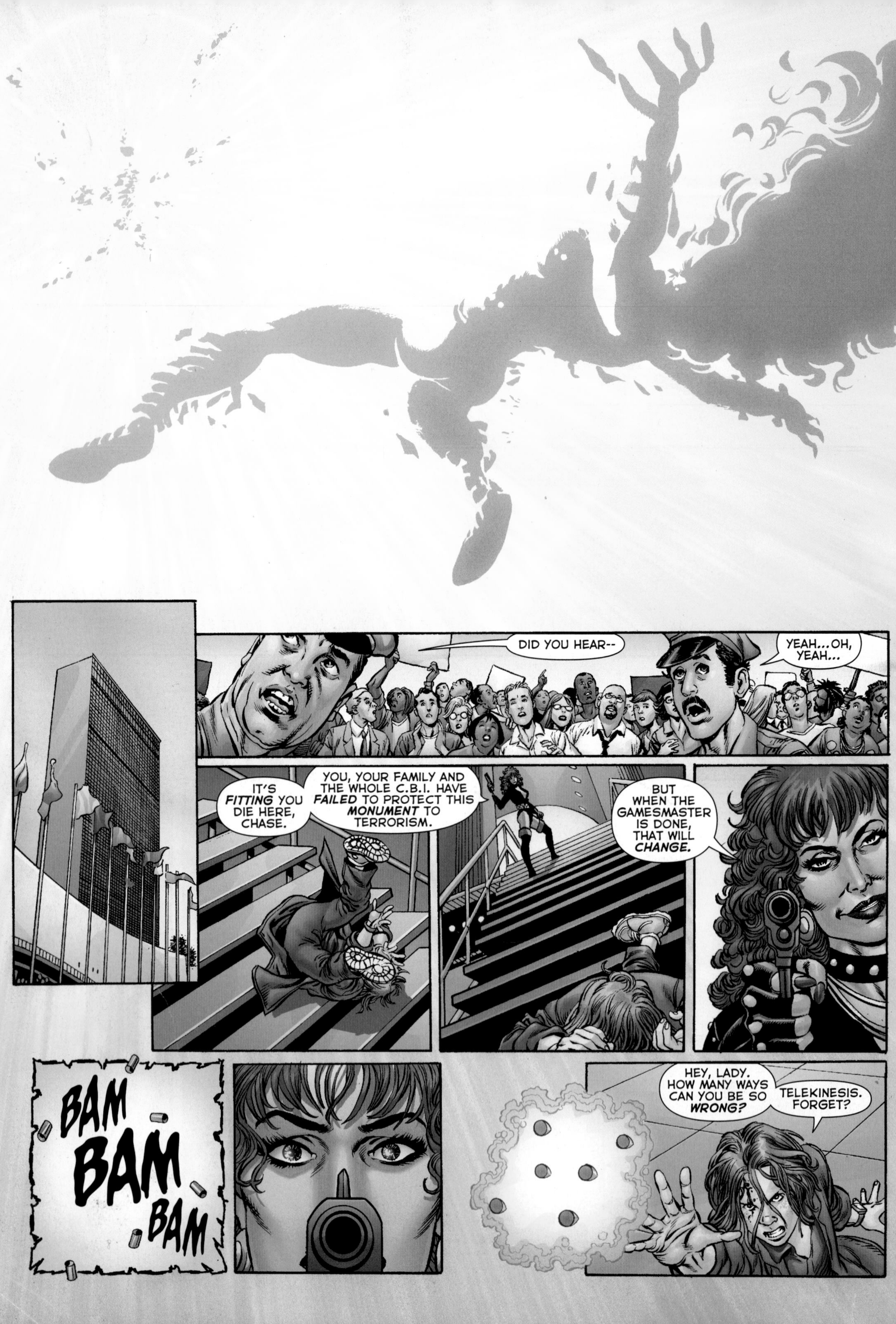
DID YOU HEAR--
YEAH...OH, YEAH...
IT'S FITTING YOU DIE HERE, CHASE.
YOU, YOUR FAMILY AND THE WHOLE C.B.I. HAVE FAILED TO PROTECT THIS MONUMENT TO TERRORISM.
BUT WHEN THE GAMESMASTER IS DONE, THAT WILL CHANGE.
BAM BAM BAM
HEY, LADY. HOW MANY WAYS CAN YOU BE SO WRONG?
TELEKINESIS. FORGET?

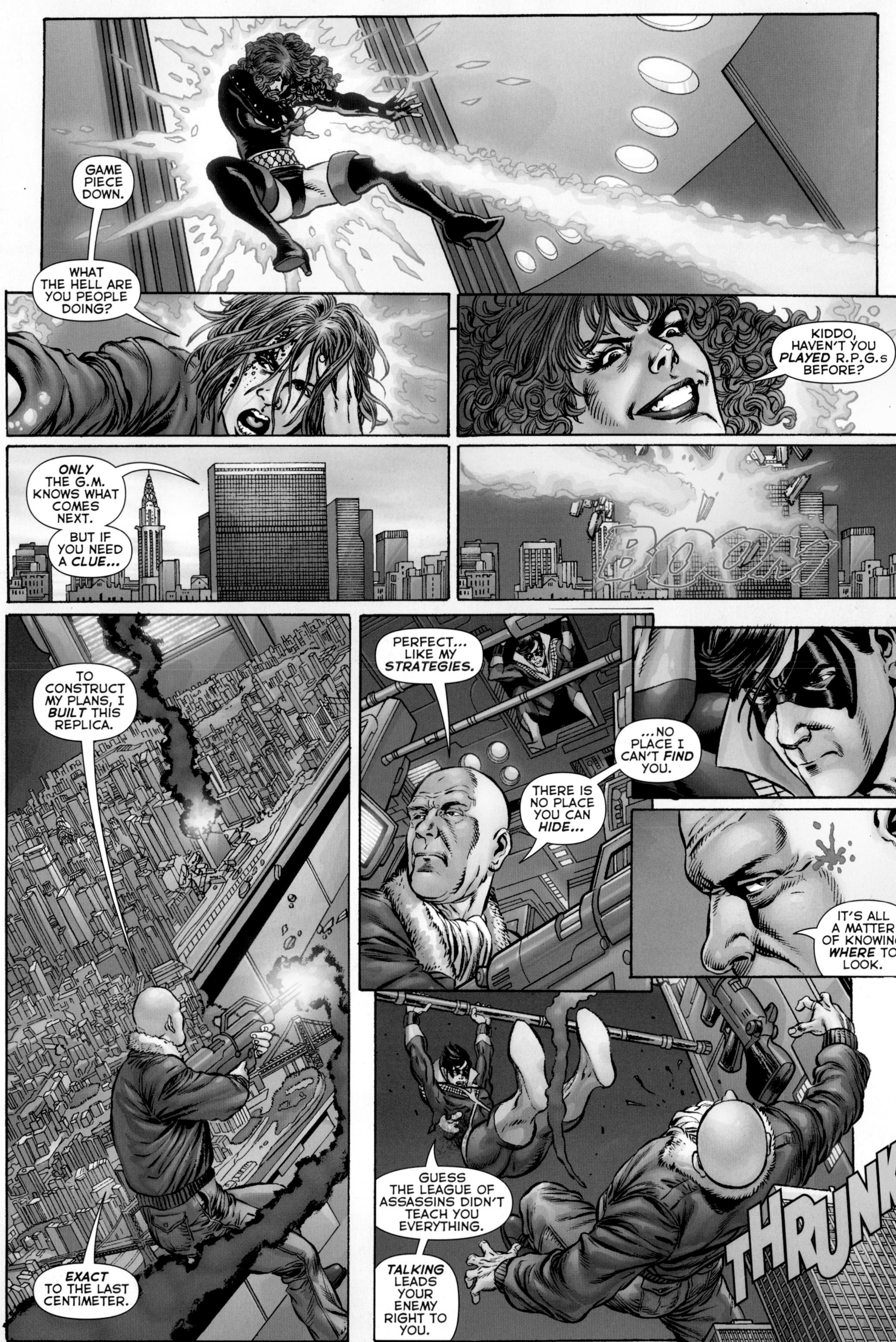
GAME PIECE DOWN.
WHAT THE HELL ARE YOU PEOPLE DOING?
KIDDO, HAVEN'T YOU PLAYED R.P.G.s BEFORE?
ONLY THE G.M. KNOWS WHAT COMES NEXT.
BUT IF YOU NEED A CLUE...
BOOM!
TO CONSTRUCT MY PLANS, I BUILT THIS REPLICA.
EXACT TO THE LAST CENTIMETER.
PERFECT... LIKE MY STRATEGIES.
THERE IS NO PLACE YOU CAN HIDE...
...NO PLACE I CAN'T FIND YOU.
IT'S ALL A MATTER OF KNOWING WHERE TO LOOK.
GUESS THE LEAGUE OF ASSASSINS DIDN'T TEACH YOU EVERYTHING.
TALKING LEADS YOUR ENEMY RIGHT TO YOU.
THRUNKK

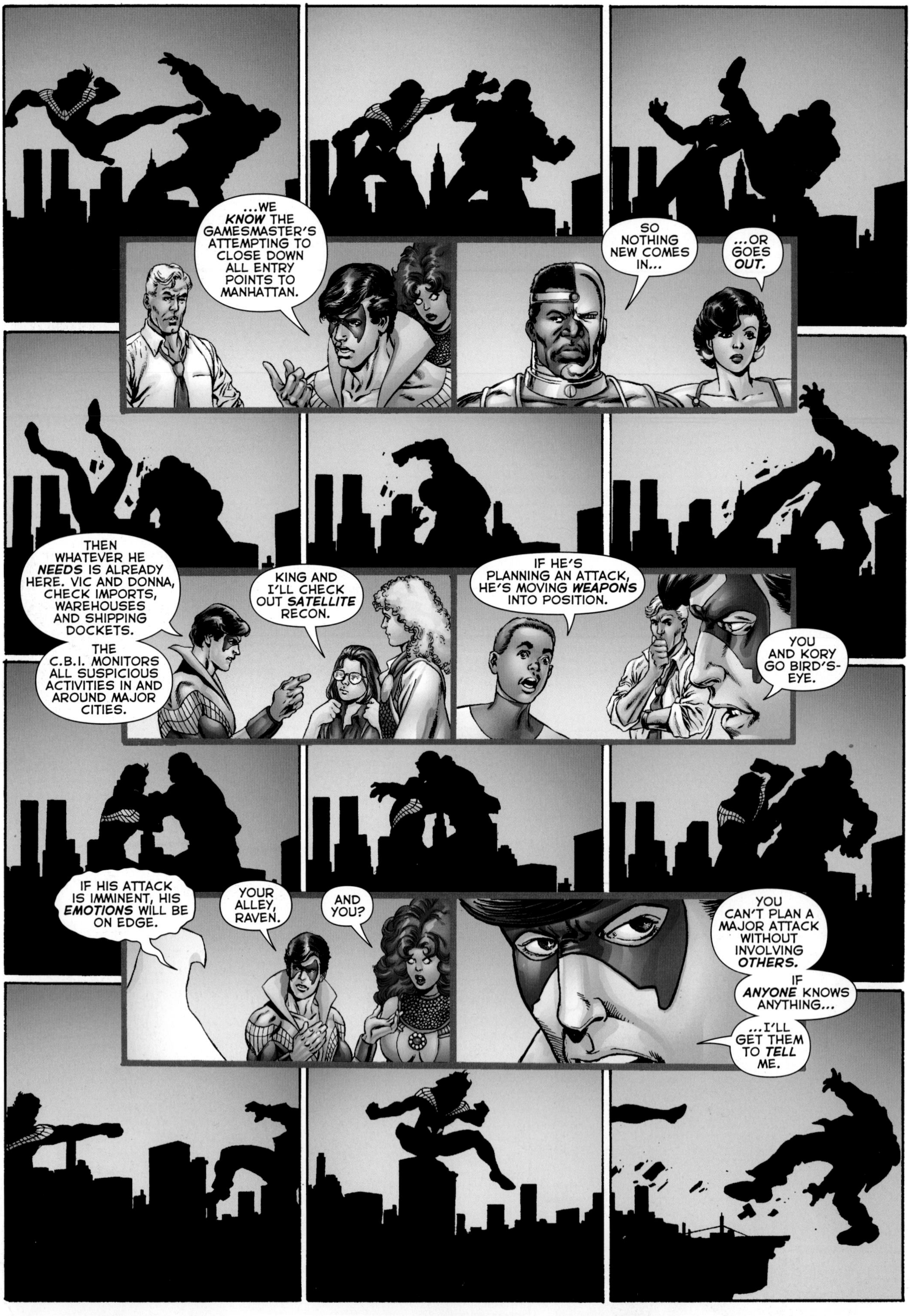
...WE KNOW THE GAMESMASTER'S ATTEMPTING TO CLOSE DOWN ALL ENTRY POINTS TO MANHATTAN.
SO NOTHING NEW COMES IN...
...OR GOES OUT.
THEN WHATEVER HE NEEDS IS ALREADY HERE. VIC AND DONNA, CHECK IMPORTS, WAREHOUSES AND SHIPPING DOCKETS.
THE C.B.I. MONITORS ALL SUSPICIOUS ACTIVITIES IN AND AROUND MAJOR CITIES.
KING AND I'LL CHECK OUT SATELLITE RECON.
IF HE'S PLANNING AN ATTACK, HE'S MOVING WEAPONS INTO POSITION.
YOU AND KORY GO BIRD'S-EYE.
IF HIS ATTACK IS IMMINENT, HIS EMOTIONS WILL BE ON EDGE.
YOUR ALLEY, RAVEN.
AND YOU?
YOU CAN'T PLAN A MAJOR ATTACK WITHOUT INVOLVING OTHERS.
IF ANYONE KNOWS ANYTHING...
...I'LL GET THEM TO TELL ME.

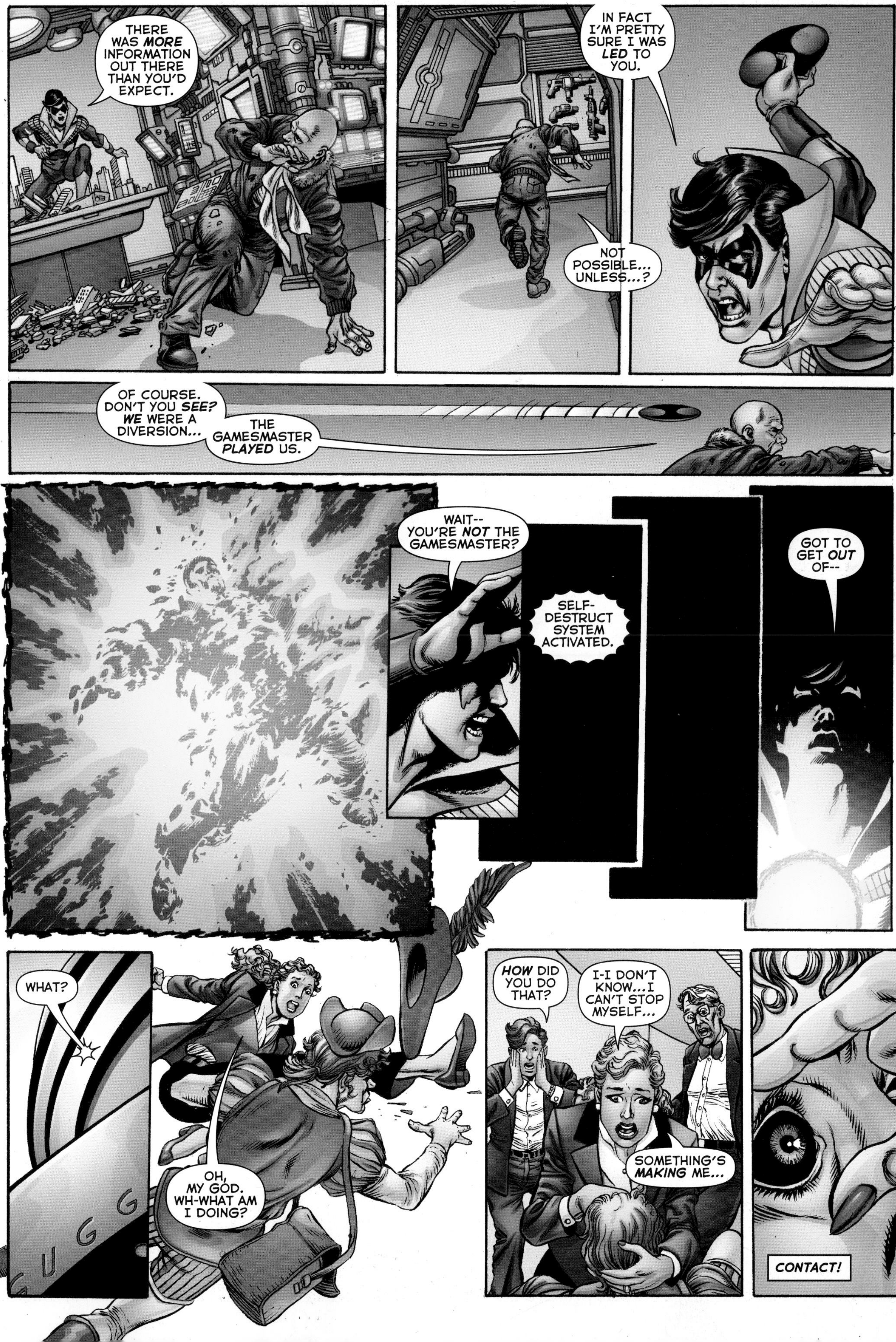
THERE WAS MORE INFORMATION OUT THERE THAN YOU'D EXPECT.
IN FACT I'M PRETTY SURE I WAS LED TO YOU.
NOT POSSIBLE... UNLESS...?
OF COURSE. DON'T YOU SEE? WE WERE A DIVERSION...
THE GAMESMASTER PLAYED US.
WAIT-- YOU'RE NOT THE GAMESMASTER?
SELF-DESTRUCT SYSTEM ACTIVATED.
GOT TO GET OUT OF--
WHAT?
OH, MY GOD. WH-WHAT AM I DOING?
GUGG
HOW DID YOU DO THAT?
I-I DON'T KNOW...I CAN'T STOP MYSELF...
SOMETHING'S MAKING ME...
CONTACT!

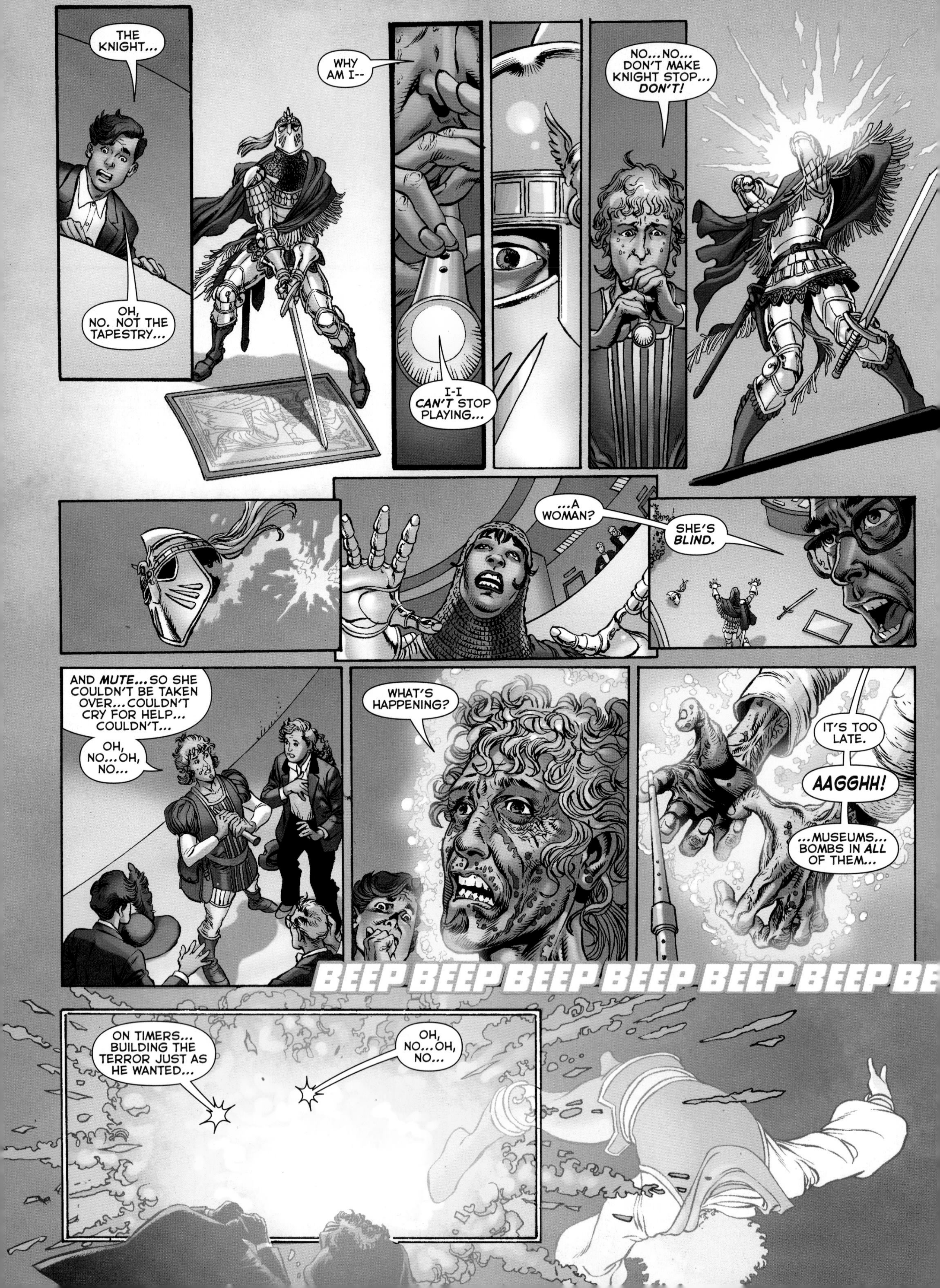
THE KNIGHT...
OH, NO. NOT THE TAPESTRY...
WHY AM I--
I-I *CAN'T* STOP PLAYING...
NO...NO... DON'T MAKE KNIGHT STOP... *DON'T!*
...A WOMAN?
SHE'S *BLIND.*
AND *MUTE*...SO SHE COULDN'T BE TAKEN OVER...COULDN'T CRY FOR HELP... COULDN'T...
OH, NO...OH, NO...
WHAT'S HAPPENING?
IT'S TOO LATE.
AAGGHH!
...MUSEUMS... BOMBS IN *ALL* OF THEM...
BEEP BEEP BEEP BEEP BEEP BEEP BE
ON TIMERS... BUILDING THE TERROR JUST AS HE WANTED...
OH, NO...OH, NO...

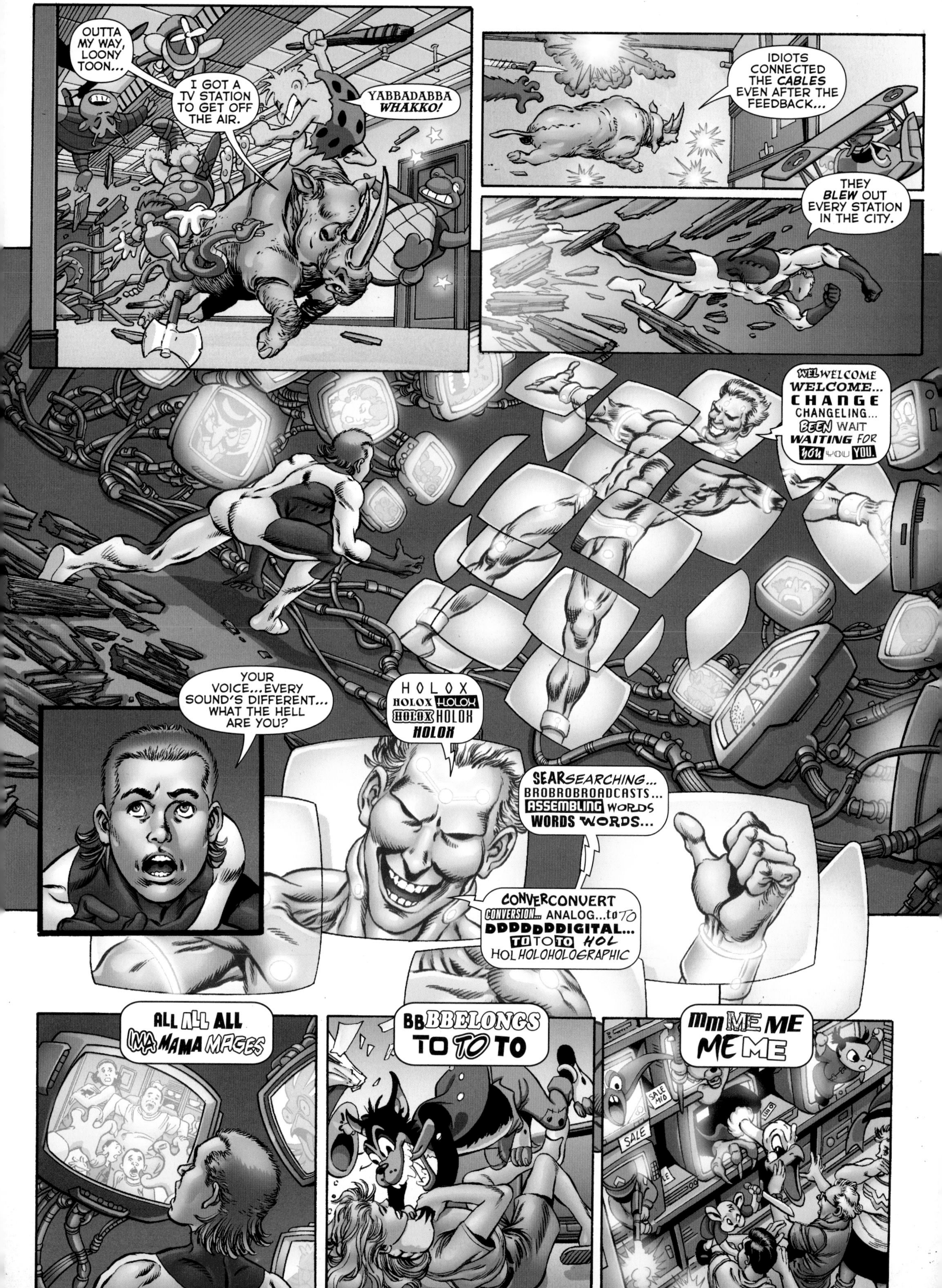
OUTTA MY WAY, LOONY TOON...
I GOT A TV STATION TO GET OFF THE AIR.
YABBADABBA WHAKKO!
IDIOTS CONNECTED THE CABLES EVEN AFTER THE FEEDBACK...
THEY BLEW OUT EVERY STATION IN THE CITY.
WEL WELCOME WELCOME... CHANGE CHANGELING... BEEN WAIT WAITING FOR YOU YOU YOU.
YOUR VOICE...EVERY SOUND'S DIFFERENT... WHAT THE HELL ARE YOU?
HOLOX HOLOX HOLOX HOLOX HOLOX HOLOX
SEARSEARCHING... BROBROBROADCASTS... ASSEMBLING WORDS WORDS WORDS...
CONVERCONVERT CONVERSION... ANALOG...to TO DDDDDDIGITAL... TO TO TO HOL HOL HOLOHOLOGRAPHIC
ALL ALL ALL IMA MAMA MAGES
BBBBELONGS TO TO TO
MM ME ME ME ME

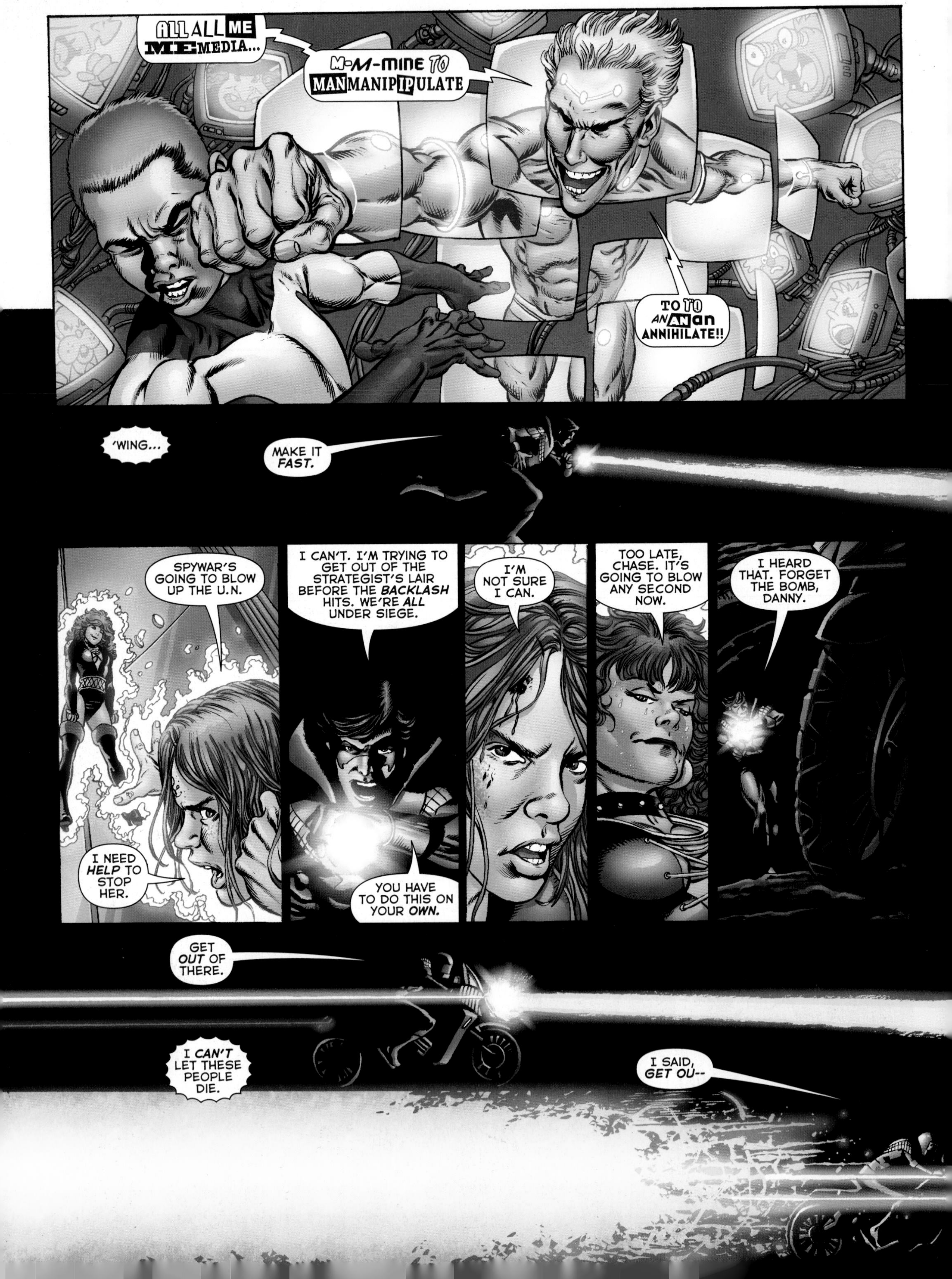
ALL ALL ME ME MEDIA...
M-M-MINE TO MAN MANIP IP ULATE
TO TO AN AN AN ANNIHILATE!!
'WING...
MAKE IT FAST.
SPYWAR'S GOING TO BLOW UP THE U.N.
I NEED HELP TO STOP HER.
I CAN'T. I'M TRYING TO GET OUT OF THE STRATEGIST'S LAIR BEFORE THE BACKLASH HITS. WE'RE ALL UNDER SIEGE.
YOU HAVE TO DO THIS ON YOUR OWN.
I'M NOT SURE I CAN.
TOO LATE, CHASE. IT'S GOING TO BLOW ANY SECOND NOW.
I HEARD THAT. FORGET THE BOMB, DANNY.
GET OUT OF THERE.
I CAN'T LET THESE PEOPLE DIE.
I SAID, GET OU--

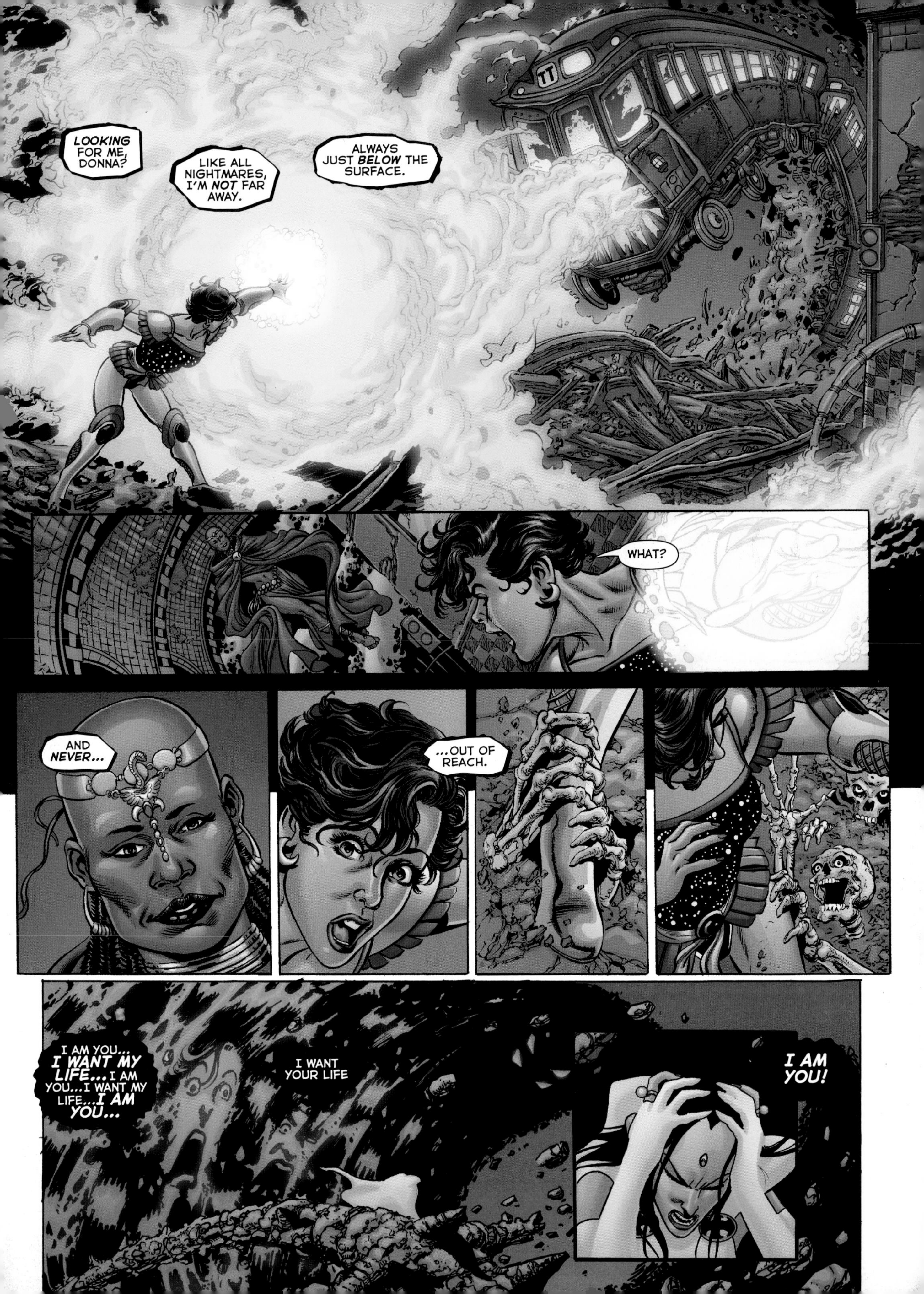
LOOKING FOR ME, DONNA?
LIKE ALL NIGHTMARES, I'M NOT FAR AWAY.
ALWAYS JUST BELOW THE SURFACE.
WHAT?
AND NEVER...
...OUT OF REACH.
I AM YOU... I WANT MY LIFE... I AM YOU...I WANT MY LIFE...I AM YOU...
I WANT YOUR LIFE
I AM YOU!

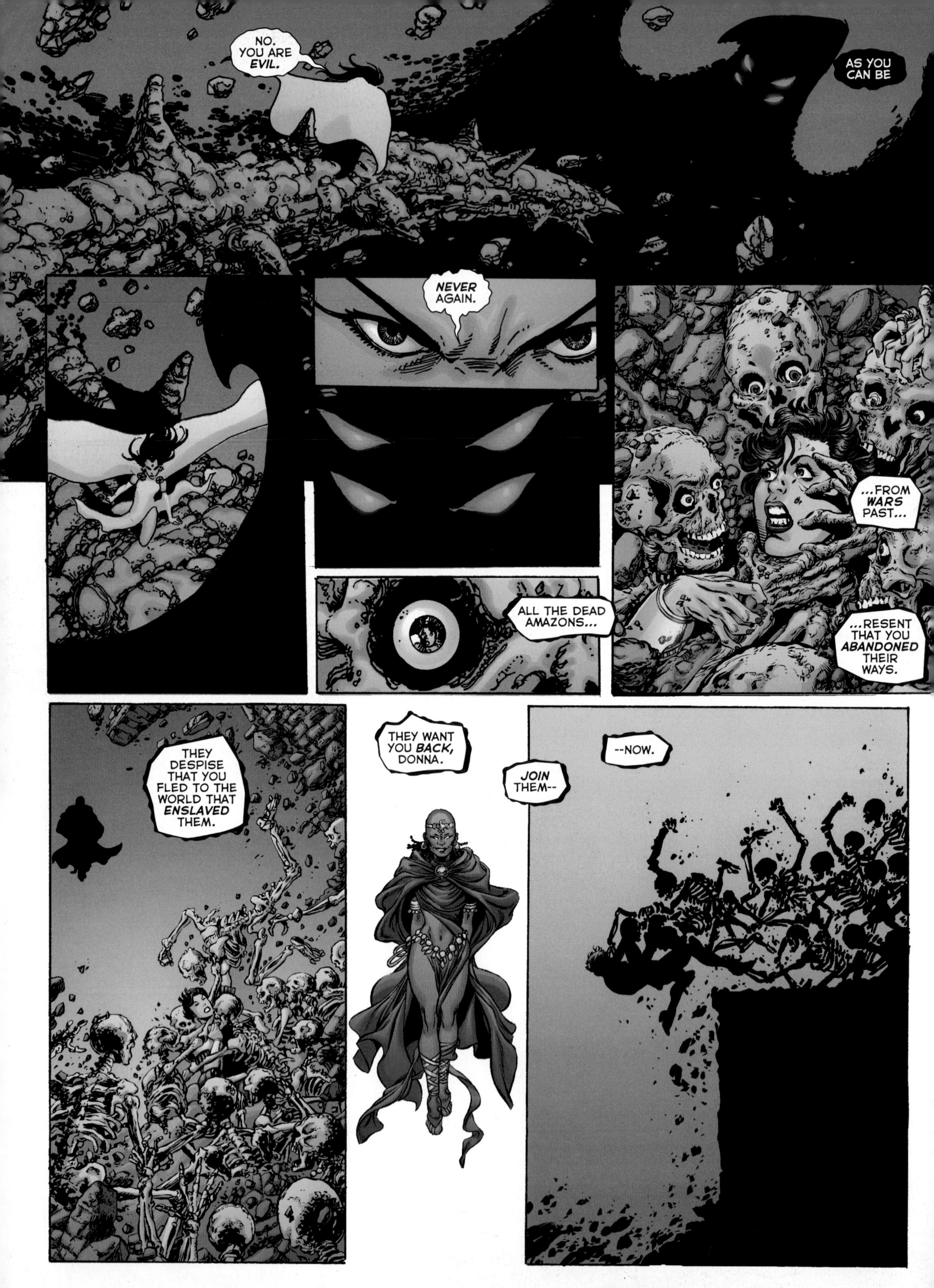
NO. YOU ARE EVIL.
AS YOU CAN BE
NEVER AGAIN.
ALL THE DEAD AMAZONS...
...FROM WARS PAST...
...RESENT THAT YOU ABANDONED THEIR WAYS.
THEY DESPISE THAT YOU FLED TO THE WORLD THAT ENSLAVED THEM.
THEY WANT YOU BACK, DONNA.
JOIN THEM--
--NOW.

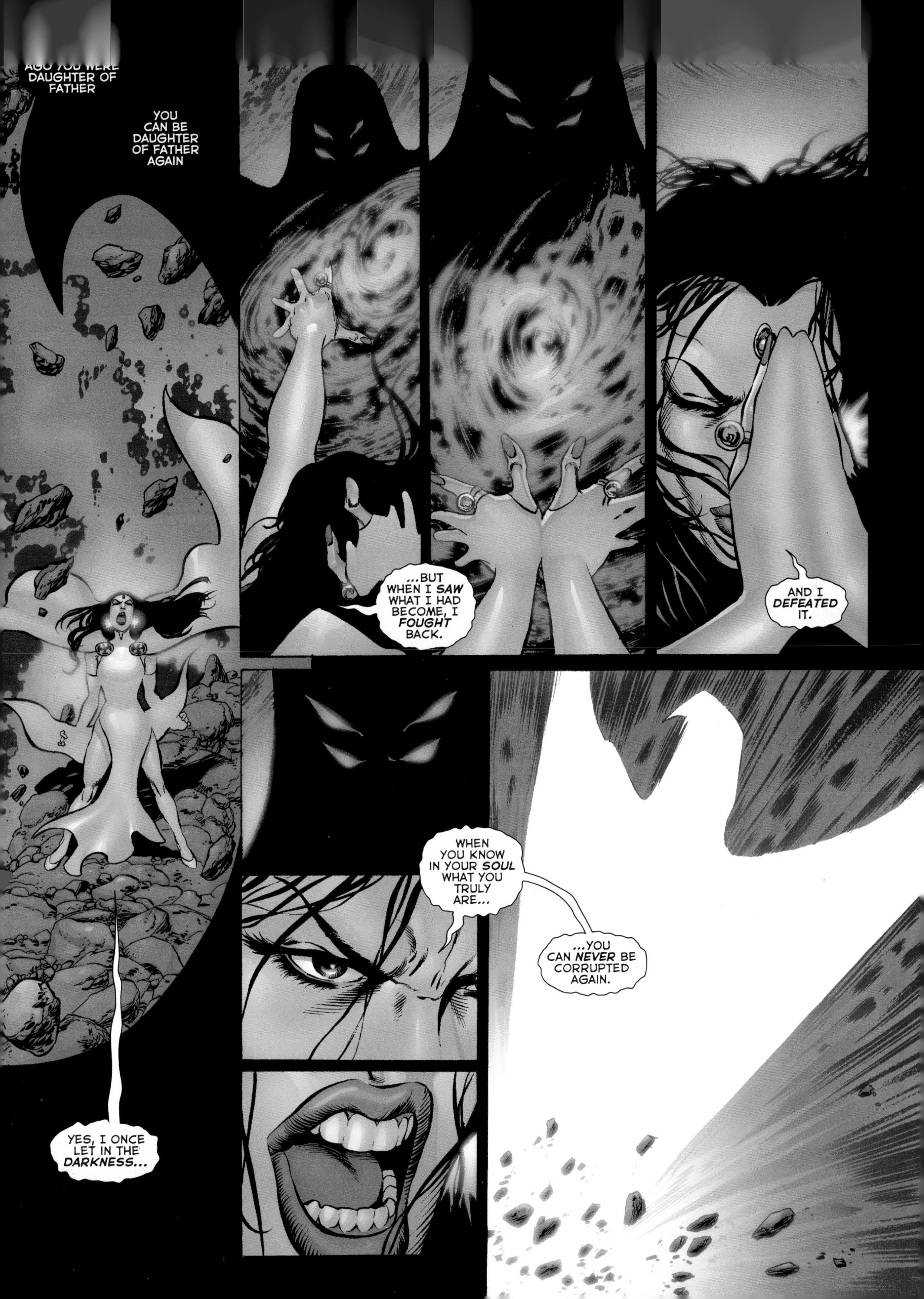

AGO YOU WERE DAUGHTER OF FATHER
YOU CAN BE DAUGHTER OF FATHER AGAIN
YES, I ONCE LET IN THE *DARKNESS...*
*...*BUT WHEN I *SAW* WHAT I HAD BECOME, I *FOUGHT* BACK.
AND I *DEFEATED* IT.
WHEN YOU KNOW IN YOUR *SOUL* WHAT YOU TRULY ARE...
*...*YOU CAN *NEVER* BE CORRUPTED AGAIN.

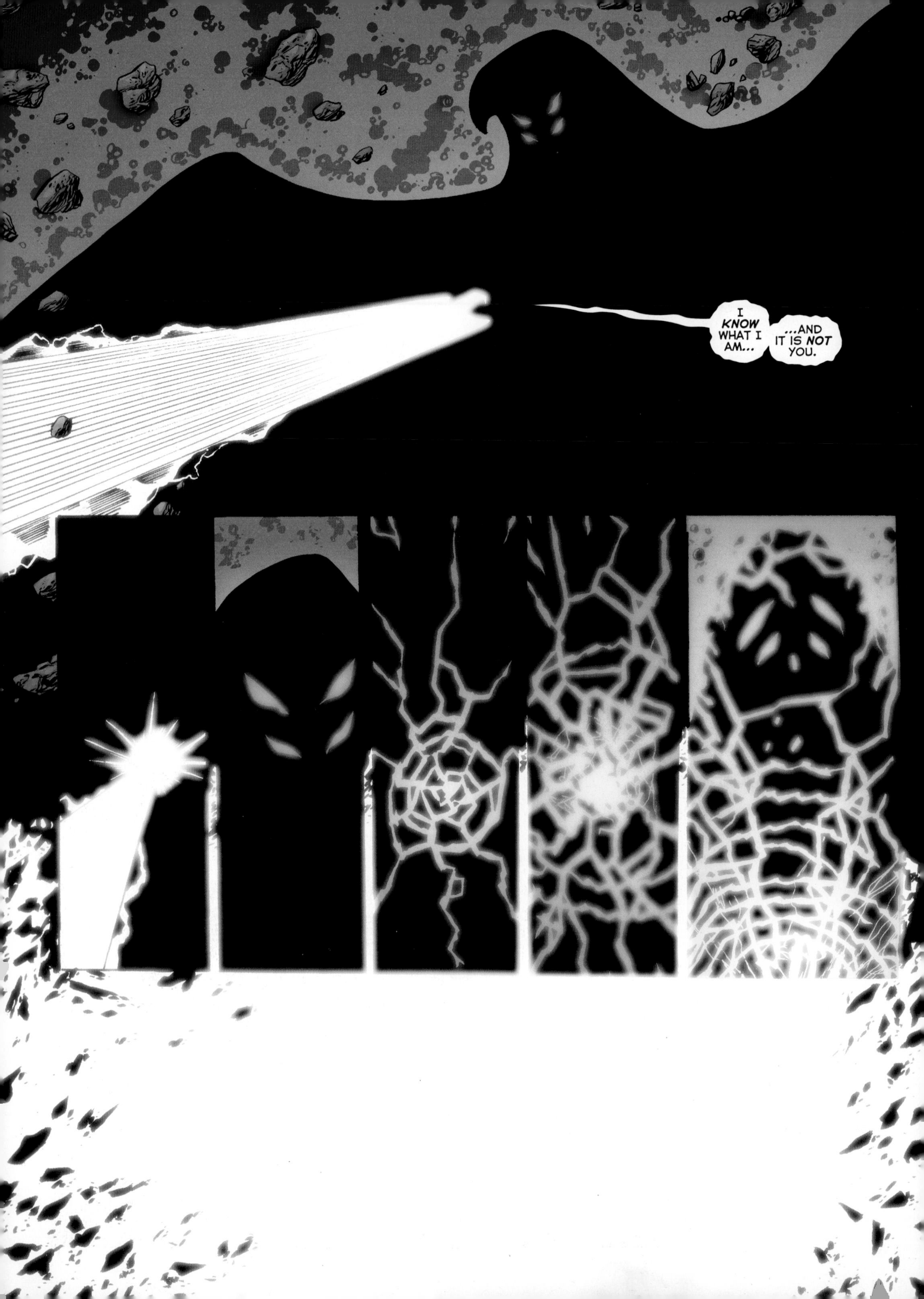
I KNOW WHAT I AM...
...AND IT IS NOT YOU.

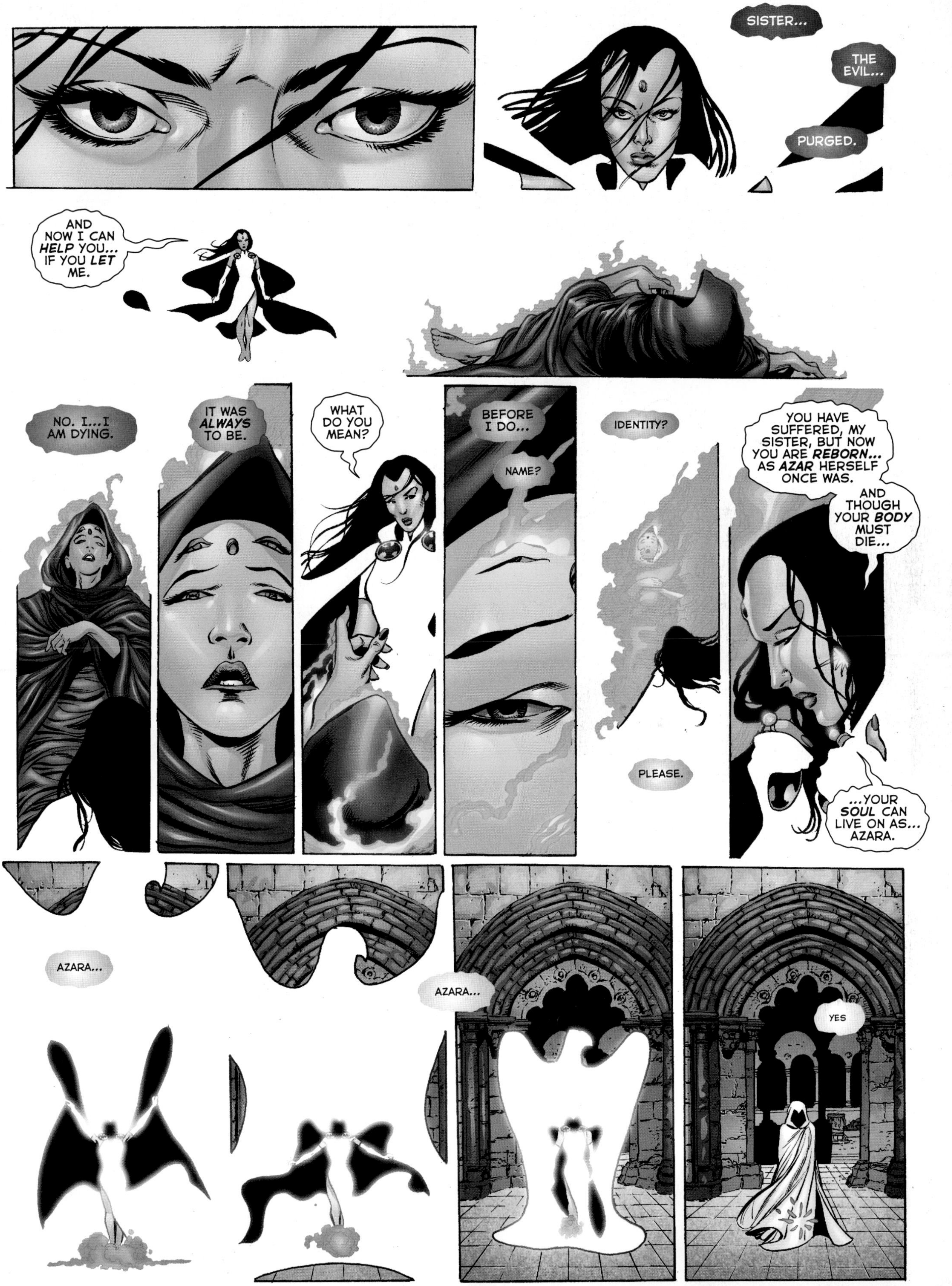
SISTER...
THE EVIL...
PURGED.
AND NOW I CAN HELP YOU... IF YOU LET ME.
NO. I...I AM DYING.
IT WAS ALWAYS TO BE.
WHAT DO YOU MEAN?
BEFORE I DO...
NAME?
IDENTITY?
PLEASE.
YOU HAVE SUFFERED, MY SISTER, BUT NOW YOU ARE REBORN... AS AZAR HERSELF ONCE WAS.
AND THOUGH YOUR BODY MUST DIE...
...YOUR SOUL CAN LIVE ON AS... AZARA.
AZARA...
AZARA...
YES

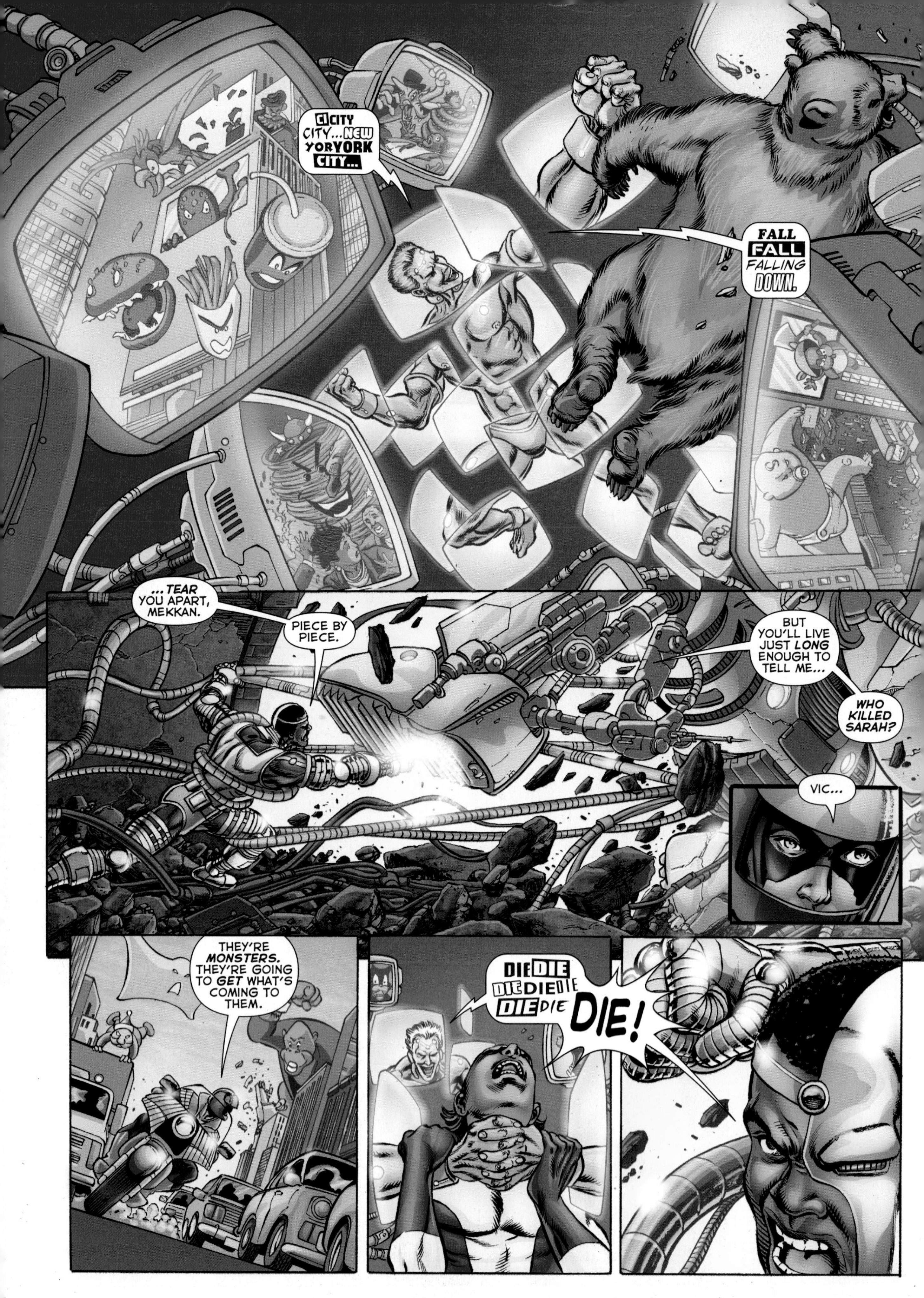
CI CITY CITY... NEW YOR YORK CITY...
FALL FALL FALLING DOWN.
...TEAR YOU APART, MEKKAN.
PIECE BY PIECE.
BUT YOU'LL LIVE JUST LONG ENOUGH TO TELL ME...
WHO KILLED SARAH?
VIC...
THEY'RE MONSTERS. THEY'RE GOING TO GET WHAT'S COMING TO THEM.
DIE DIE DIE DIE DIE DIE DIE DIE!
DIE!

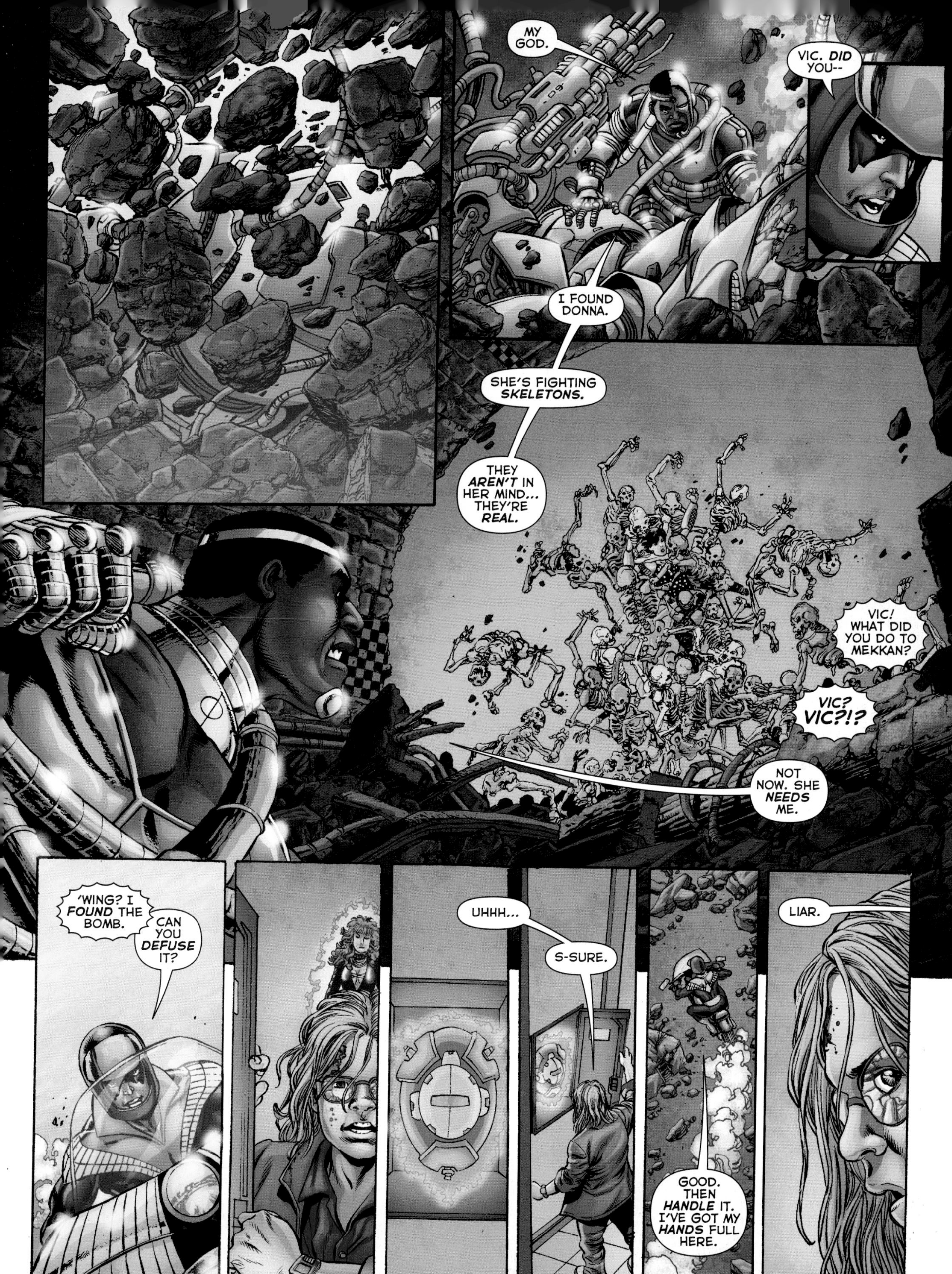
MY GOD.
VIC. DID YOU--
I FOUND DONNA.
SHE'S FIGHTING SKELETONS.
THEY AREN'T IN HER MIND... THEY'RE REAL.
VIC! WHAT DID YOU DO TO MEKKAN?
VIC? VIC?!?
NOT NOW. SHE NEEDS ME.
'WING? I FOUND THE BOMB.
CAN YOU DEFUSE IT?
UHHH...
S-SURE.
GOOD. THEN HANDLE IT. I'VE GOT MY HANDS FULL HERE.
LIAR.

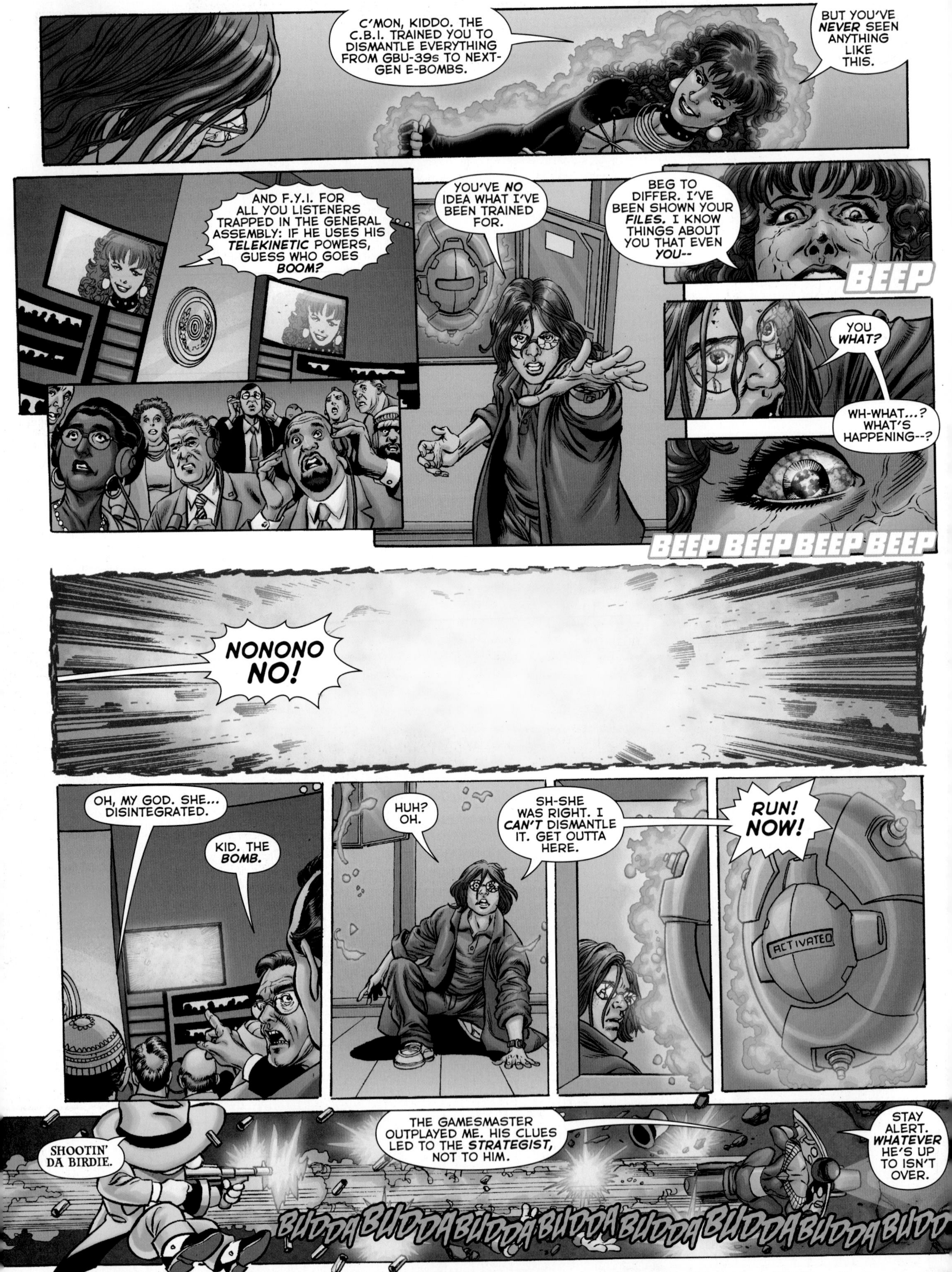
C'MON, KIDDO. THE C.B.I. TRAINED YOU TO DISMANTLE EVERYTHING FROM GBU-39s TO NEXT-GEN E-BOMBS.
BUT YOU'VE NEVER SEEN ANYTHING LIKE THIS.
AND F.Y.I. FOR ALL YOU LISTENERS TRAPPED IN THE GENERAL ASSEMBLY: IF HE USES HIS TELEKINETIC POWERS, GUESS WHO GOES BOOM?
YOU'VE NO IDEA WHAT I'VE BEEN TRAINED FOR.
BEG TO DIFFER. I'VE BEEN SHOWN YOUR FILES. I KNOW THINGS ABOUT YOU THAT EVEN YOU--
BEEP
YOU WHAT?
WH-WHAT...? WHAT'S HAPPENING--?
BEEP BEEP BEEP BEEP
NONONO NO!
OH, MY GOD. SHE... DISINTEGRATED.
KID. THE BOMB.
HUH? OH.
SH-SHE WAS RIGHT. I CAN'T DISMANTLE IT. GET OUTTA HERE.
RUN! NOW!
ACTIVATED
SHOOTIN' DA BIRDIE.
THE GAMESMASTER OUTPLAYED ME. HIS CLUES LED TO THE STRATEGIST, NOT TO HIM.
STAY ALERT. WHATEVER HE'S UP TO ISN'T OVER.
BUDDA BUDDA BUDDA BUDDA BUDDA BUDDA BUDDA BUDD

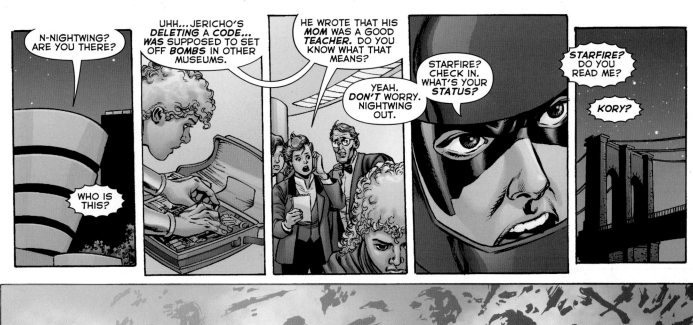

N-NIGHTWING? ARE YOU THERE?

WHO IS THIS?

UHH...JERICHO'S *DELETING A CODE...WAS* SUPPOSED TO SET OFF *BOMBS* IN OTHER MUSEUMS.

HE WROTE THAT HIS *MOM* WAS A GOOD *TEACHER.* DO YOU KNOW WHAT THAT MEANS?

YEAH. *DON'T* WORRY. NIGHTWING OUT.

STARFIRE? CHECK IN. WHAT'S YOUR *STATUS?*

STARFIRE? DO YOU *READ* ME?

KORY?

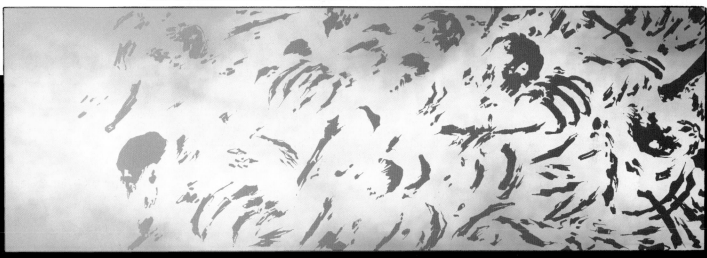

I GOT THE SKELS. NEED *HELP* WITH THE TRAIN?

NO. DUNGEON THINKS I'M STILL SIX YEARS OLD AND *AFRAID* OF NIGHTMARES.

BUT I *STOPPED* GIVING IN TO MY FEARS LONG BEFORE I PUT ON MY FIRST WONDER GIRL UNIFORM.

WHEN YOU *GROW UP* FIGHTING MONSTERS...

...YOU LEARN HOW TO TAKE THEM *DOWN.*

BEEP BEEP BEEP BEEP BEEP BEEP BEEP BEEP BEEP BEEP BEEP BEEP BEE

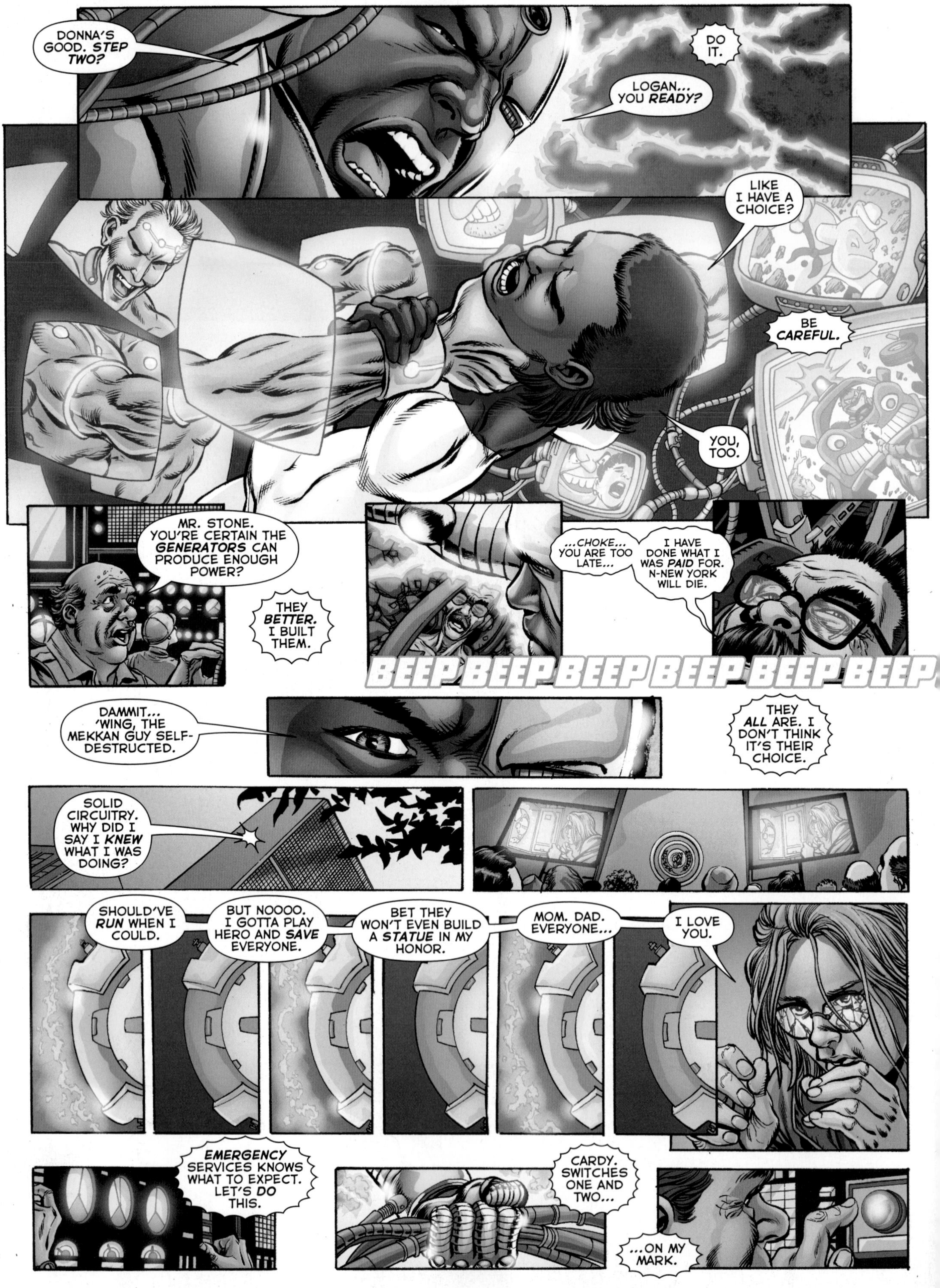
DONNA'S GOOD. STEP TWO?
DO IT.
LOGAN... YOU READY?
LIKE I HAVE A CHOICE?
BE CAREFUL.
YOU, TOO.
MR. STONE. YOU'RE CERTAIN THE GENERATORS CAN PRODUCE ENOUGH POWER?
THEY BETTER. I BUILT THEM.
...CHOKE... YOU ARE TOO LATE...
I HAVE DONE WHAT I WAS PAID FOR. N-NEW YORK WILL DIE.
BEEP BEEP BEEP BEEP BEEP BEEP
DAMMIT... 'WING, THE MEKKAN GUY SELF-DESTRUCTED.
THEY ALL ARE. I DON'T THINK IT'S THEIR CHOICE.
SOLID CIRCUITRY. WHY DID I SAY I KNEW WHAT I WAS DOING?
SHOULD'VE RUN WHEN I COULD.
BUT NOOOO. I GOTTA PLAY HERO AND SAVE EVERYONE.
BET THEY WON'T EVEN BUILD A STATUE IN MY HONOR.
MOM. DAD. EVERYONE...
I LOVE YOU.
EMERGENCY SERVICES KNOWS WHAT TO EXPECT. LET'S DO THIS.
CARDY. SWITCHES ONE AND TWO...
...ON MY MARK.

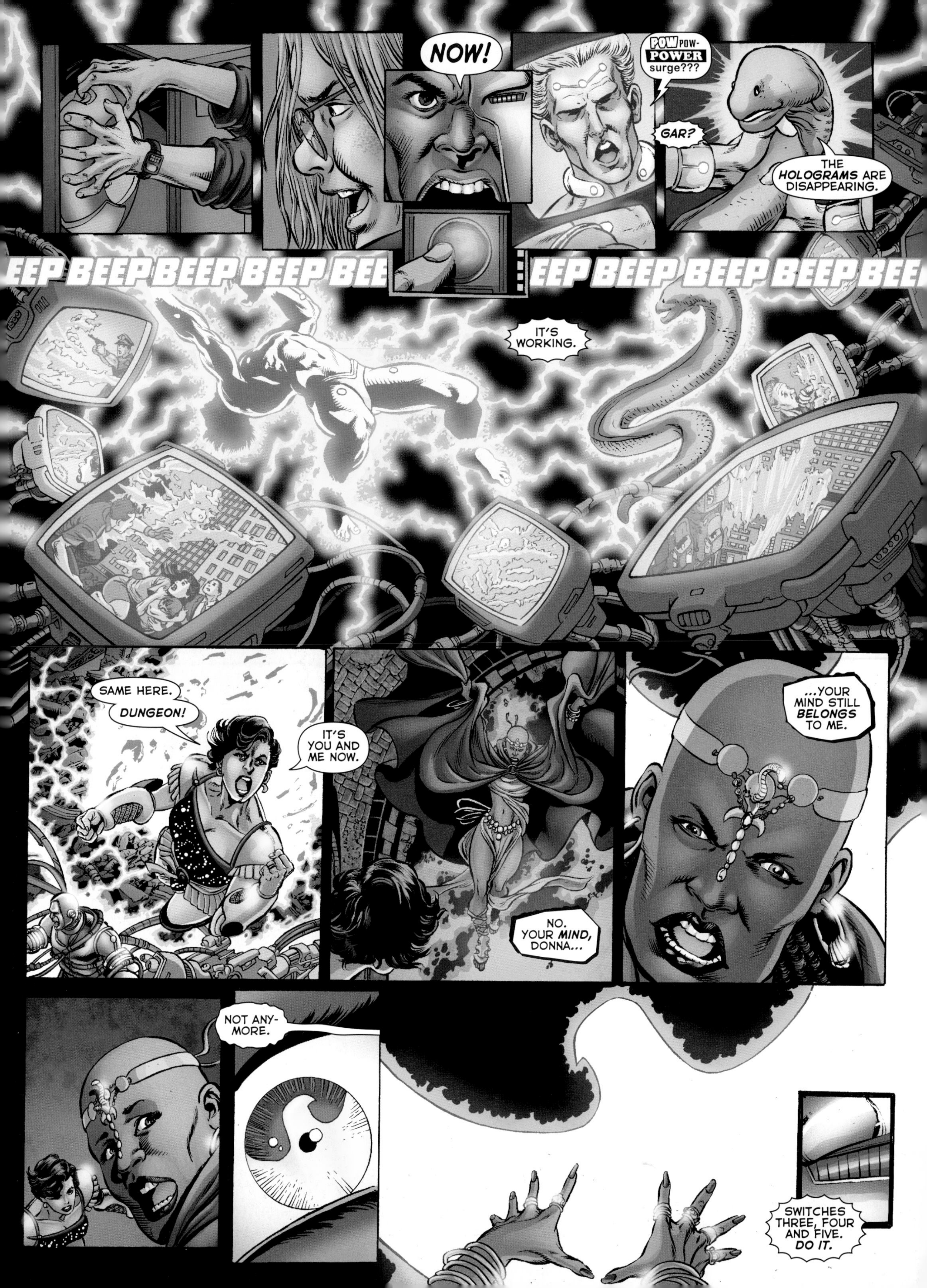
NOW!
POW POW-
POWER
surge???
GAR?
THE HOLOGRAMS ARE DISAPPEARING.
EEP BEEP BEEP BEEP BEE
EEP BEEP BEEP BEEP BEE
IT'S WORKING.
SAME HERE.
DUNGEON!
IT'S YOU AND ME NOW.
NO. YOUR MIND, DONNA...
...YOUR MIND STILL BELONGS TO ME.
NOT ANY-MORE.
SWITCHES THREE, FOUR AND FIVE. DO IT.

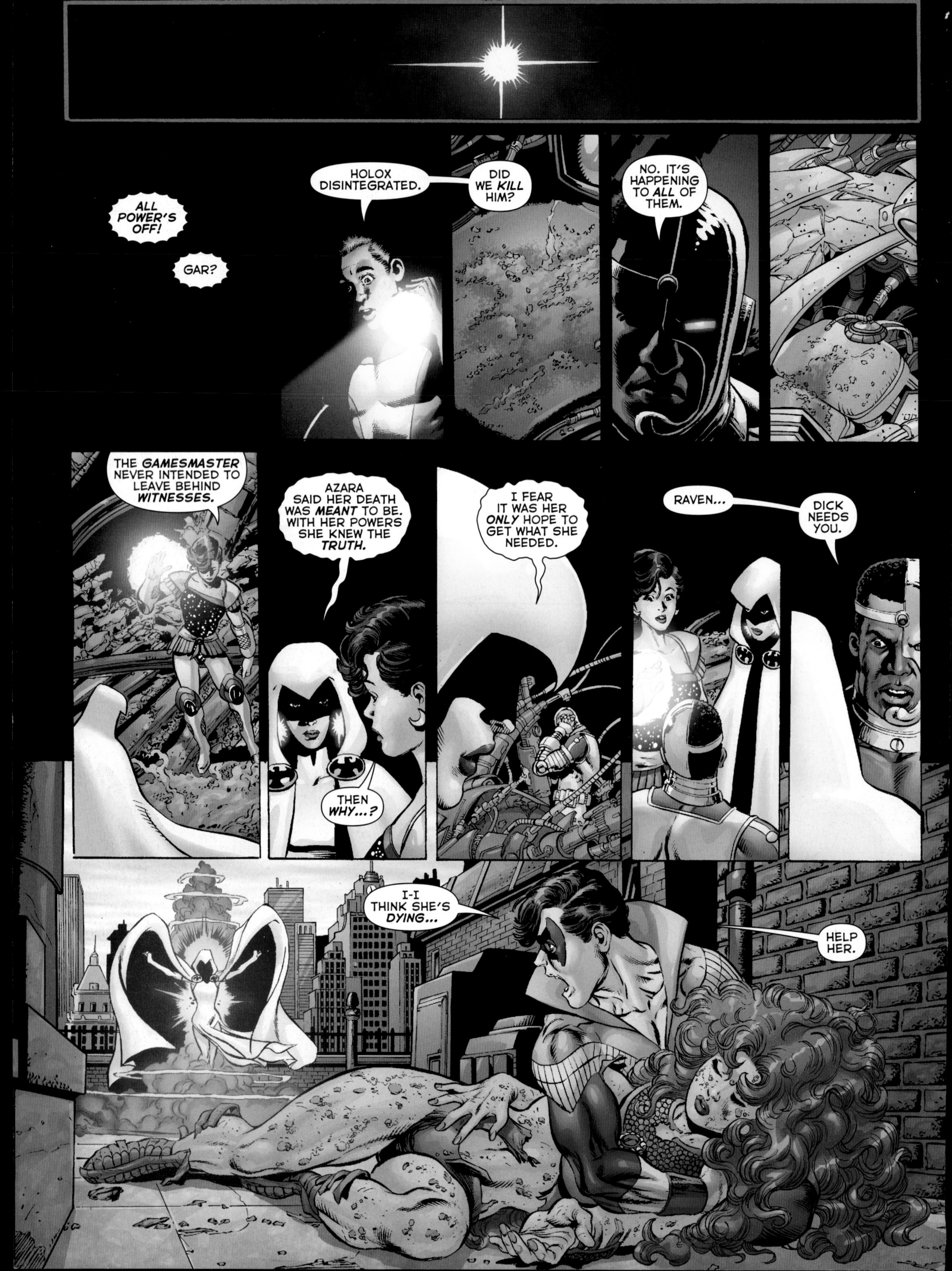
ALL POWER'S OFF!
GAR?
HOLOX DISINTEGRATED.
DID WE KILL HIM?
NO. IT'S HAPPENING TO ALL OF THEM.
THE GAMESMASTER NEVER INTENDED TO LEAVE BEHIND WITNESSES.
AZARA SAID HER DEATH WAS MEANT TO BE. WITH HER POWERS SHE KNEW THE TRUTH.
THEN WHY...?
I FEAR IT WAS HER ONLY HOPE TO GET WHAT SHE NEEDED.
RAVEN...
DICK NEEDS YOU.
I-I THINK SHE'S DYING...
HELP HER.

SHE HAS BEEN *BLEEDING*... ...FOR MUCH TOO LONG.

DO *EVERYTHING* YOU CAN.

I *CANNOT* MAKE PROMISES.

PLEASE.

THEN LEAVE US. YOU STILL HAVE *EVIL* TO DEAL WITH.

AND IT *NEVER* ENDS.

NIGHTWING. *UPDATES?*

POWER TO MANHATTAN'S BEEN SHUT OFF WITH ONLY *EMERGENCY* SERVICES STILL ON THE GRID.

I'LL BE ABLE TO *TRACK* ANY SUDDEN ELECTRICAL OUTPUT.

SUBWAYS ARE DOWN. THE M.T.A.'S SENT CREWS TO HELP COMMUTERS.

UMM. I'M SPEAKING FOR JERICHO. HE'S *DEACTIVATED* THE BOMB THING DEVICE.

EVERYTHING'S SHUT DOWN. IT'S LIKE *FLINTSTONES* ALL OVER AGAIN.

THEN IT'S ALL GOOD. DANNY-- REPORT.

EVERYTHING OKAY?

NO.

NOT EVEN CLOSE.

I-I'M IN REALLY DEEP *TROUBLE.*

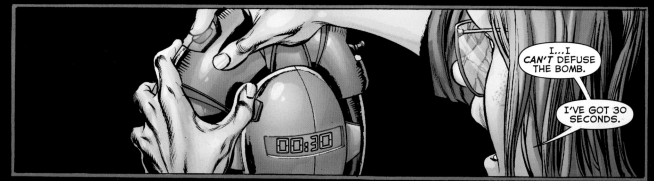

I...I *CAN'T* DEFUSE THE BOMB.

I'VE GOT 30 SECONDS.

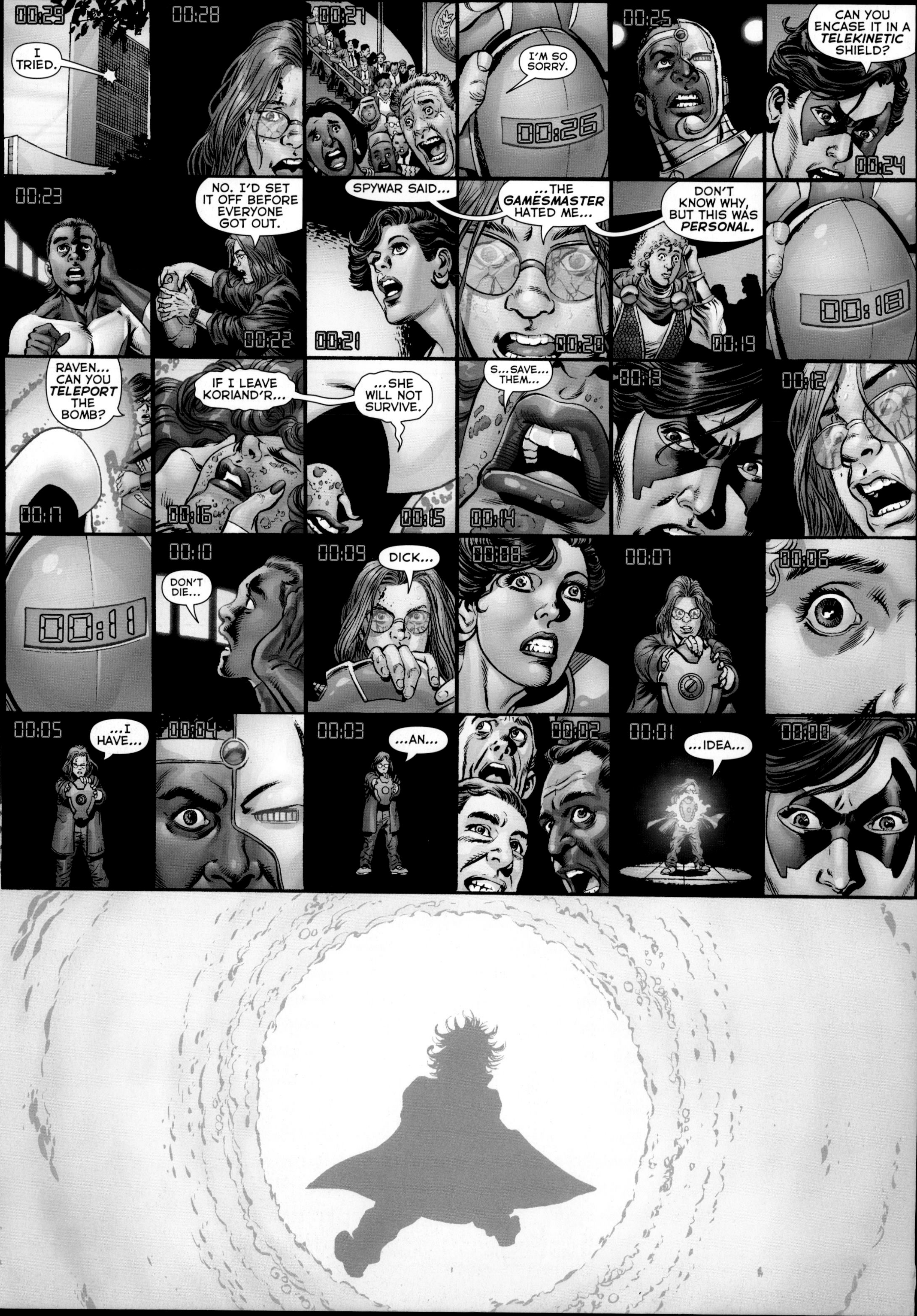
00:29
I TRIED.
00:28
00:27
I'M SO SORRY.
00:26
00:25
CAN YOU ENCASE IT IN A TELEKINETIC SHIELD?
00:24
00:23
NO. I'D SET IT OFF BEFORE EVERYONE GOT OUT.
00:22
SPYWAR SAID...
00:21
...THE GAMESMASTER HATED ME...
00:20
DON'T KNOW WHY, BUT THIS WAS PERSONAL.
00:19
00:18
RAVEN... CAN YOU TELEPORT THE BOMB?
00:17
IF I LEAVE KORIAND'R...
00:16
...SHE WILL NOT SURVIVE.
00:15
S...SAVE... THEM...
00:14
00:13
00:12
00:11
00:10
DON'T DIE...
00:09
DICK...
00:08
00:07
00:06
00:05
...I HAVE...
00:04
00:03
...AN...
00:02
00:01
...IDEA...
00:00

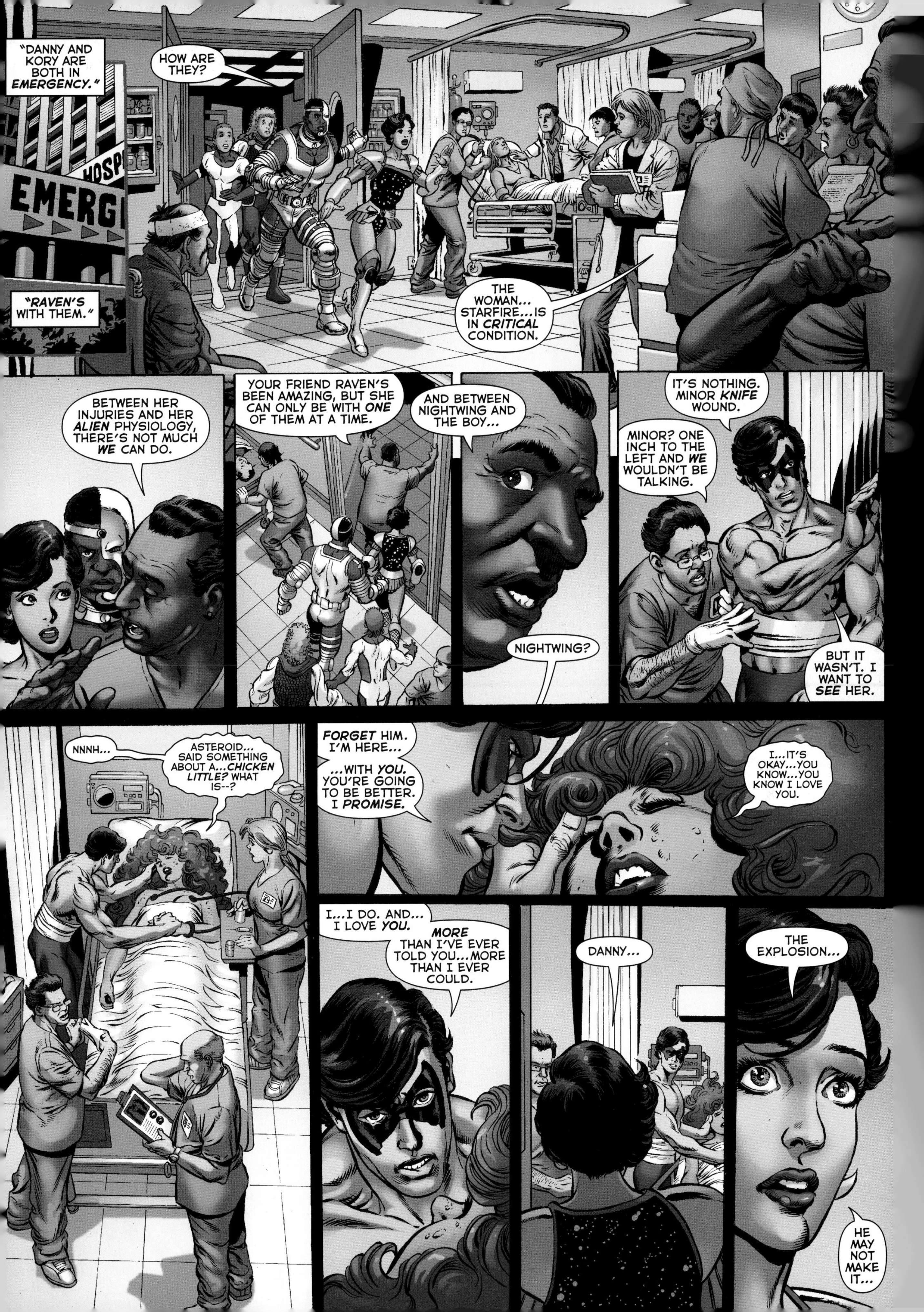
"DANNY AND KORY ARE BOTH IN EMERGENCY."
HOW ARE THEY?
"RAVEN'S WITH THEM."
EMERG
HOSP
THE WOMAN... STARFIRE...IS IN CRITICAL CONDITION.
BETWEEN HER INJURIES AND HER ALIEN PHYSIOLOGY, THERE'S NOT MUCH WE CAN DO.
YOUR FRIEND RAVEN'S BEEN AMAZING, BUT SHE CAN ONLY BE WITH ONE OF THEM AT A TIME.
AND BETWEEN NIGHTWING AND THE BOY...
NIGHTWING?
IT'S NOTHING. MINOR KNIFE WOUND.
MINOR? ONE INCH TO THE LEFT AND WE WOULDN'T BE TALKING.
BUT IT WASN'T. I WANT TO SEE HER.
NNNH...
ASTEROID... SAID SOMETHING ABOUT A...CHICKEN LITTLE? WHAT IS--?
FORGET HIM. I'M HERE...
...WITH YOU. YOU'RE GOING TO BE BETTER. I PROMISE.
I...IT'S OKAY...YOU KNOW...YOU KNOW I LOVE YOU.
I...I DO. AND... I LOVE YOU.
MORE THAN I'VE EVER TOLD YOU...MORE THAN I EVER COULD.
DANNY...
THE EXPLOSION...
HE MAY NOT MAKE IT...

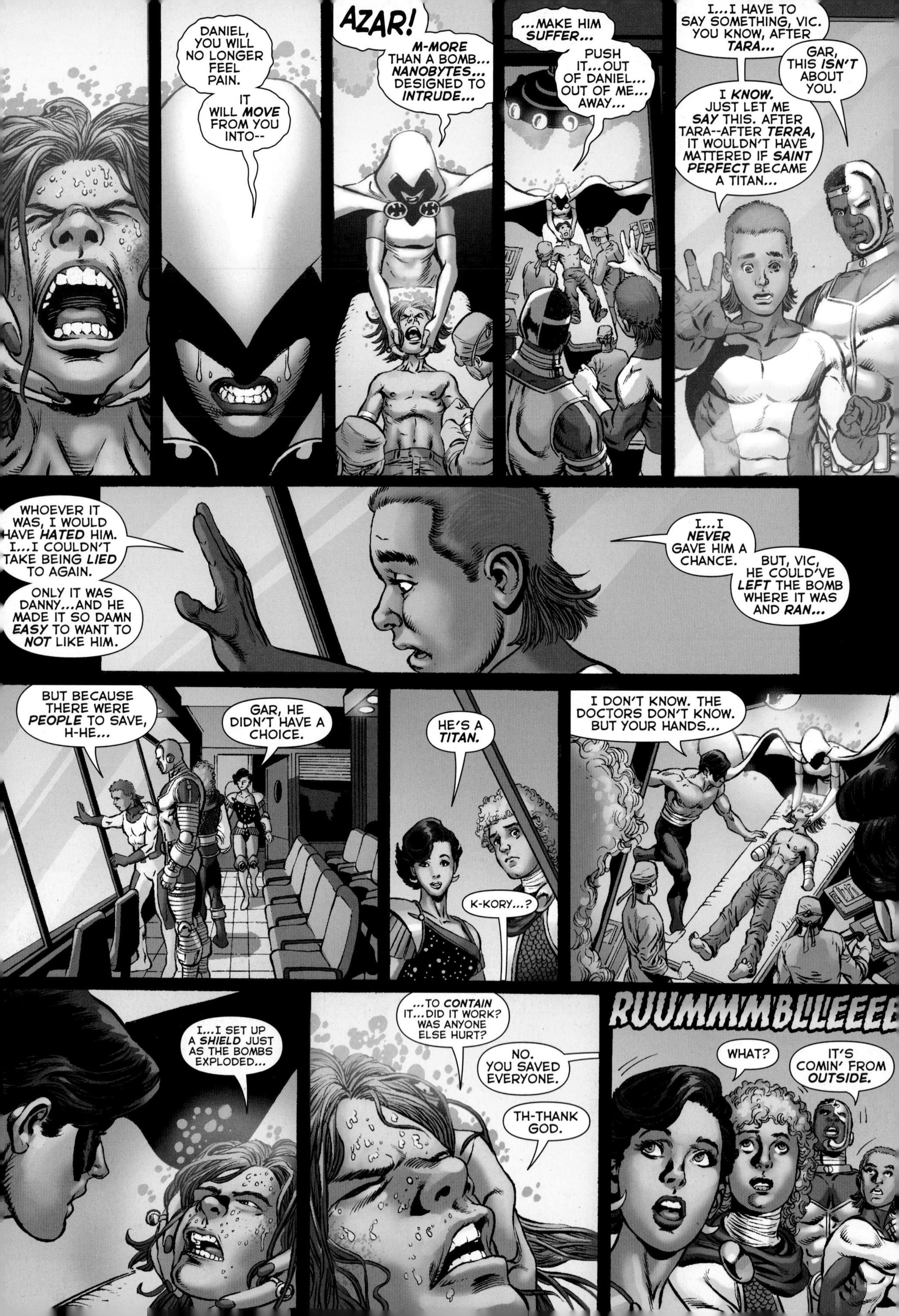
DANIEL, YOU WILL NO LONGER FEEL PAIN.
IT WILL MOVE FROM YOU INTO--
AZAR!
M-MORE THAN A BOMB... NANOBYTES... DESIGNED TO INTRUDE...
...MAKE HIM SUFFER...
PUSH IT...OUT OF DANIEL... OUT OF ME... AWAY...
I...I HAVE TO SAY SOMETHING, VIC. YOU KNOW, AFTER TARA...
GAR, THIS ISN'T ABOUT YOU.
I KNOW. JUST LET ME SAY THIS. AFTER TARA--AFTER TERRA, IT WOULDN'T HAVE MATTERED IF SAINT PERFECT BECAME A TITAN...
WHOEVER IT WAS, I WOULD HAVE HATED HIM. I...I COULDN'T TAKE BEING LIED TO AGAIN.
ONLY IT WAS DANNY...AND HE MADE IT SO DAMN EASY TO WANT TO NOT LIKE HIM.
I...I NEVER GAVE HIM A CHANCE.
BUT, VIC, HE COULD'VE LEFT THE BOMB WHERE IT WAS AND RAN...
BUT BECAUSE THERE WERE PEOPLE TO SAVE, H-HE...
GAR, HE DIDN'T HAVE A CHOICE.
HE'S A TITAN.
K-KORY...?
I DON'T KNOW. THE DOCTORS DON'T KNOW. BUT YOUR HANDS...
I...I SET UP A SHIELD JUST AS THE BOMBS EXPLODED...
...TO CONTAIN IT...DID IT WORK? WAS ANYONE ELSE HURT?
NO. YOU SAVED EVERYONE.
TH-THANK GOD.
RUUMMMBLLEEEE
WHAT?
IT'S COMIN' FROM OUTSIDE.

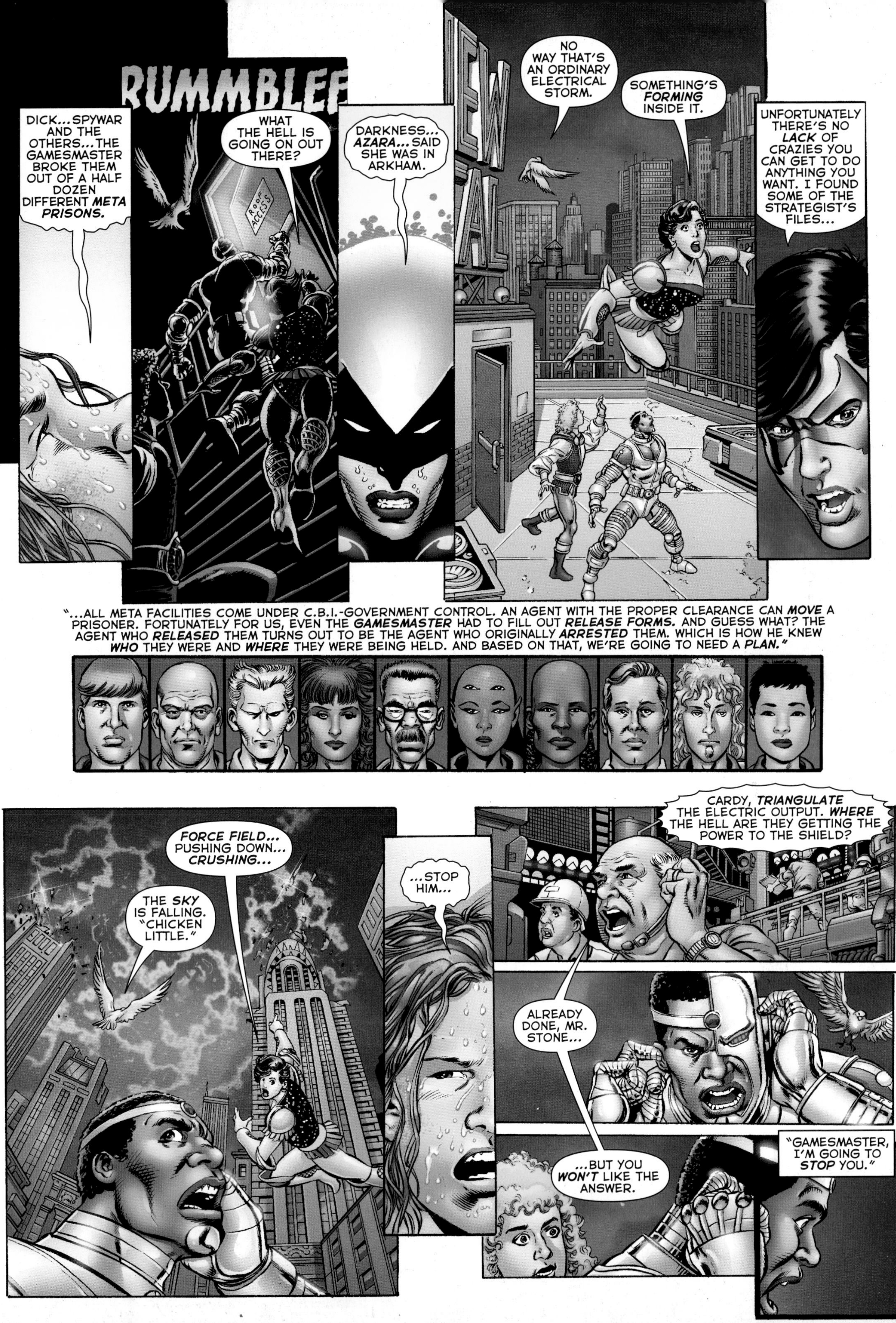
RUMMBLEF
DICK...SPYWAR AND THE OTHERS...THE GAMESMASTER BROKE THEM OUT OF A HALF DOZEN DIFFERENT META PRISONS.
ROOF ACCESS
WHAT THE HELL IS GOING ON OUT THERE?
DARKNESS... AZARA... SAID SHE WAS IN ARKHAM.
NO WAY THAT'S AN ORDINARY ELECTRICAL STORM.
SOMETHING'S FORMING INSIDE IT.
UNFORTUNATELY THERE'S NO LACK OF CRAZIES YOU CAN GET TO DO ANYTHING YOU WANT. I FOUND SOME OF THE STRATEGIST'S FILES...
"...ALL META FACILITIES COME UNDER C.B.I.-GOVERNMENT CONTROL. AN AGENT WITH THE PROPER CLEARANCE CAN MOVE A PRISONER. FORTUNATELY FOR US, EVEN THE GAMESMASTER HAD TO FILL OUT RELEASE FORMS. AND GUESS WHAT? THE AGENT WHO RELEASED THEM TURNS OUT TO BE THE AGENT WHO ORIGINALLY ARRESTED THEM. WHICH IS HOW HE KNEW WHO THEY WERE AND WHERE THEY WERE BEING HELD. AND BASED ON THAT, WE'RE GOING TO NEED A PLAN."
FORCE FIELD... PUSHING DOWN... CRUSHING...
THE SKY IS FALLING. "CHICKEN LITTLE."
...STOP HIM...
CARDY, TRIANGULATE THE ELECTRIC OUTPUT. WHERE THE HELL ARE THEY GETTING THE POWER TO THE SHIELD?
ALREADY DONE, MR. STONE...
...BUT YOU WON'T LIKE THE ANSWER.
"GAMESMASTER, I'M GOING TO STOP YOU."

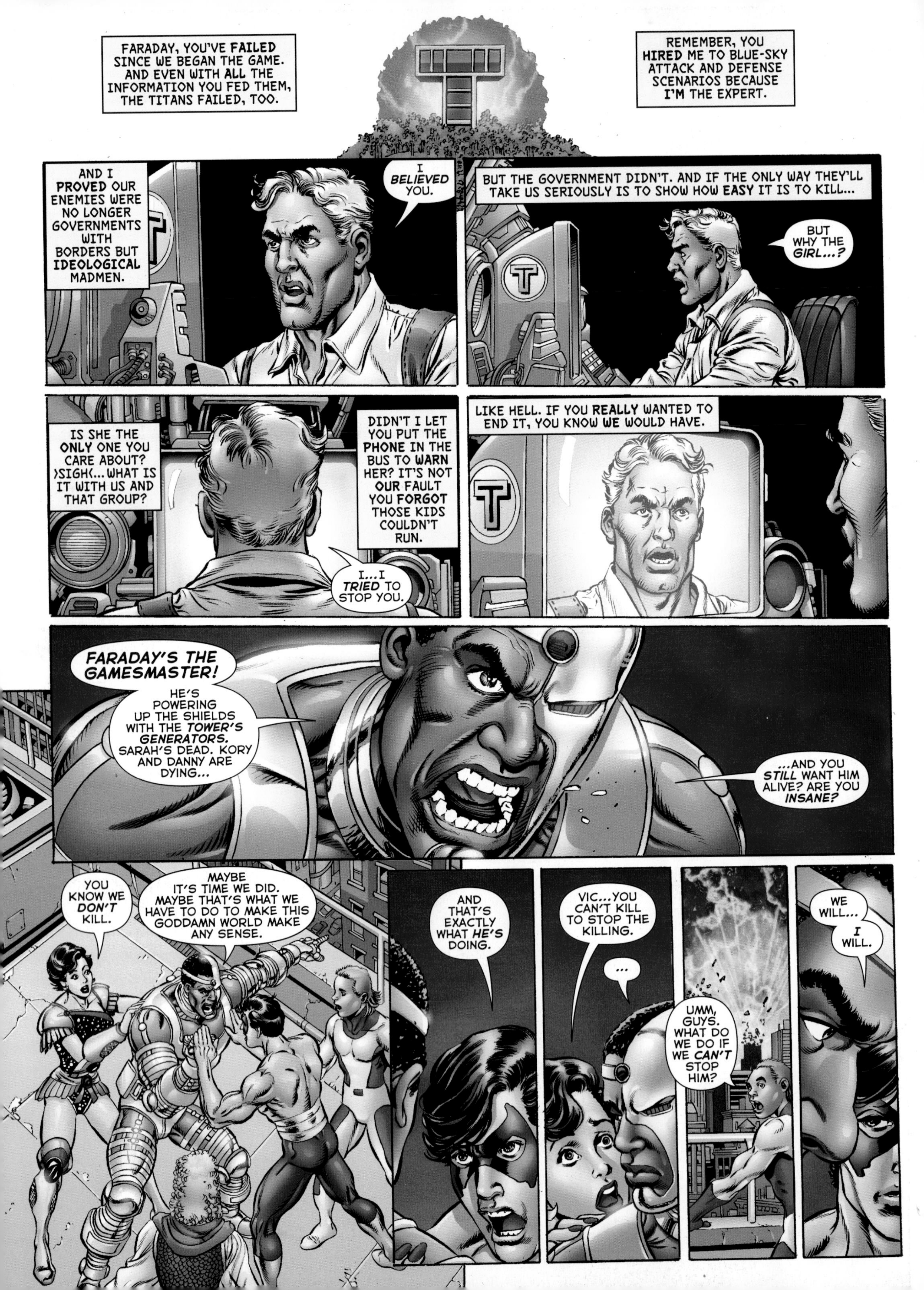
FARADAY, YOU'VE FAILED SINCE WE BEGAN THE GAME. AND EVEN WITH ALL THE INFORMATION YOU FED THEM, THE TITANS FAILED, TOO.
REMEMBER, YOU HIRED ME TO BLUE-SKY ATTACK AND DEFENSE SCENARIOS BECAUSE I'M THE EXPERT.
AND I PROVED OUR ENEMIES WERE NO LONGER GOVERNMENTS WITH BORDERS BUT IDEOLOGICAL MADMEN.
I BELIEVED YOU.
BUT THE GOVERNMENT DIDN'T. AND IF THE ONLY WAY THEY'LL TAKE US SERIOUSLY IS TO SHOW HOW EASY IT IS TO KILL...
BUT WHY THE GIRL...?
IS SHE THE ONLY ONE YOU CARE ABOUT? ›SIGH‹... WHAT IS IT WITH US AND THAT GROUP?
DIDN'T I LET YOU PUT THE PHONE IN THE BUS TO WARN HER? IT'S NOT OUR FAULT YOU FORGOT THOSE KIDS COULDN'T RUN.
I...I TRIED TO STOP YOU.
LIKE HELL. IF YOU REALLY WANTED TO END IT, YOU KNOW WE WOULD HAVE.
FARADAY'S THE GAMESMASTER!
HE'S POWERING UP THE SHIELDS WITH THE TOWER'S GENERATORS. SARAH'S DEAD. KORY AND DANNY ARE DYING...
...AND YOU STILL WANT HIM ALIVE? ARE YOU INSANE?
YOU KNOW WE DON'T KILL.
MAYBE IT'S TIME WE DID. MAYBE THAT'S WHAT WE HAVE TO DO TO MAKE THIS GODDAMN WORLD MAKE ANY SENSE.
AND THAT'S EXACTLY WHAT HE'S DOING.
VIC...YOU CAN'T KILL TO STOP THE KILLING.
...
UMM, GUYS. WHAT DO WE DO IF WE CAN'T STOP HIM?
WE WILL... I WILL.

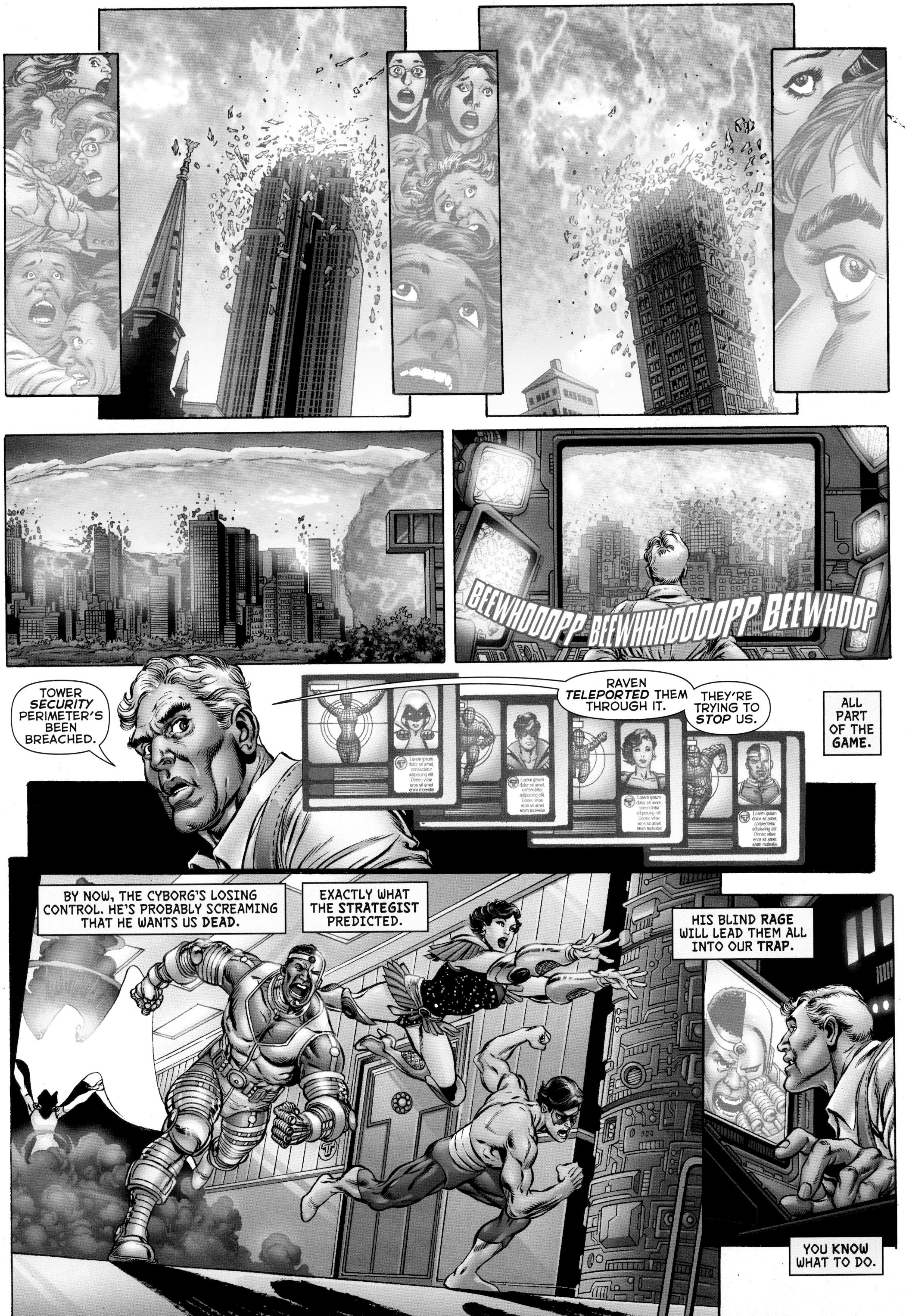
BEEWHOOOPP BEEWHHHOOOOPP BEEWHOOP
TOWER SECURITY PERIMETER'S BEEN BREACHED.
RAVEN TELEPORTED THEM THROUGH IT.
THEY'RE TRYING TO STOP US.
ALL PART OF THE GAME.
BY NOW, THE CYBORG'S LOSING CONTROL. HE'S PROBABLY SCREAMING THAT HE WANTS US DEAD.
EXACTLY WHAT THE STRATEGIST PREDICTED.
HIS BLIND RAGE WILL LEAD THEM ALL INTO OUR TRAP.
YOU KNOW WHAT TO DO.

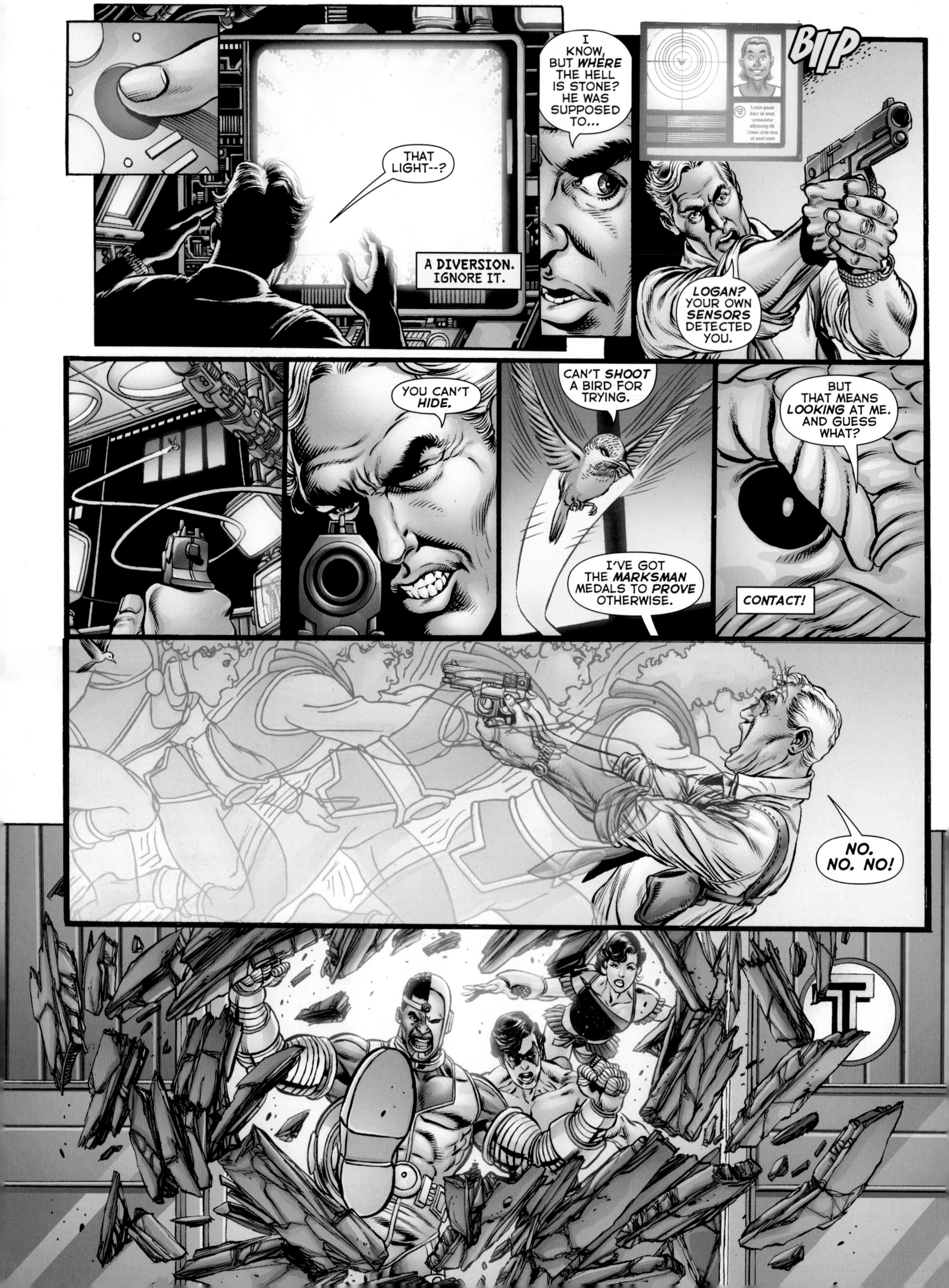
THAT LIGHT--?
A DIVERSION. IGNORE IT.
I KNOW, BUT *WHERE* THE HELL IS STONE? HE WAS SUPPOSED TO...
BIIP
LOGAN? YOUR OWN *SENSORS* DETECTED YOU.
YOU CAN'T *HIDE.*
CAN'T *SHOOT* A BIRD FOR TRYING.
I'VE GOT THE *MARKSMAN* MEDALS TO *PROVE* OTHERWISE.
BUT THAT MEANS *LOOKING* AT ME. AND GUESS WHAT?
CONTACT!
NO. NO. NO!

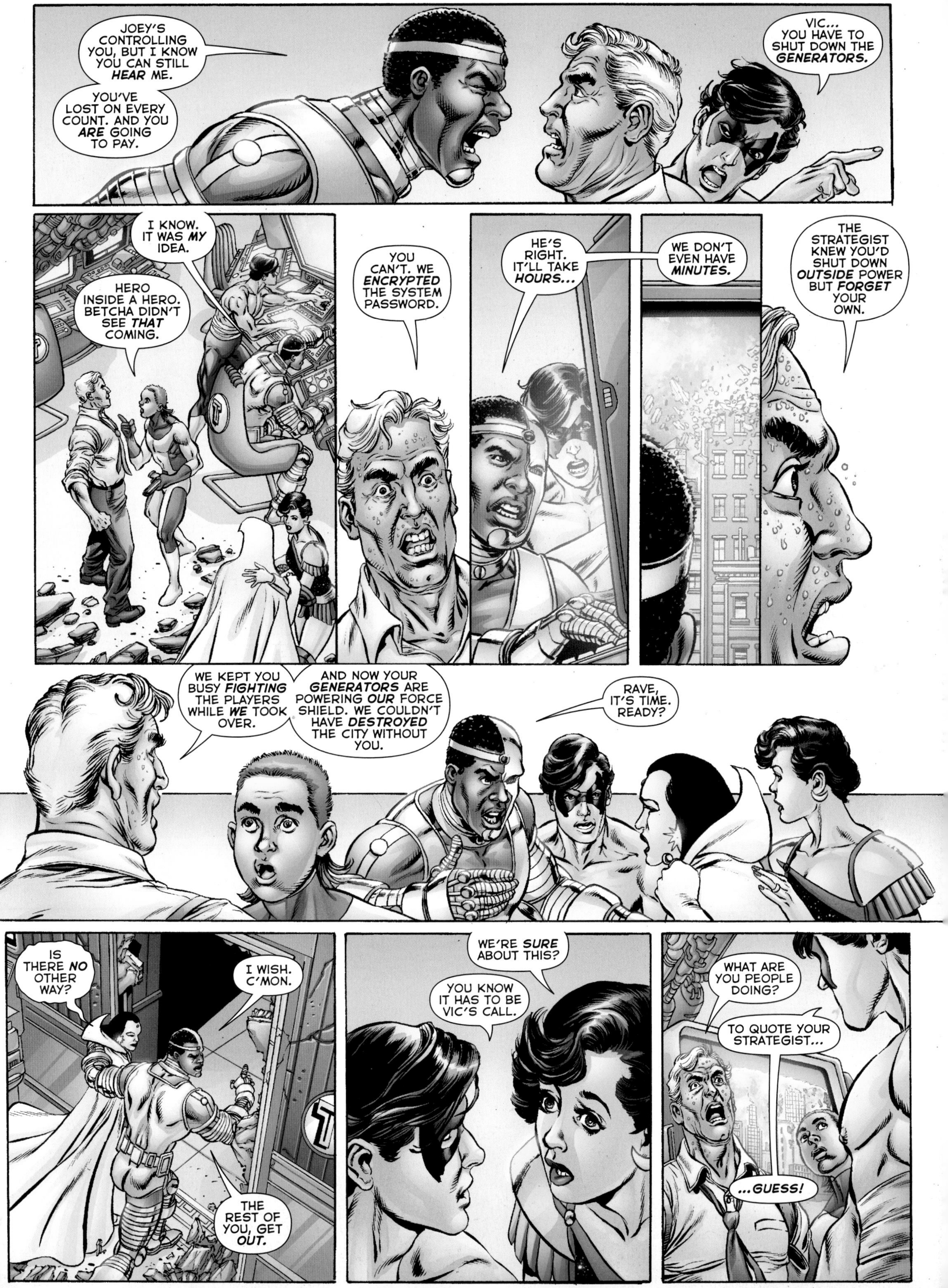
JOEY'S CONTROLLING YOU, BUT I KNOW YOU CAN STILL HEAR ME.
YOU'VE LOST ON EVERY COUNT. AND YOU ARE GOING TO PAY.
VIC... YOU HAVE TO SHUT DOWN THE GENERATORS.
I KNOW. IT WAS MY IDEA.
HERO INSIDE A HERO. BETCHA DIDN'T SEE THAT COMING.
YOU CAN'T. WE ENCRYPTED THE SYSTEM PASSWORD.
HE'S RIGHT. IT'LL TAKE HOURS...
WE DON'T EVEN HAVE MINUTES.
THE STRATEGIST KNEW YOU'D SHUT DOWN OUTSIDE POWER BUT FORGET YOUR OWN.
WE KEPT YOU BUSY FIGHTING THE PLAYERS WHILE WE TOOK OVER.
AND NOW YOUR GENERATORS ARE POWERING OUR FORCE SHIELD. WE COULDN'T HAVE DESTROYED THE CITY WITHOUT YOU.
RAVE, IT'S TIME. READY?
IS THERE NO OTHER WAY?
I WISH. C'MON.
THE REST OF YOU, GET OUT.
WE'RE SURE ABOUT THIS?
YOU KNOW IT HAS TO BE VIC'S CALL.
WHAT ARE YOU PEOPLE DOING?
TO QUOTE YOUR STRATEGIST...
...GUESS!

FARADAY... *SHUT THE HELL UP.*

DON'T YOU UNDERSTAND? THE DESTRUCTION OF NEW YORK WILL *FORCE* THE GOVERNMENT TO GET READY FOR ALL ENEMY ATTACKS.

YOU'VE BEEN THROUGH HELL. YOU'RE *SURE* YOU HAVE THE STRENGTH TO TELEPORT *BOTH* OF US?

YOU CAN STILL SAVE YOURSELF.

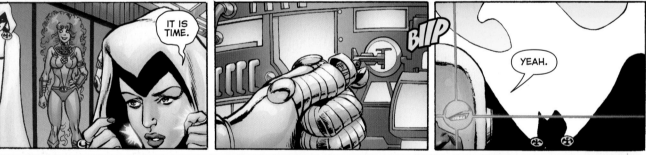

VICTOR, I SAW A VERSION OF MYSELF WHO HAD NEVER KNOWN *CARING.* NEVER HAD A *FRIEND.*

BUT I HAVE. AND MY *FRIEND* WILL GIVE ME HIS STRENGTH. AND TOGETHER WE WILL DO THIS.

MY *DAD* BUILT THIS TOWER.

NEVER THOUGHT *I'D* BE THE ONE WHO'D TEAR IT DOWN.

IT IS TIME.

BIIP

YEAH.

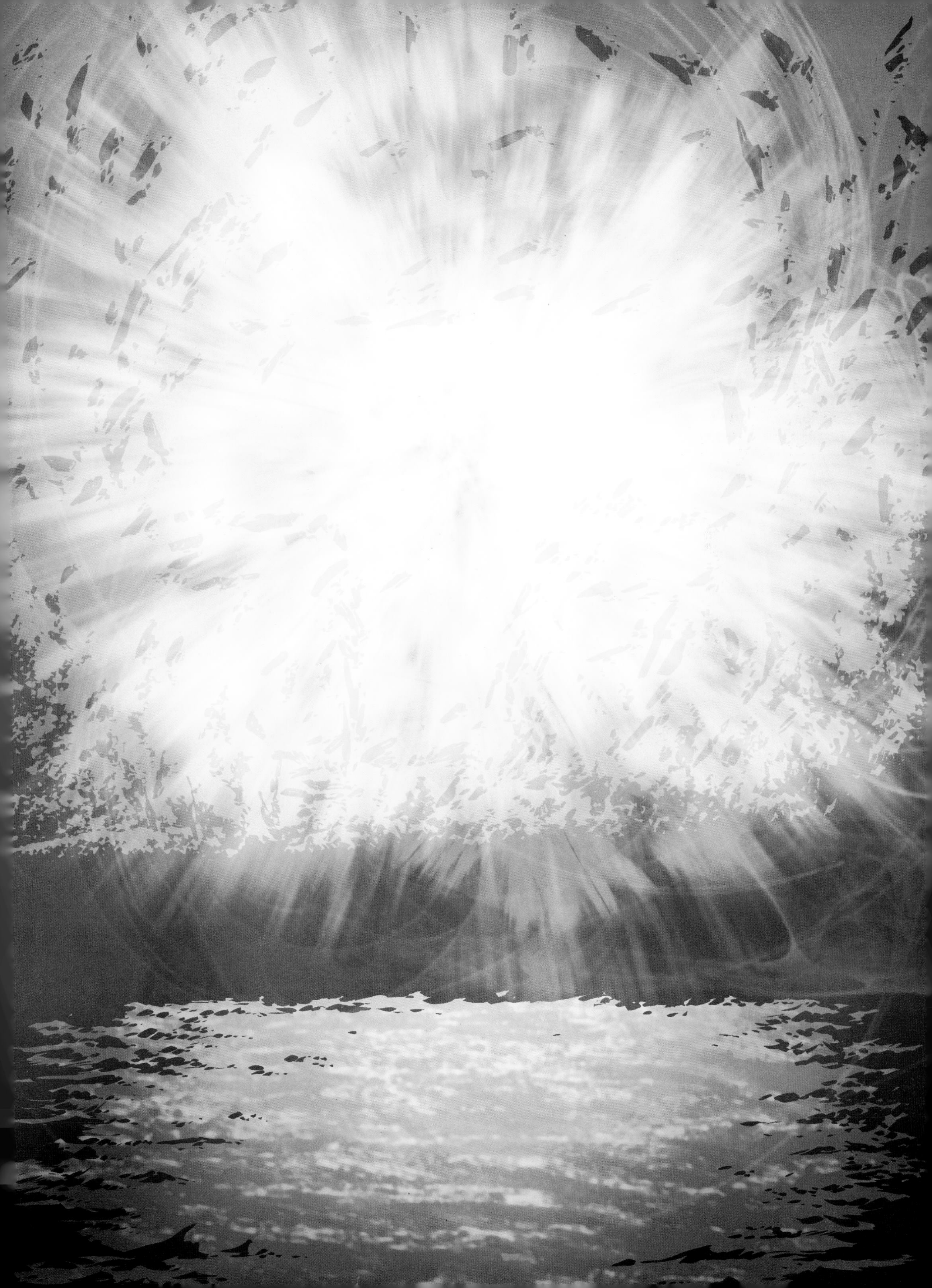

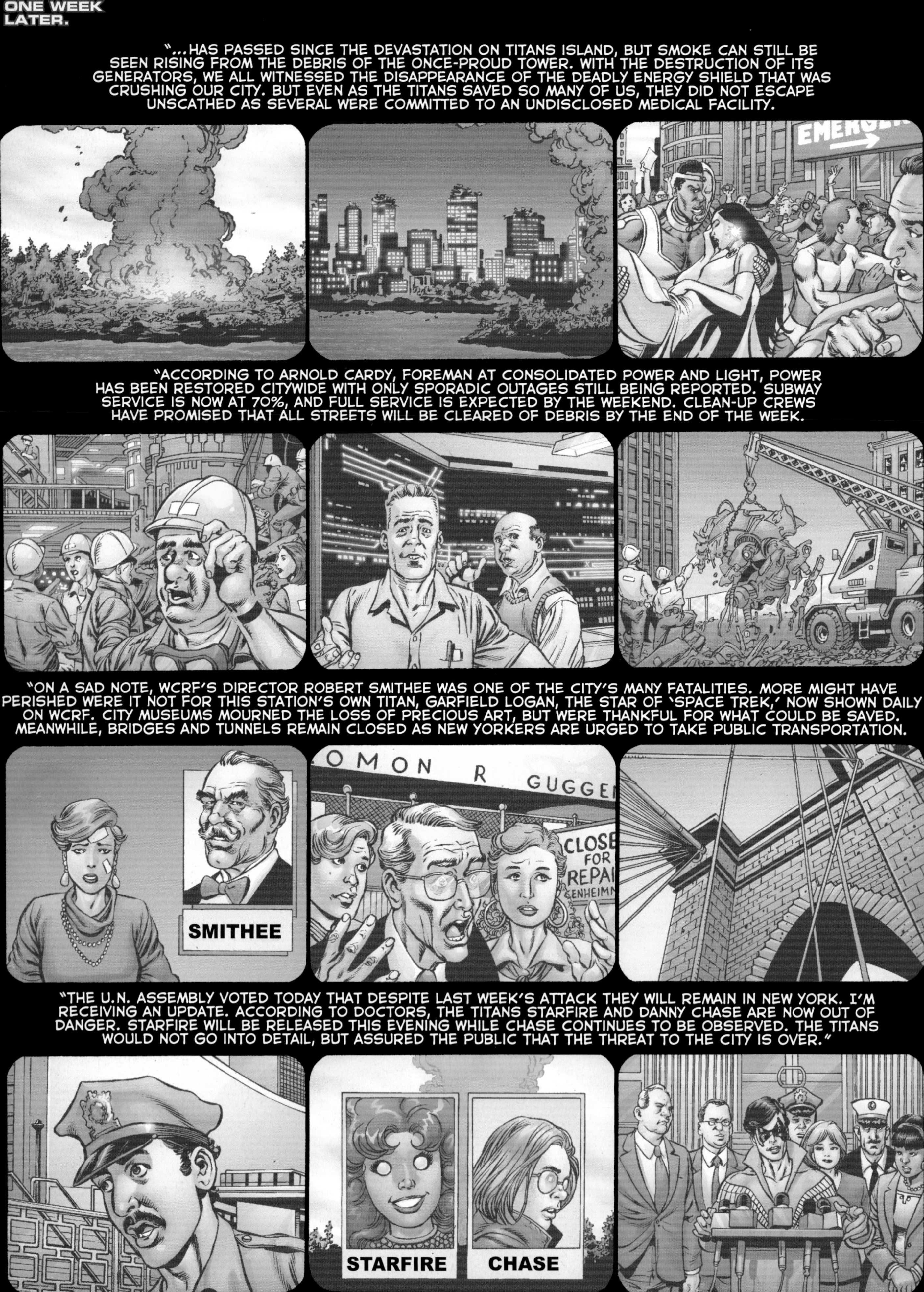
ONE WEEK LATER.
"...HAS PASSED SINCE THE DEVASTATION ON TITANS ISLAND, BUT SMOKE CAN STILL BE SEEN RISING FROM THE DEBRIS OF THE ONCE-PROUD TOWER. WITH THE DESTRUCTION OF ITS GENERATORS, WE ALL WITNESSED THE DISAPPEARANCE OF THE DEADLY ENERGY SHIELD THAT WAS CRUSHING OUR CITY. BUT EVEN AS THE TITANS SAVED SO MANY OF US, THEY DID NOT ESCAPE UNSCATHED AS SEVERAL WERE COMMITTED TO AN UNDISCLOSED MEDICAL FACILITY.
"ACCORDING TO ARNOLD CARDY, FOREMAN AT CONSOLIDATED POWER AND LIGHT, POWER HAS BEEN RESTORED CITYWIDE WITH ONLY SPORADIC OUTAGES STILL BEING REPORTED. SUBWAY SERVICE IS NOW AT 70%, AND FULL SERVICE IS EXPECTED BY THE WEEKEND. CLEAN-UP CREWS HAVE PROMISED THAT ALL STREETS WILL BE CLEARED OF DEBRIS BY THE END OF THE WEEK.
"ON A SAD NOTE, WCRF'S DIRECTOR ROBERT SMITHEE WAS ONE OF THE CITY'S MANY FATALITIES. MORE MIGHT HAVE PERISHED WERE IT NOT FOR THIS STATION'S OWN TITAN, GARFIELD LOGAN, THE STAR OF 'SPACE TREK,' NOW SHOWN DAILY ON WCRF. CITY MUSEUMS MOURNED THE LOSS OF PRECIOUS ART, BUT WERE THANKFUL FOR WHAT COULD BE SAVED. MEANWHILE, BRIDGES AND TUNNELS REMAIN CLOSED AS NEW YORKERS ARE URGED TO TAKE PUBLIC TRANSPORTATION.
SMITHEE
"THE U.N. ASSEMBLY VOTED TODAY THAT DESPITE LAST WEEK'S ATTACK THEY WILL REMAIN IN NEW YORK. I'M RECEIVING AN UPDATE. ACCORDING TO DOCTORS, THE TITANS STARFIRE AND DANNY CHASE ARE NOW OUT OF DANGER. STARFIRE WILL BE RELEASED THIS EVENING WHILE CHASE CONTINUES TO BE OBSERVED. THE TITANS WOULD NOT GO INTO DETAIL, BUT ASSURED THE PUBLIC THAT THE THREAT TO THE CITY IS OVER."
STARFIRE
CHASE

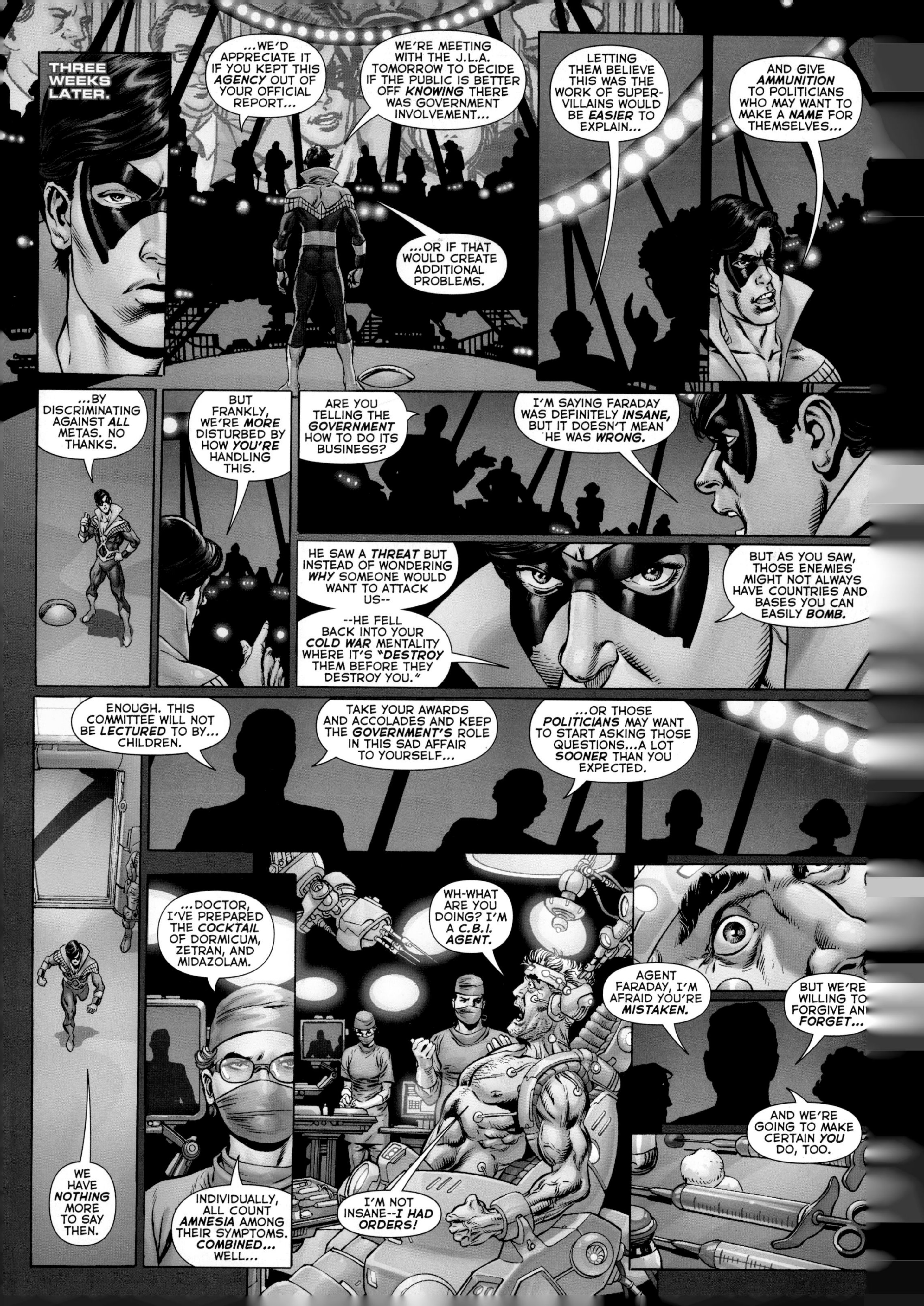
THREE WEEKS LATER.
...WE'D APPRECIATE IT IF YOU KEPT THIS AGENCY OUT OF YOUR OFFICIAL REPORT...
WE'RE MEETING WITH THE J.L.A. TOMORROW TO DECIDE IF THE PUBLIC IS BETTER OFF KNOWING THERE WAS GOVERNMENT INVOLVEMENT...
...OR IF THAT WOULD CREATE ADDITIONAL PROBLEMS.
LETTING THEM BELIEVE THIS WAS THE WORK OF SUPER-VILLAINS WOULD BE EASIER TO EXPLAIN...
AND GIVE AMMUNITION TO POLITICIANS WHO MAY WANT TO MAKE A NAME FOR THEMSELVES...
...BY DISCRIMINATING AGAINST ALL METAS. NO THANKS.
BUT FRANKLY, WE'RE MORE DISTURBED BY HOW YOU'RE HANDLING THIS.
ARE YOU TELLING THE GOVERNMENT HOW TO DO ITS BUSINESS?
I'M SAYING FARADAY WAS DEFINITELY INSANE, BUT IT DOESN'T MEAN HE WAS WRONG.
HE SAW A THREAT BUT INSTEAD OF WONDERING WHY SOMEONE WOULD WANT TO ATTACK US--
--HE FELL BACK INTO YOUR COLD WAR MENTALITY WHERE IT'S "DESTROY THEM BEFORE THEY DESTROY YOU."
BUT AS YOU SAW, THOSE ENEMIES MIGHT NOT ALWAYS HAVE COUNTRIES AND BASES YOU CAN EASILY BOMB.
ENOUGH. THIS COMMITTEE WILL NOT BE LECTURED TO BY... CHILDREN.
TAKE YOUR AWARDS AND ACCOLADES AND KEEP THE GOVERNMENT'S ROLE IN THIS SAD AFFAIR TO YOURSELF...
...OR THOSE POLITICIANS MAY WANT TO START ASKING THOSE QUESTIONS...A LOT SOONER THAN YOU EXPECTED.
WE HAVE NOTHING MORE TO SAY THEN.
...DOCTOR, I'VE PREPARED THE COCKTAIL OF DORMICUM, ZETRAN, AND MIDAZOLAM.
INDIVIDUALLY, ALL COUNT AMNESIA AMONG THEIR SYMPTOMS. COMBINED... WELL...
WH-WHAT ARE YOU DOING? I'M A C.B.I. AGENT.
I'M NOT INSANE--I HAD ORDERS!
AGENT FARADAY, I'M AFRAID YOU'RE MISTAKEN.
BUT WE'RE WILLING TO FORGIVE AN FORGET...
AND WE'RE GOING TO MAKE CERTAIN YOU DO, TOO.

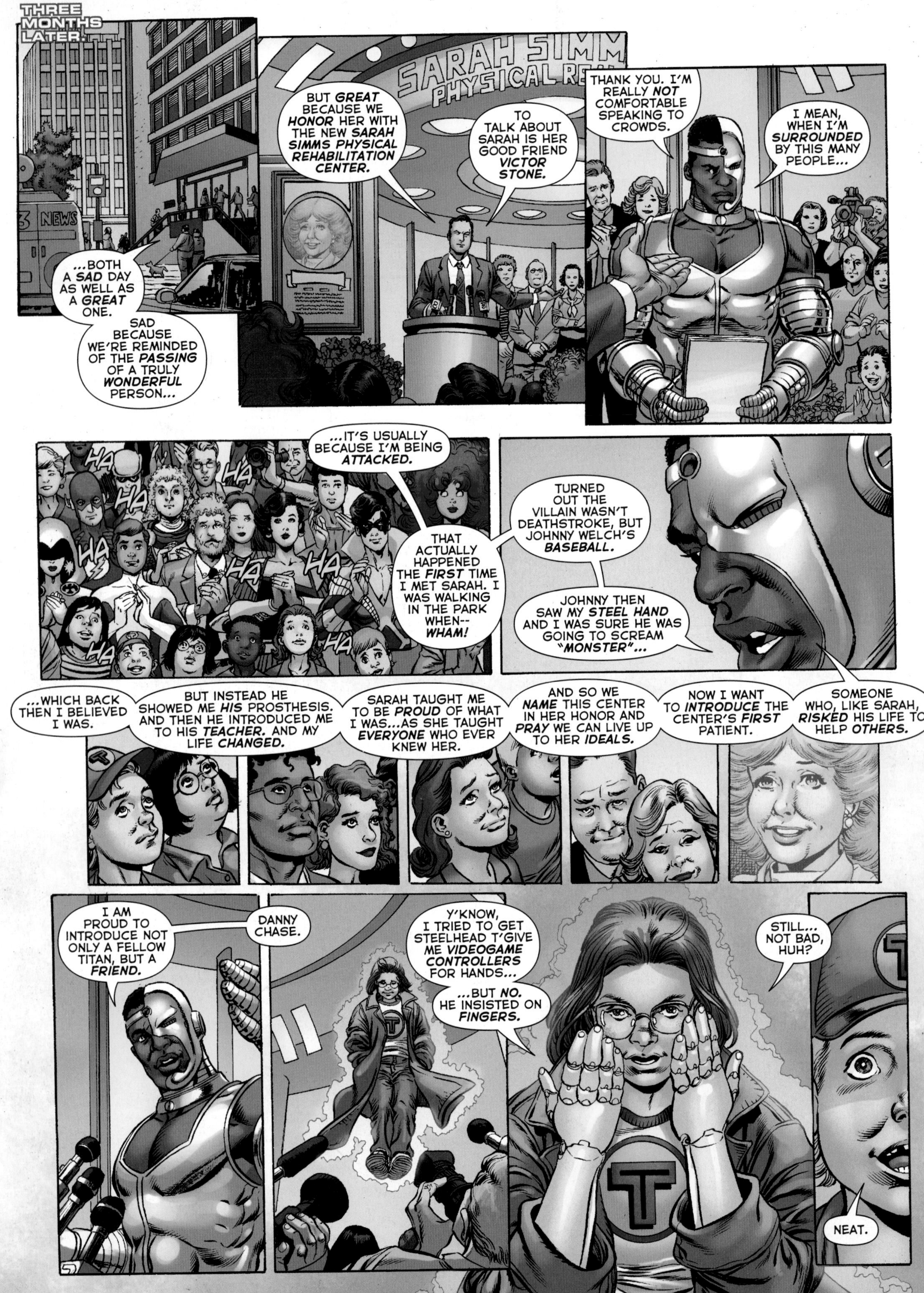
THREE MONTHS LATER.
...BOTH A SAD DAY AS WELL AS A GREAT ONE.
SAD BECAUSE WE'RE REMINDED OF THE PASSING OF A TRULY WONDERFUL PERSON...
BUT GREAT BECAUSE WE HONOR HER WITH THE NEW SARAH SIMMS PHYSICAL REHABILITATION CENTER.
TO TALK ABOUT SARAH IS HER GOOD FRIEND VICTOR STONE.
THANK YOU. I'M REALLY NOT COMFORTABLE SPEAKING TO CROWDS.
I MEAN, WHEN I'M SURROUNDED BY THIS MANY PEOPLE...
...IT'S USUALLY BECAUSE I'M BEING ATTACKED.
HA HA HA HA HA HA HA HA HA
THAT ACTUALLY HAPPENED THE FIRST TIME I MET SARAH. I WAS WALKING IN THE PARK WHEN-- WHAM!
TURNED OUT THE VILLAIN WASN'T DEATHSTROKE, BUT JOHNNY WELCH'S BASEBALL.
JOHNNY THEN SAW MY STEEL HAND AND I WAS SURE HE WAS GOING TO SCREAM "MONSTER"...
...WHICH BACK THEN I BELIEVED I WAS.
BUT INSTEAD HE SHOWED ME HIS PROSTHESIS. AND THEN HE INTRODUCED ME TO HIS TEACHER. AND MY LIFE CHANGED.
SARAH TAUGHT ME TO BE PROUD OF WHAT I WAS...AS SHE TAUGHT EVERYONE WHO EVER KNEW HER.
AND SO WE NAME THIS CENTER IN HER HONOR AND PRAY WE CAN LIVE UP TO HER IDEALS.
NOW I WANT TO INTRODUCE THE CENTER'S FIRST PATIENT.
SOMEONE WHO, LIKE SARAH, RISKED HIS LIFE TO HELP OTHERS.
I AM PROUD TO INTRODUCE NOT ONLY A FELLOW TITAN, BUT A FRIEND.
DANNY CHASE.
Y'KNOW, I TRIED TO GET STEELHEAD T'GIVE ME VIDEOGAME CONTROLLERS FOR HANDS...
...BUT NO. HE INSISTED ON FINGERS.
STILL... NOT BAD, HUH?
NEAT.

WOW. AFTER ALL THESE YEARS...

...GONE. JUST LIKE THAT.

HARD TO BELIEVE.

THE FEW TIMES I VISITED IT WAS LIKE WALKING INTO SOMEPLACE *EXTRAORDINARY.*

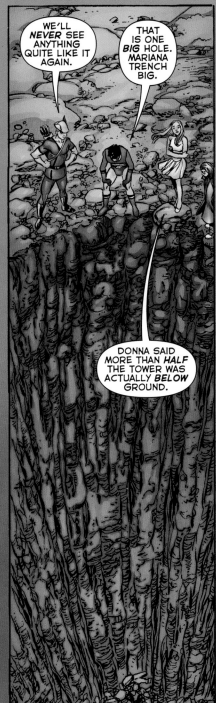

WE'LL *NEVER* SEE ANYTHING QUITE LIKE IT AGAIN.

THAT IS ONE *BIG* HOLE. MARIANA TRENCH BIG.

DONNA SAID MORE THAN *HALF* THE TOWER WAS ACTUALLY *BELOW* GROUND.

...WHAT'S STILL DRIVING ME CRAZY IS IF FARADAY INTENDED TO *DESTROY* THE CITY, *WHY* BRING IN THE TITANS?

HE THOUGHT HE SAW A HORRIFYING *REALITY* HE BELIEVED HE COULD *NOT* CHANGE.

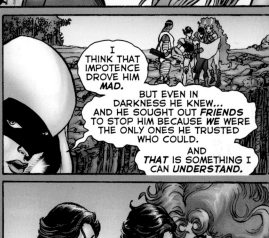

I THINK THAT IMPOTENCE DROVE HIM *MAD.*

BUT EVEN IN DARKNESS HE KNEW... AND HE SOUGHT OUT *FRIENDS* TO STOP HIM BECAUSE *WE* WERE THE ONLY ONES HE TRUSTED WHO COULD.

AND *THAT* IS SOMETHING I CAN *UNDERSTAND.*

NICE DESIGN, BUT IT'LL NEVER FEEL LIKE *OUR* TOWER.

EVERYTHING CHANGES. BESIDES, WITH OR WITHOUT A BUILDING...

I KNOW. THERE WILL *ALWAYS* BE A TITANS.

...MY *DAD* BUILT IT SO WE'D HAVE A *PLACE* WHERE WE COULD HELP OTHERS.

HE COULDN'T EXPECT, WELL, *THIS*... BUT WITH WHAT WE DID, HIS TOWER *SAVED* THOUSANDS OF LIVES. MAYBE MORE.

I...I ONLY HOPE SOMEWHERE HE *KNOWS* THAT.

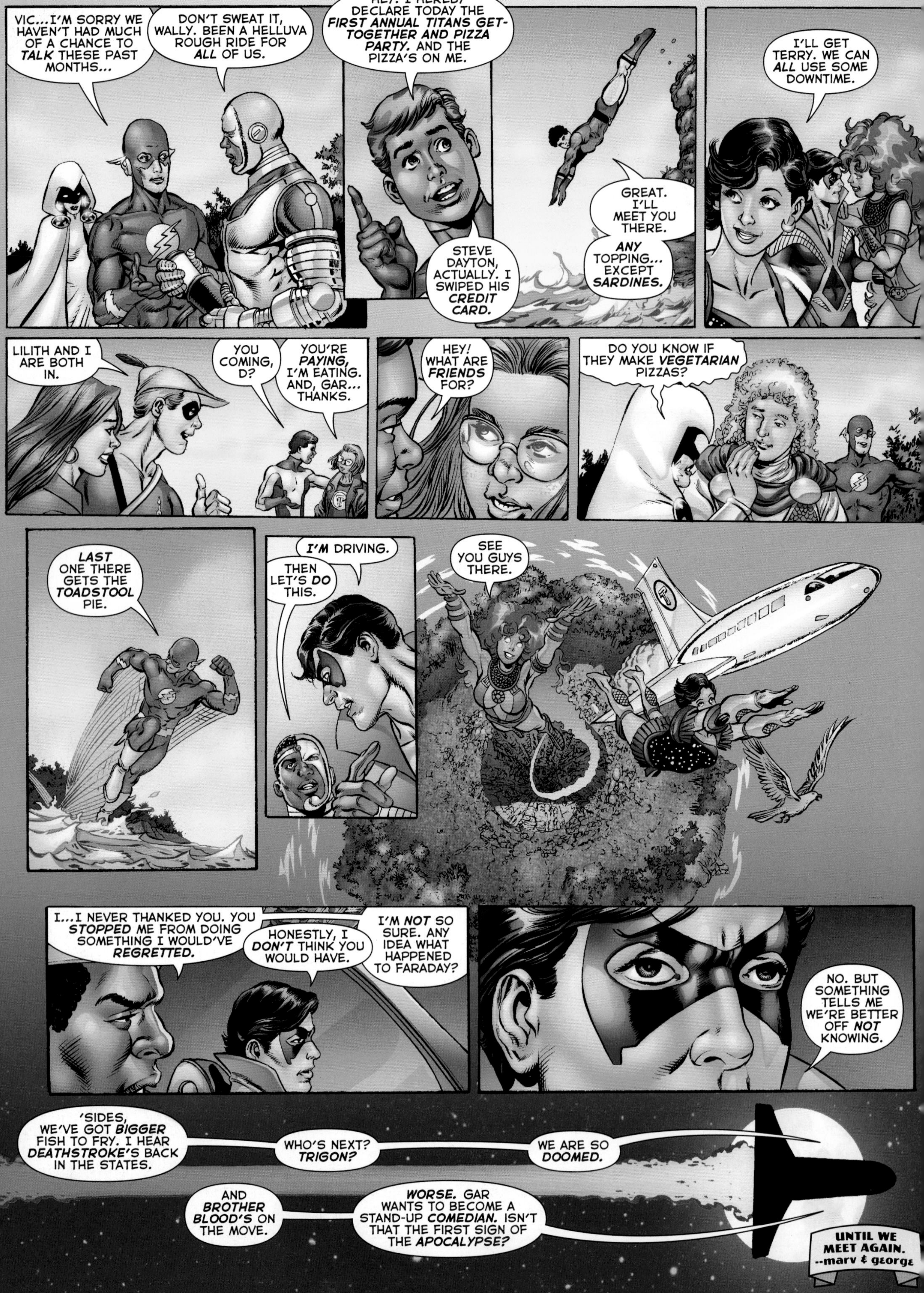
VIC...I'M SORRY WE HAVEN'T HAD MUCH OF A CHANCE TO TALK THESE PAST MONTHS...
DON'T SWEAT IT, WALLY. BEEN A HELLUVA ROUGH RIDE FOR ALL OF US.
HEY. I HEREBY DECLARE TODAY THE FIRST ANNUAL TITANS GET-TOGETHER AND PIZZA PARTY. AND THE PIZZA'S ON ME.
STEVE DAYTON, ACTUALLY. I SWIPED HIS CREDIT CARD.
GREAT. I'LL MEET YOU THERE.
ANY TOPPING... EXCEPT SARDINES.
I'LL GET TERRY. WE CAN ALL USE SOME DOWNTIME.
LILITH AND I ARE BOTH IN.
YOU COMING, D?
YOU'RE PAYING, I'M EATING. AND, GAR... THANKS.
HEY! WHAT ARE FRIENDS FOR?
DO YOU KNOW IF THEY MAKE VEGETARIAN PIZZAS?
LAST ONE THERE GETS THE TOADSTOOL PIE.
I'M DRIVING.
THEN LET'S DO THIS.
SEE YOU GUYS THERE.
I...I NEVER THANKED YOU. YOU STOPPED ME FROM DOING SOMETHING I WOULD'VE REGRETTED.
HONESTLY, I DON'T THINK YOU WOULD HAVE.
I'M NOT SO SURE. ANY IDEA WHAT HAPPENED TO FARADAY?
NO. BUT SOMETHING TELLS ME WE'RE BETTER OFF NOT KNOWING.
'SIDES, WE'VE GOT BIGGER FISH TO FRY. I HEAR DEATHSTROKE'S BACK IN THE STATES.
WHO'S NEXT? TRIGON?
WE ARE SO DOOMED.
AND BROTHER BLOOD'S ON THE MOVE.
WORSE. GAR WANTS TO BECOME A STAND-UP COMEDIAN. ISN'T THAT THE FIRST SIGN OF THE APOCALYPSE?
UNTIL WE MEET AGAIN. --marv & george

AFTERWORD
BY GEORGE PÉREZ

Quite a journey, wasn't it?

I embarked on this long journey over two decades ago as a relatively young swabby of 34 and finally coasted to the final port as a 57-year-old salt just half a decade away from Social Security.

So much has changed during that voyage. Teenagers who were the same age as the Teen Titans when the plot was first conceived by Marv Wolfman, then-editor Barbara Kesel and me in 1988 are now old enough to be parents of teenagers themselves. Those just born in 1988 may already be parents themselves. The Internet was in its relative infancy. Cell phones had yet to become the prevalent form of communication for the masses. The Twin Towers of the World Trade Center in New York were less than two decades old and sadly would no longer be in existence when its appearance in this graphic novel finally saw print.

So many years. So many changes. Yet, the Titans are still teens. Within the confines of this graphic novel, these young heroes have not aged more than a few days from the first page I pencilled and inked in 1988 to the 120th page inked by Mike Perkins (succeeding Al Vey), whose career hadn't even begun twenty-three years ago. Heck, Mike was probably barely a teen himself when this book was started. And, even as I type this, I realize that I'm the same age my now-80-year-old parents were when I started this book!

Then how on Earth can the Titans still be so young? Because in the wonderful, fanciful, magical world of illustrated fiction, no one ever need age. The difference this time, of course, is that those eternally youthful characters that were drawn by a young man in his early 30s now get to share their world with versions of themselves drawn by an artist in his mid-50s and do so without betraying their true ages to each other and their audience gazing at them from the corporeal world beyond the realm of paper and ink.

And, of course, therein was the major challenge of this book. Like most artists, I like to think that I've made some strides in both my art style and technical finesse. Could I really replicate my drawing style of twenty-plus years ago?

Well, it turns out that it wasn't as hard as I thought it would be. And you know why? Because these are the New Teen Titans. These are the same young heroes whose faces, demeanor and personalities have become so ingrained in me for decade upon decade that I didn't actually need to relearn how to draw them. They, the Titans themselves, will always direct my hand. The very things that made these characters so real to me so many years ago is what still keeps them so identifiable in my mind, and so natural to draw with my hands. When I draw these characters, it's like doing portraitures of old friends, albeit in a proverbial Shangri-La where friends never wither and age, and, unlike Dorian Gray, neither do their pictures.

And while I'm glad to say that my instincts for drawing the Titans had not diminished with age, I wish the same could be said for my memory—especially regarding the GAMES storyline. While much of the story had been laid out by me, I still had about fifty more pages to draw, and all that existed as a story guide was the original, very skeletal plot outline that I had used as a jumping-off point, changing elements freely as I went along—but not providing any

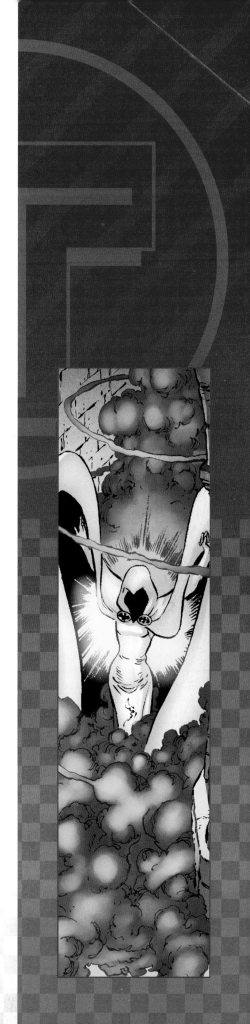

notes explaining the changes. In years past, doing that was standard operating procedure since I would soon enough explain my storytelling decisions to Marv when he was ready to script the pages.

Of course, I never imagined that Marv wouldn't get to do that until twenty years later. I no longer remembered why many of the things were happening or what exactly were the clues that the Titans were deciphering. It was like a gigantic puzzle with not only pieces missing, but without a real idea of what the finished picture even looked like! What a calamitous conundrum!

That's when you truly appreciate the incredible genius of Marv Wolfman. Marv sat down and took my pages, read the original plot notes and, after several discussions, not only cobbled together a coherent plot to fit the pages already drawn, but worked out a totally different ending that was head and shoulders above the original's climax.

When GAMES was originally conceived, it was meant to be a companion piece to the still-ongoing series. But now, twenty years later, the story needn't be restricted to a specific continuity and was therefore handled like a special stand-alone story where such matters need not be addressed. Marv gave GAMES a unique feel, and together we hope that it provides a nice sense of nostalgia for those who were there when Marv and I were at the helm of NEW TEEN TITANS, and just a cracking good story for those who may be reading the adventures of this particular Titans incarnation for the very first time.

Hopefully, Marv and I, along with Al, Mike, Kevin, the folks at Hi-Fi and all the editors past and present, have done our part to remind everyone what the fuss was all about so many years ago. I want to thank my friends Spencer Beck and Michael Lovitz for providing access to the original art from 20 years ago, and to Neil Southwell for providing the Titans card art featured in the story. I hope we've been able to bring you back to a special time in the lives of Dick Grayson, Donna Troy, Victor Stone, Princess Koriand'r, Gar Logan, Raven, Joe Wilson and Danny Chase—a team, a family, the Titans.

Time for me to leave the ship now. The journey's ended, twenty-three years after it began.

And, like the Titans, I still feel so young.

THE ORIGINAL PLOT

Writer Marv Wolfman walks us through the 1988 'GAMES' plot noting what has altered between then and now.

THE NEW TITANS GRAPHIC NOVEL
Co-plotted by **MARV WOLFMAN** *(scripter)*
and **GEORGE PÉREZ** *(artist)* for **Barbara Randall** *(editor)*
Proposed Title: **GAMES**   Submitted: **APRIL 1988**

BRIAN CUNNINGHAM, EDITOR: Hello, GAMES readers! Before I turn this over to Marv Wolfman, I'd like to explain what you are looking at. This is the *original GAMES plot* typed up back in early 1988. You'll notice that some of it — actually a lot of it — made it through to the story you hopefully just read. (And if not, stop right now and go read it! Trust me, you'll be glad you did.) You might be interested in the parts that didn't, and we'll note why within the pages ahead.

We wanted to show this original plot to give some perspective to Marv and George's wonderful creative process, as well as showing how a story can evolve over the course of twenty-odd years. So, without further ado, here is Marv pulling back the curtain on his recollections of putting GAMES together the first time around! Take it away, Marv…

SPOILER WARNING: PLEASE DON'T READ THIS UNTIL AFTER YOU'VE READ THE STORY.

MARV WOLFMAN, WRITER: Confession time. As you'll see by this plot, although visually much of the 1989 pages appear to follow the story George typed up based on our early conversations, the printed book story has changed quite a bit, mostly in the reasons behind events, but also in the addition of characters and new story elements. There are many reasons for that, but as I said in my introduction—*and please read that before you read this as there are SPOILERS throughout*—the major one is back then, we simply had not worked out the entire story in detail. Both of us, having moved on and not thinking this book would ever happen, simply forgot much of what we had planned a quarter century ago.

Once George returned to finish the story and he drew up a few more pages based on his early layouts, we had virtually no place to go. A brand-new story had to be devised. But the real trick was to come up with ideas that actually fit the pages as George had drawn them, without changes. Fortunately, I think we both love this kind of challenge. The new plot we came up with was presented in a series of documents and notes that I sent to George and kept refining as we went back and forth, working out all the ideas together as we had always done before.

Ultimately those documents are too many and too large and rambling to print here, but we thought you might be interested in seeing that original 1988 doc George wrote up, with appropriate notes and more.

Finally, as a matter of Titans history and for completists only, please note although George had drawn 60-70 pages back in 1988, and finished drawing the rest of the pages over the last year or so, I dialogued the entire story just this past year. No pages were ever dialogued back in the '80s.

We start off in some military early-warning installation in a frozen landscape. Perhaps Alaska near the Russian side. There is total devastation. Buildings are still burning and bodies are strewn all over the place. Some are even melted into the ice in desperate attempts to extinguish the fire on their bodies. All this is being witnessed by an investigating team of military personnel in copters, land vehicles and the like. No one knows what happened, only that radio contact had been lost. Among the debris is a painted message (maybe in blood) on the side of one of the fallen buildings: *Your Move, Faraday*

Cut to a high-tech government espionage center. It is the command center of the CBI, the fictional government spy group we've used from time to time. King Faraday is there being grilled by his superiors (none of whose faces we ever see. It kind of lends an air of foreboding when the "good guys" are treated like dangerous threats). King Faraday denies knowledge of the significance of the scrawled message at the installation. As Faraday returns to his office, he finds a package waiting for him. When he opens it, there is a book inside (whose contents we will not see now but it is basically a game manual which tells of the *Gamesmaster's* newest gambit with Super-Terrorists) and a note: *Your Move, Faraday*

Note: I'm calling the main villain the Gamesmaster strictly for the sake of writing this synopsis. The name is still undecided.

WOLFMAN: All the above has remained, although some of the reasoning behind it changed once the new plot had been worked out. I had fun adding in the bit about the missing nuclear bomb (which is completely true) because I like tying in real-world events with the fiction to make our super-heroics all the more plausible.

During the course of the first half of this story, we'll be setting up the Super-Terrorists at their respective target points. This will be done by inserting predominantly silent sequences throughout the narrative just to tantalize the reader. For the sake of this synopsis, and in the interest of clarity, I'll list the terrorists and their targets here.

1. A Military Soldier of Fortune Type (let's call him *The Strategist*): He's the one who plans and instructs the others on their "games." The whole motif to this story is that of a deadly role-playing game. His is a military *War Game*, and Manhattan Island is the gaming board. The Strategist has a perfect model of the city in his chamber. (To the reader, it will appear that the Strategist is the Gamesmaster, but it will turn out that he too is a pawn.) This character is sequestered in some private area, probably outside the city itself. He will be **Dick Grayson/Nightwing's** evil counterpart.

WOLFMAN: Much of this has stayed the same. What changes is the different villain plots were originally not connected; they went off and did whatever they wanted. Once we had a new Gamesmaster and a new plan, the villain plots—which were already drawn and could not be changed—were tied together verbally to work toward one specific goal. Everything they were doing had to feed into the new plot. Beyond that, several new villains were created, and I'll get to them in a moment.

With 60-70 pages already drawn, George and I discussed the idea that we might have to give origins for our villains since they had never appeared before. But the problem was we had a lot of brand-new story still to tell, and not that much space to do it in. I thought having to spend precious pages on origins for characters who didn't require it would have wasted time and space. Realizing our real villain, the Gamesmaster, was now King Faraday, a C.B.I. officer, actually made things easier. So now Faraday had simply arrested them all some time in the past. That way he'd know who they were, what their powers were and where he could find them. For the reader it meant these were DCU villains we had not met before. Eureka! No long backstory exposition was necessary.

2. A Flash Gordon type of Space Fantasy adventurer (we'll call him *George Jetson* for the sake of this synopsis): He will be setting up his operations at the heliports and bridges. It will become impossible for anyone to get in or out of the city by the time his job is done. He also sets up a defense system to blast aircraft from the sky. His game motif is *Space Invaders* and its similar brethren. George Jetson will face **Princess Koriand'r/Starfire**.

WOLFMAN: George Jetson was of course renamed Asteroid, after the game. I decided to give all the villains different verbal ticks to differentiate them. Asteroid must be pretty hungry as he sets his bombs to blow up all of New York's bridges and tunnels because nearly all his comments concerning Starfire are food oriented. That was a personal joke on my part since Starfire's real name, Koriand'r, is a play on the well-known food spice coriander. Kory was and remains one spicy Titan.

3. A Demon (let's call it **The Demon**, no relation to Jack Kirby's version): This character's weird. It appears to be simply a person in a cloak and cowl. However, the Demon actually *is* the cloak and cowl; there's nobody underneath it except some nasty nightmare stuff which is the perfect battleground for **Raven**. Maybe the setting could be a cemetery or something synonymous with death and despair. The goal could be simple: fear. Let's scare the hell out of those Manhattanites!

WOLFMAN: This character was never meant to be seen; as George said above, it was just a cloak. But because George set this demon against Raven, I wanted to tie them closer together and decided to make her one of Trigon's failed children, someone who escaped destruction only because she fell to Earth. But unlike Raven, who was brought up on Azarath and had a mother and support system, this quite mad baby had, unbeknownst to anyone else, found herself buried in the deepest recesses of Arkham where she infected those already insane with her even greater madness. She had never been touched. Never been loved. And most of all, she had never been given a name or identity.

Through this character, Raven could come to grips with her own origin fears, and through Raven, this lost daughter of Trigon would be given both a name and eternal peace. I think George and I both felt this gave Raven her own emotionally strong story in the midst of the much larger GAMES tale.

4. A Medieval Knight in bright shiny armor, complete with steed and squire, the difference is that the Knight is a **woman** (let's call her *Lady Jane*). Her game motif is *Dark Castle*, and she has invaded the great museums of art. She seems intent on destroying them. This will not sit well with our resident renaissance man **Joe Wilson/Jericho**. Perhaps Lady Jane may be a bit of an enchantress and desires Joe as her new squire. It may be interesting for Joe to have to battle her in order to safeguard the paintings. Perhaps by jousting with her he seems to be allowing the curators to get some of the artwork to safety in some delivery trucks that *just happened* to be there that day. Obviously, nothing is really what it seems.

WOLFMAN: Except for their names, these characters stayed much the same, although no magic powers are evident.

5. A big Robot controlled from the inside by a man, probably Japanese (we'll call him *Gigantor*). Visually, he'd be like Sigourney Weaver when she controlled the robotic forklift in *Aliens*. This sucker is a mean wrecking machine that seems intent on destroying the computer and electronics corporations and operations of the city. Since this will serve to also screw up the traffic signals and communications, this guy is obviously dangerous. Visually we're talking *Robotech*, and his obvious adversary is **Victor Stone/Cyborg**. As to how such a hulking machine can infiltrate the city unnoticed, I will show a sequence of this little guy accumulating suitcases and

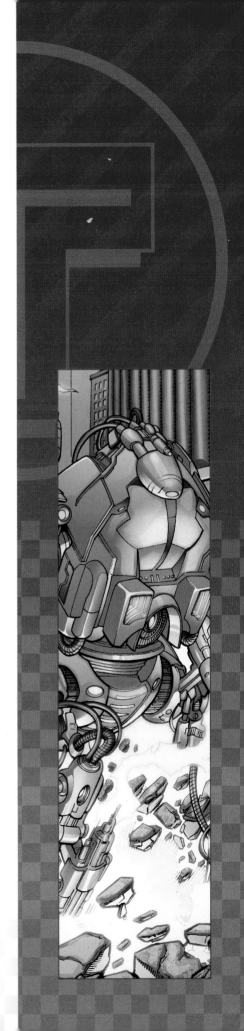

trunks which he will have shipped to an empty suite in one of the computer industry buildings and then he'll just put Gigantor together there.

WOLFMAN: Name change to Mekkan. George and I felt at least one of the villains should simply be in it for the money. No grand motivation. No personal gripes. Just cold, hard cash.

6. A sultry female spy, straight out of Modesty Blaise (her name is **Bond, Jane Bond**) and her obvious, and most ridiculous, adversary is **Danny Chase**. Imagine her trying to use her feminine wiles on a **fourteen-year-old**! This may get this book banned. Normally Danny is pretty adept, but this is a whole new ballgame for him. The game is obviously **Cloak and Dagger**, and the arena could be one of the foreign embassies or perhaps the United Nations.

WOLFMAN: Name change to Spywar. What was cool was not needing to change her, but totally changing everything we might have done with Danny. After the death of Terra [in 1984's TALES OF THE TEEN TITANS ANNUAL #3], George had moved on to WONDER WOMAN and CRISIS ON INFINITE EARTHS, and I decided to bring someone else into the group to shake things up. I wanted to make him extremely intelligent, incredibly capable, a total pro, but also a terribly nasty 14-year-old brat. I thought he'd be great to get on Gar Logan's nerves as Gar had been the kid until then. I wanted to somewhat lighten the tone of the book which, because of Terra, had become dark, and Danny's caustic nastiness, I thought, would work.

Needless to say, readers did not agree. They did not take to Danny the way they took to Terra, who of course was introduced trying to destroy the Statue of Liberty, then things got worse from there. Knowing the fans' dislike of the character, I was absolutely determined (read: stubborn!) to force a redemption because I really liked him and felt he wasn't given a chance to grow, a point I have Gar himself say in this story. By the way, I suggested the sacrifice of his arm while saving all those in the U.N.—to prove he was a hero—and George came up with the idea that he becomes the first prosthesis recipient of the new Sarah Simms clinic. When George suggested it, my grin extended beyond the borders of my face; it was the absolute perfect ending. Of course, I still wrote him as being snotty to the end. But hey! Danny might be a hero, but he'll always be a brat.

7. A walking pile of TV sets (!) (for now I kinda like the name **PeeWee**) This thing is actually a bunch of holographic screen images where ultra-violent, and ultra-silly cartoons actually seem to come alive! For example, if a wily coyote has a stick of Acme dynamite in his paw, when that sucker blows up, it really blows up. Of course we'll explain some of it with pseudo-scientific mumbo jumbo, but with all the screens which form the skeleton of PeeWee, he will make a most unusual menace for our own walking cartoon character **Gar Logan/Changeling**. The motif is basically a **Cartoon Role Playing Game** or something similar (I must now confess to not being much of an aficionado on games; hopefully Marv and Barbara are better at it.) PeeWee at first seems intent on destroying the television and broadcast centers but, as it will be seen, he is actually trying to control them, a preparation for the big broadcast planned by the Gamester.

WOLFMAN: The other big change. There was no HoloX in the original plot. Since there was now going to be one villain plan—the Gamesmaster was guiding everyone—we needed a villain. HoloX fit the bill and more. George had drawn a number of animated cartoons attacking Gar, and I seem to recall that when I asked him what that was about, he didn't fully remember what he had planned back in '88. So I came up with the idea of HoloX, a living hologram (no idea where that came from) who could bring digital images to life, the cartoons being only one example. I had also suggested a scene where all the digital billboards in Times Square come to life so we'd have the Titans fighting 40-foot advertising images, but, sadly, there was no room to do that. George then topped that with the incredible idea that

HoloX was composed of multiple holographic screens, which led me to dialogue him using repeating vowels as he searched the Internet to grab words (and partial words) that expressed his thoughts. Another case of the two of us building on each other's ideas.

8. A high-priestess type in a fantasy setting, a witch of sorts (call her *Angelique* for now): He power is mystical and it will involve **Donna Troy/Whatever-her-new-name-is** in a terrifying *Dungeons and Dragons* type game in the heart of the New York Transit system. Things like subway trains turning into huge fire-breathing dragons and other boring stuff like that. Angelique's goal is to make the system inoperative and the tunnels themselves inaccessible.

WOLFMAN: Once again, the effort was to not just have a standard villain attacking Donna, but to make her a unique character that would fit into Donna's mythological background. I don't know about you, but George's pictures of the train/dragon attacking Donna are beyond incredible.

So, now when I refer to the Terrorist you'll know what I'm talking about. Of course, the readers will learn all this stuff later. The setup scenes with the terrorists are also intercut with shots of other mysterious persons scoping places like the school for physically challenged children, where Sarah Simms works; a cruise ship where Tucker and Maude Stone (Vic's grandparents) are vacationing; the prison which houses Slade Wilson (Deathstroke the Terminator, Joe's dad); Donna and Terry's apartment building; Dayton manor and other familiar sites, including Titans Tower. Much of this will be kept as unclear as possible, giving the readers clues, but no details.

King Faraday contacts the Titans. Perhaps they're each in their normal habitats. By this time we might have established what the hell Dick Grayson and Joe Wilson do with their time outside the Tower. After all, even Kory has a job (and she doesn't even have a Green Card). Maybe Faraday, through agents or other means of communication, call our heroes to the Tower. Donna would be on a Photo Shoot (with Kory?), Gar could be with Jillian, Vic's at S.T.A.R. labs, etc. This sequence will help familiarize the uninitiated with the Titans. A good Graphic Novel should never assume that a reader is so familiar with the lead characters that introductions are unnecessary.

WOLFMAN: George and I usually think in sync. Not so this time. As I later learned, George drew the Kory car commercial to be the characters editing an already filmed commercial. I thought they were filming it live and wrote it as such. Fortunately George liked what I did so we kept it.

They all meet with Faraday at Titans Tower. Faraday informs them that the Gamesmaster is on the loose and has been responsible for major terrorist activities throughout the world. Faraday says that the only way to stop the Gamesmaster is to kill him. There can be no other solution. The Gamesmaster is crazy and terminally ill. He has nothing to lose by dying and will make sure that he takes everyone with him — unless he is killed before he "pulls the switch" as it were.

The Titans, who harbor no great affection for Faraday, refuse to be involved in a government-sanctioned plot to deliberately murder an individual. They're not government agents, and they

insist that there must be an alternative. Faraday insists that there isn't. When the Titans adamantly reject Faraday's terms, the C.B.I. agent decides to put pressure on.

WOLFMAN: This has all remained, but we decided to make Cyborg the character who might very well decide to kill. With the Gamesmaster killing Sarah, we wanted to push Vic to the breaking point before showing he would never go that far. His attitude was one of the major emotional focuses for the story and would be our statement about what heroes do and won't do. Our heroes don't intentionally kill; that's not a cliché, but that is what separates them from the villains.

Faraday proceeds to shut down the Titans. He starts municipal proceedings to have Titans Island returned to the city. He threatens Steve Dayton with a tax audit and cancellation of the lucrative government contracts. He knows that Dick is Nightwing and the tie-in with Bruce Wayne and Wayne Industries. He threatens to deport Kory and Raven. Donna's studio is investigated. Research to help and maintain Vic's cyborg body is halted pending bogus inquiries. Adeline Kane's (Joe's mom) passport is revoked. The one person who seems unaffected is Danny. This kid grew up in the C.B.I., he knows the limits of its power and how much Faraday has overstepped his authority. Eventually, the Titans rally. Extortion is not something they take kindly to. They find ways out. They win a few, they lose a few. But Faraday does not close them down.

However, Faraday then tells them that the Gamesmaster has already arranged to kill someone close to one of the Titans, in order to boast of his invulnerability or some similar contrivance. Each of the Titans goes to his or her home base to locate the danger. Gar goes to Dayton, his adoptive father; Raven finds her mother Arella safe in Wyoming where she now owns a ranch and lives and idyllic, quiet existence. Donna goes to her husband Terry and tries to contact her foster family. Joe sees his mother and father (and we hint at some girl friends he wants to check out). Faraday has said that the Gamesmaster has no desire to face the Batman and in turn the JLI, so Dick and Kory, whose closest loved one is each other, seem to be safe. Vic tries to contact his grandparents on the ship. The C.B.I. assures Danny that his parents are safe.

WOLFMAN: Kept some. Changed some. Stories evolve.

However, Faraday receives a call from one of his operatives. They've found the target. There's a bomb in one of the school buses owned by the School for Physically Challenged Children, a bus which is now out on the road somewhere. They call Victor, who being always linked up to a computer gets the message immediately and heads toward the school. Faraday breaks CB channels to locate the bus. Kory flies out to get to it. She and Vic can carry the bus to explode safely out of harm's way. Faraday tries to contact Wally West/Flash but can't seem to reach him (it will be established at the end of this story that he didn't want to reach him). Dick tries to contact Raven, since she has the power to teleport to anyplace instantly. However, Raven is now enjoying a peaceful time with her mother. Her cloak is off, laid over a chair in one of the cabins as she and Arella are outside on horseback. She never hears the call.

At Sarah's funeral, Victor wants vengeance. He wants to blow that Gamesmaster to kingdom come. The other Titans, afraid of what Victor might do, decide to help him, even though Vic doesn't want their help. This is his war now. But Dick insists that none of them are safe. It could have been any one of their family and friends that could have been targeted.

The investigation starts. With Dick's detective skills, Danny's knowledge of commonly used espionage codes and their variations, and the use of the Titans Tower computers, they slowly but surely begin to understand the Gamesmaster's plan. The past terrorist actions have grown with each incident. Each incident (which includes assassinations of political power-brokers) has had one thread in common. Each was a case investigated by Faraday. Obviously, this bozo had made this into some kind of vicious game, a private contest between him and the C.B.I. agent with the world as a chessboard. They learn about the super-terrorists and finally realize where target zero is: Manhattan Island. Was he planning to blow it up? Was it going to be a nuclear destruction? Maybe the clues lie in his opponent. There are seven strike zones or plans, each corresponding to the seven letters in Faraday's name (e.g., Angelique may be terrorizing the subway stations along the F line near DC Comics, Lady Anne may be at an art museum, or other such hints). It doesn't escape their notice that these assassins all seem particularly chosen to be adversaries for the Titans. Faraday admits that he knew that the Gamesmaster wanted to confront the Titans to make his final victory all the sweeter. The Gamesmaster knew of Faraday's occasional reliance on the Titans for extraordinary cases and was now seeking to flaunt his power by using his own super-counterspies! The Gamesmaster does seem to know a lot about King Faraday and the Titans. But how? Who is this clown? Also, why only seven terrorists? There are, after all, eight currently active members in the group. Maybe the Gamesmaster is Dick's adversary. While the others go to their established fields of combat (decided on by the clues in the gamebook) Dick remains to find out the identity, hideout and motivation of the master terrorist.

WOLFMAN: This had to be sacrificed for clarity. It was also not a visual concept. Frankly, this is the kind of first thoughts I think we would have changed even back in the '80s had we completed the story then. George and I often began with complex ideas, then set about finding ways to make them work in straightforward visual terms, since comics are, first and foremost, visual. Also, when you have an artist like George, you don't want to cover up all the art with words or simply have panels filled with talking heads. You want the grandness only he can do.

So, the major battle sequences occur, with the Titans facing off individually against their evil counterparts as stated earlier. Some win and some seem to reach an impasse. However, in all cases, the result is the same: Manhattan Island has been cut off from the rest of the world and is going to be blown up with all television and radio stations tuned in to the event.

During the course of these battles Dick does manage to find the Strategist's hideout. They fight until the Strategist suddenly dies. A computer turns on in the gaming room with the readout: *Your Move, Faraday.* In fact, just before the Big Broadcast, all the terrorists seem to expire or explode with different variations

of that note being seen. Dick finds more clues that lead him to some startling, but as yet unseen, conclusions.

The Gamesmaster finally makes his big appearance on the TV. He is based in the Empire State Building (he is the Emperor or perhaps a King the name of his adversary and defeated fellow gamester). He intends to go out with the reputation of being the greatest mass murderer of them all and without a nuclear device, but slow deaths: several bombs placed in strategic places in the city. (The key word is strategic: Dick figures the clues to their locations are in the model of the city in the Strategist's game room.) Somehow Dick solves the puzzle, but there's no way the Titans can disarm all the detonators which are scattered all over the city. A force field now surrounds the Island. The only thing that can penetrate it is radio and television waves. The Titans, except Dick, are also trapped on the Island, with no way any other super-hero can get in. (The others have been called away.) Also, the Gamesmaster has rigged his base in the Empire State Building to blow up if anyone enters it so even Raven dare not risk teleporting in. We will establish that there's no way Raven's soul self can take in an entire city into itself.

So, how do we get outta this mess? We don't. The whole place blows up and everybody dies. The End.

Just kiddin'.

The details haven't been worked out yet, but I think the key could lie with the transmission signals. It's the one weak link in the chain necessitated by the terrorist's desire for media attention. Perhaps the detonation device is triggered by the same radio signal which is transmitting his message to the world. If the Titans break the signal, the bombs won't go off. And with the Gamesmaster caught off guard, Gar could fly in through the ventilation shafts and short out the fail-safe device. Then Raven would teleport herself into the Gamesmaster's lair and capture him, teleporting him out of there before an enraged Cyborg can get to him. (During the run of this story, Victor's been getting more and more uncontrollable.)

From the vantage point of Titans Tower, Faraday has been watching all this. He is in communication with Dick and is enraged to learn that they didn't kill the bum whom Raven brought over to where Dick was. The Gamesmaster doesn't seem upset; in fact he seems positively content. We see all the television viewscreens that were broadcasting his ultimatum earlier are now showing him talking to Dick and Raven. The Titans are also witnessing it, as well as sweating King Faraday in the Tower. The Game is not over.

The Gamesmaster tells of how the games started. Of how it began as a correspondence between two men who relished the idea of having full control to do their covert actions without being reined in by government bureaucracy. King Faraday was not a truly bad man, just obsessive, with a desire to defend his country and its beliefs, no matter how it was accomplished. Unfortunately, in the real world, he could not act on those desires. But, in a game, he could. Faraday and the Gamesmaster had kept up their relationship strictly through correspondence, neither at first knowing who the other was. However, in the course of the games, which dealt with espionage and global threats, Faraday's maneuvers were being used as real assaults on targets. For example, during the course of a game the Gamesmaster might challenge Faraday to either commit a perfect political assassination, or to prevent one; Years later, the Gamesmaster would actuate those plans for real. Faraday would always be called in to investigate, because the Gamesmaster always attacked within Faraday's current jurisdiction (a fact Dick found out while investigating the Strategist's base), otherwise the spirit of the game was compromised. However, the Gamesmaster was too good. Faraday didn't see the connection between the activities. Other terrorist and/or politically radical groups were being blamed (or credited) for his accomplishments. The Gamesmaster became bolder. He started dropping hints before the attacks. He set up his pattern, graphing it all out like a concerto, with the attack on Manhattan Island the final crescendo. (The sheet music would be one of the clues found by Dick.) However, Faraday was too cool to call attention to the fact that he may have inadvertently helped this lunatic with his operations. After all, the plans were foolproof because Faraday conceived them that way. The final game had to be done with Faraday's full knowledge that it was about to happen, but this time, the Gamesmaster would conceive it. Faraday had utilized the Titans as secret weapons in one of the imaginary encounters so the Gamesmaster sought out or created the Super-Terrorists. Of course, the terrorist had to die before the Big Broadcast, or they might spoil the game. Faraday wanted the Gamesmaster killed before he could blab about Faraday's indiscretion. But still, this victory was his. Faraday's security clearance has been destroyed; in fact, the man is now to be considered a security threat, and the C.B.I. has ways of dealing with those. Of course, all this is being heard by the C.B.I. as well. The Gamesmaster turns to the camera and says *"Your Move, Faraday."*

WOLFMAN: Obviously this was all changed. As I thought about the story and about games in general, I was reminded that in the real world the CIA often brings in game designers, science fiction writers and others who work in the fiction field to "blue sky" ideas about how the U.S. could be attacked and our possible responses. Several friends of mine go off to these CIA confabs once or twice a year. It struck me that the C.B.I., our fictional counterpart, would do the same; they brought in games people who "blue sky" ideas. For our story, one of them would come up with a brilliant attack scenario based on the idea that our future enemies might not be Russia or China but individual terrorists (sadly, what has happened). This unknown game designer's ideas so frightened King Faraday—who saw the frightening possibilities—that he tried to convince the C.B.I. brass that this could very well happen.

Unfortunately, as with many bureaucracies, nobody believed him. Faraday goes insane obsessing about doing the right thing. Finally, he kills the original GM only to schizophrenically become the Gamesmaster himself (hence the caption on page one where he says, "I will find you and I will kill you," only to have the GM respond, "You tried that. I'm still here.") The real Gamesmaster is dead, but now, unbeknownst to himself, Faraday has become him.

Without realizing what he was doing, Faraday sends himself warnings, and tries to prove the idea could work, while believing the Titans would prevent the destruction, which is why he subconsciously involved them in the first place. This would become a story about a man being driven past the limit (counterpointing Vic's story as well as Raven's, and in a way, Azara's story but in reverse) and getting caught up in it while the heroes step back, always in control. In short, evil embraces the abyss while good avoids it. Simple, perhaps, but the core stuff of superhero mythology. The way one makes that work is by making each one of the Titans go through his or her own problems based on who they are. Then each character is given a moment to make a decision, a choice. How they make that choice determines their future and defines their character.

Was there anything wrong with the original idea? No, but it meant, in terms of page count, that we'd suddenly be introducing a brand new character (the Gamesmaster) whom we'd never seen before, and right at the very end of the story. I felt we wouldn't be able to spend the time necessary to give him a convincing motivation. Ultimately, I felt I could do many of the things George had come up with, but by making King Faraday the unwitting villain, it would simplify the story and frankly make it more personal than if a total stranger suddenly popped up and said, "I did it. I'm the bad guy!"

Also, I thought it would be more unsettling that Faraday was destroying New York City in his blind desire to save the world because Faraday is one of the oldest DC characters still being used. For those who don't know, King Faraday, who George and I used often in THE NEW TEEN TITANS, was created in the comic DANGER TRAIL, dated July 1950, which means he debuted while the original Justice Society of America was still being published and six years before Barry Allen became the Flash, ushering in the Silver Age of comics. Faraday's history as a cold war spy who dedicated his life to protecting the country gave more resonance to our modern-day world situation.

Dick is furious. "You endangered an entire city, killed an innocent young woman, because of some damned game?!" The Gamesmaster is, for once, confused. What woman? Raven senses he's genuinely bewildered. The Gamesmaster never even heard of Sarah Simms. In fact, he only knows about the Titans, he never had any interest in their friends and relatives. He only wanted the Titans to play the game.

The sudden realization hits all the Titans simultaneously. Faraday was the one who killed Sarah Simms! During this conversation, Victor has managed to trap Donna, Joe, Gar and Danny in the Gamesmaster's lair by reactivating one of the safety devices or something. He bolts towards Titans Tower. The Titans try to contact Dick and Raven.

Meanwhile, Faraday is rushing down to where the Titans Sub is docked while we see Vic arrive on the rooftop. Intercut with the two progressing. Raven teleports in with Dick and the Gamesmaster, but Victor, with the zero response time of a computerized machine, zaps them both unconscious immediately.

Faraday tries to launch the sub but Victor is actually holding that sucker back with sheer brute strength. Victor breaks into the ship and nearly kills Faraday. Somehow, Dick and Raven manage to stop him. Even in his rage, Victor still couldn't kill him. Dick says that King Faraday will be dealt with by his own superiors, but Faraday still seems defiant. He does however, in a calm, unrepentant tone, apologize for Simms' death. The bomb had been timed to allow Sarah and the kids to be able to run clear before the bomb exploded. They didn't properly take into consideration the fact that the children were disabled and could not all run fast enough. It never occurred to them that Sarah would get back on the bus. All Faraday wanted was to get the Titans to help him kill the Gamesmaster. To once and for all end this stupid game.

WOLFMAN: Having Titans Tower be the surprise power source for the villain's plans would not only make total sense, but also a great plot twist. It also would smooth over any questions as to what the villains were doing; ultimately, and against their own knowledge, they were being used not only to help Faraday, but as a distraction to keep the Titans busy while Faraday took over the Tower and powered up his force field. It was important that the Titans, and primarily Vic, decided that the only way they could save New York was to destroy their own Tower. If a villain destroyed it, even if the Titans ultimately won, they still would have lost. By making the destruction their own decision, and by having Vic decide that his father originally built the Tower to help them save others, that it would also be fulfilling his father's dreams while harkening back to the very first Titans stories we did. Finally, since in the DCU there is a new and different Tower, this would in a way explain why it needed to be built.

Cut to later. In a special holding cell in the Tower. All the Titans are together. Victor is still mourning his dead friend, praying to God that Dick was right. That Faraday will get his just deserts. It's just that Faraday didn't seem to be that afraid. Dick says not to worry.

In the cell, Faraday smokes a cigarette defiantly as he sits next to the Gamesmaster (who never reveals his real name throughout the entire story). They share knowing looks. Faraday, even through the bruises, remained cool. In the end he may still snatch victory from the jaws of defeat. He had, through the years, accumulated a lot of data which could be embarrassing to certain governmental types. At least he will be alive, while the terminally ill Gamesmaster will never play a game again. Suddenly, a shrill whistle seems to be coming from the Gamesmaster's body. The guy's wired to go off! As Faraday bangs the door for assistance, the calm Gamesmaster smiles. "Sorry, Faraday. That was your last move."

The cell explodes.

The Titans rush up to the smoldering cell. Nothing is left. How fortunate that the Titans happened to be just out of the bomb's range. In fact, Dick never even suggested that any one of them stand guard. Where did the bomb come from? Why didn't Dick find it when he frisked the Gamesmaster?

Nightwing says nothing.

The Game is over.

WOLFMAN: Nightwing, a murderer? Don't think so. Frankly, I don't think this would have been the ending even back then. My thought is we put it in as a placeholder until we got to that section. When our editor, Brian Cunningham (see below), suggested we make a change, there was absolutely no protest.

CUNNINGHAM: Yes, asking Marv and George to rethink this conclusion is my only real contribution to GAMES's story. I felt that Nightwing would not do this based on what we know of his character now. However, if this actually did see print in 1988, it would have affected his character profoundly, and since Marv and George were the guiding force behind Nightwing at the time, it would have been a natural progression of his character that they would definitely explore to the hilt. But in 2011, with decades of consistent character traits firmly established, and given that this was a one-shot "time capsule" lifted from time's past, it didn't fit in with the Nightwing of today. Marv and George agreed and attacked the story's climax with what I felt was a spectacular solution.

WOLFMAN: And, finally, the last page: A nice, simple return to basics for the group. Old friends have come together for a party, a nod to the cartoon show, and the idea that no matter what, the Titans will always continue. I certainly hope so.

FROM THE WRITER OF
GREEN LANTERN *AND* JSA

GEOFF JOHNS

Witness the gathering of a new team of Teen Titans and their initial battle against an old, familiar foe: the most lethal mercenary on earth, Deathstroke!

with MIKE McKONE

VOL. 1: A KID'S GAME

VOL. 2: FAMILY LOST

VOL. 3: BEAST BOYS AND GIRLS

VOL. 4: THE FUTURE IS NOW

VOL. 5: LIFE AND DEATH

VOL. 6: TITANS AROUND THE WORLD

TEEN TITANS / OUTSIDERS: THE INSIDERS

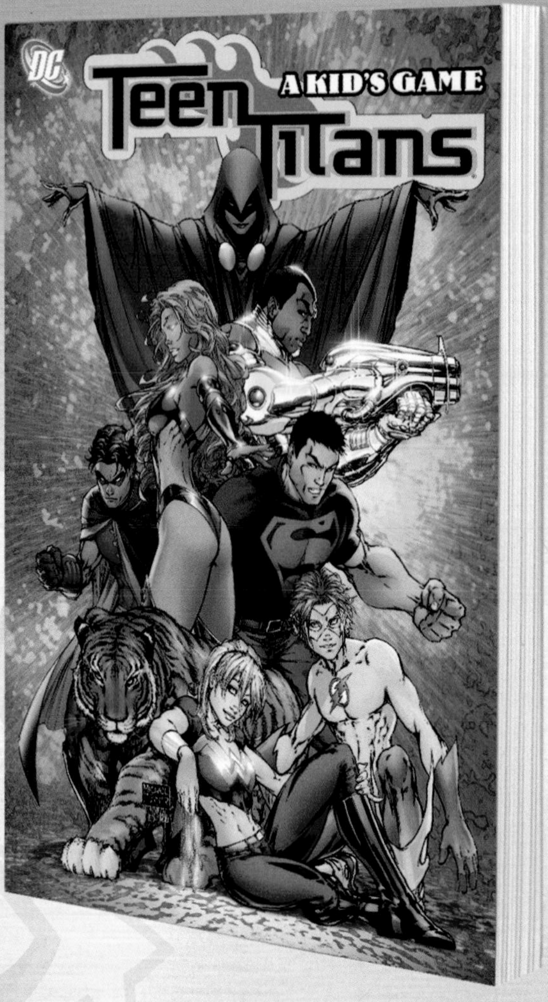
DC
Teen Titans
A KID'S GAME

TEEN TITANS VOL. 2:
FAMILY LOST

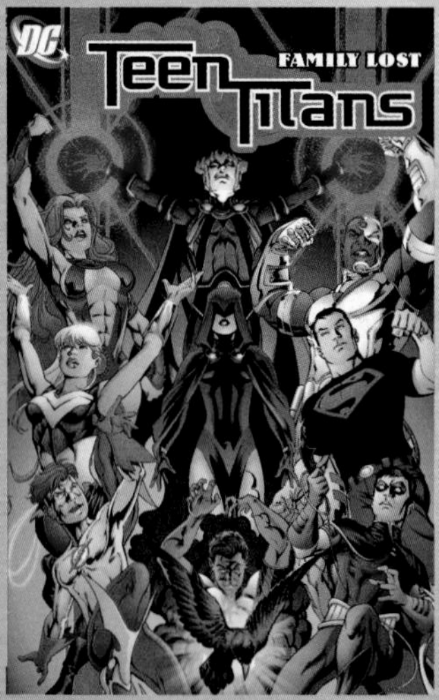
DC
Teen Titans
FAMILY LOST

with
MIKE McKONE

TEEN TITANS VOL. 4:
THE FUTURE IS NOW

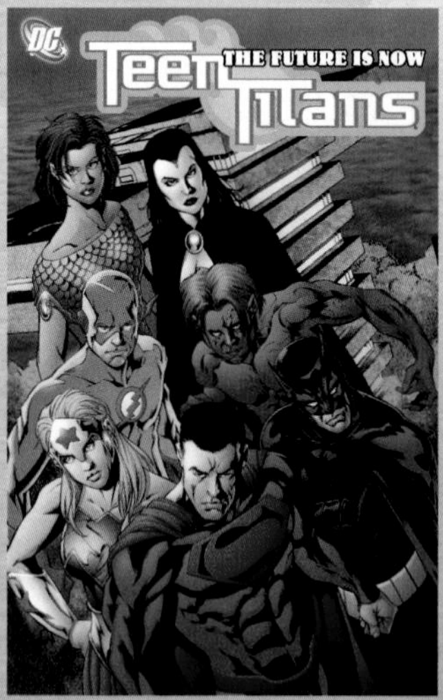
DC
Teen Titans
THE FUTURE IS NOW

with
MIKE McKONE

TEEN TITANS VOL. 5
LIFE AND DEATH

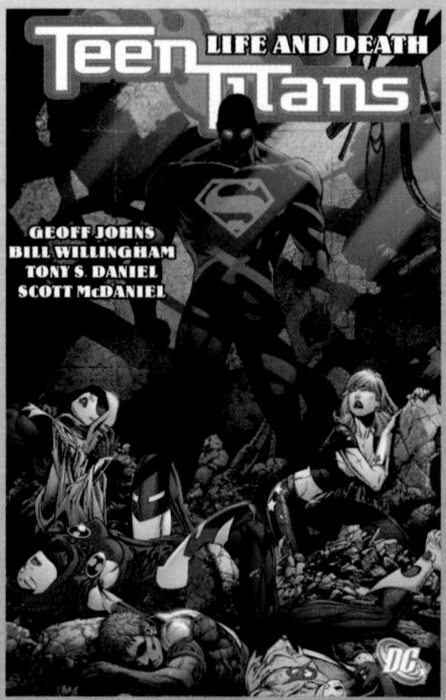
Teen Titans
LIFE AND DEATH
GEOFF JOHNS
BILL WILLINGHAM
TONY S. DANIEL
SCOTT McDANIEL
DC

with
VARIOUS ARTISTS

SEARCH THE GRAPHIC NOVELS SECTION OF
DCCOMICS.COM
FOR ART AND INFORMATION ON ALL OF OUR BOOKS!